Social & Economic Studies within the Framework of Emerging
Global Developments - Volume 5

T0291220

Kemal Cebeci / Muhammed Veysel Kaya (eds.)

Social & Economic Studies within the Framework of Emerging Global Developments - Volume 5

PETER LANG

Berlin - Bruxelles - Chennai - Lausanne - New York - Oxford

Library of Congress Cataloging-in-Publication
A record in the CIP catalog has been requested for this book.
of the Library of Congress.

Bibliographic information published by the Deutsche Nationalbibliothek
The Deutsche Nationalbibliothek collects this publication in the Deutsche Nationalbibliografie; detailed bibliographic data are available on the Internet at .Nationalbibliografie; detailed bibliographic data are available on the Internet at http://dnb.d-nb.de.

ISBN 978-3-631-91392-5 (Print)
E-ISBN 978-3-631-91471-7 (E-PDF)
E-ISBN 978-3-631-91709-1 (E-PUB)
DOI.10.3726/b21780

© 2024 Peter Lang Group AG, Lausanne
Published by Peter Lang GmbH, Berlin, Germany

info@peterlang.com - www.peterlang.com

Foreword

This book is the fifth series of the "Social & Economic Studies within the Framework of Emerging Global Developments." Fifth volume includes empirical and theoretical original papers written by researchers from different countries and universities. The target audience of this book is researchers, students and academics interested in business, economics and social sciences.

Marecki and Wojcik (Chapter 1) try to discuss whether non-bank financial services are either a threat or a promising way for the future . Their findings indicate that non-bank financial services are threats to the economy. **Marecki and Wojcik** (Chapter 2) investigate to determine the COVID-19's influence. They look at aspects including the number of new cases and fatalities brought on by COVID-19, specialized activities, and the broader monetary climate when determining the impact on the Bucharest Stock Trading (BET) records. **Challoumis** compares the cycle of money with the rewarding taxes and without the impact factor of the rest rewarding impact factors.. **Spyropoulos, Andras, Dritsas and Polychronidou** examine the perceptions of Start-Up founders, using Graph Theory and Mutual Information.

Braslina et al. analyse diverse theoretical foundations from various scientific disciplines that influence the process of innovative product development. **Pekanov** evaluates the potential of biomass-based energy production both as a sustainable and economically viable alternative to traditional fossil fuel-based energy generation. **Gunesch** examines pervading paradoxes in cultural and art economics from historical, economic, sociopolitical and psychological perspectives. **Trifu** combines a survey on the opinions related to the activity of company departments and HR specialists, presented in information in the media, with the experiences of managers, entrepreneurs and the public, related to how the characteristics, skills, specific knowledge of workers should be brought to a denominator common to across contribute and benefit the entire company/ organization.

Lajcin focuses on managerial personality and its typical traits, which should be studied and taken into account before a person is selected for a managerial position. **Ahmad and Mohebi** investigate how students in public high schools see e-learning and the difficulties in implementing it. They employ secondary data in the context of an exploratory sequential mixed-method interpretivism paradigm. The results of this study demonstrate the necessity for cautious adoption of e-learning.

Mohebi and AlHammadi assess Kenyan pre-service and in-service teachers' views on online training effectiveness and satisfaction. **Mohebi and Shaya** examine the existing literature on ESD, learning organizations and higher education, then offer a novel approach to strengthen the capabilities of higher education systems of embedding ESD in ways that facilitates meaningful transformation within the educational system, rather than simply the incorporation of sustainability-focused content.

Hamburg and Sommer review some cybersecurity educational frameworks and cybersecurity training strategies particularly for employers and employees in SMEs by improving their awareness and investigating best approaches to create attractive cybersecurity education and training programs. **Harahap et al.** research child marriages in Indonesia. **Jokhadze** creates a guideline, based on existing theoretical knowledge in the direction of change management benefiting various practical cases in management, which will help organizations in the diagnostic process of the big picture of where they are now and what type of changes are necessary and/or mandatory to became more flexible. **Danescu et al.** investigate the link between corporate social responsibility and financial performance of companies moderated by corporate governance in a context where integrated reporting is the main provider of information for stakeholder decisions and is the premise of scientific approaches.

Table of Contents

List of Contributers

Susri Adeni
Communication Science, Bengkulu University, Indonesia

Machyudin Agung Harahap
Communication Science, Universitas Pembangunan Nasional Veteran Jakarta,
Indonesia

Dawood Ahmad
Department of Education, The University of Faisalabad, Pakistan

Mariam AlHammadi
College of Education, Zayed University, Dubai, United Arab Emirates (UAE)

Christos Andras
Department of Industrial Engineering and Management, International Hellenic
University, Thessaloniki, Greece

Anda Batraga
University of Latvia, Latvia

Liga Braslina
University of Latvia, Latvia

Girts Braslins
University of Latvia, Latvia

Constantinos Challoumis
National and Kapodistrian University of Athens (N.K.U.A.), Greece

Laviniu Constantinescu
University 1 December 1918 Alba Iulia, Romania

Tatiana Danescu
George Emil Palade University of Medicine, Pharmacy, Science, and
Technology of Targu Mures, Romania

Michalis Dritsas
CEO, Elevate Greece S.A.

Konrad Gunesch
London Centre for Interdisciplinary Research, London, United Kingdom

Ileana Hamburg
Institut Arbeit und Technik, Westfälische Hochschule, Germany,
Munscheidstraße 14, 45886 Gelsenkirchen, Germanyhamburg@iat.eu

Arifin Saleh Harahap
Communication Science, Esa Unggul University, Indonesia

Ilona Jokhadze
Administrative Department, At LTB Company, Georgian American University,
Georgia

Katrina Kellerte
University of Latvia, Latvia

Daniel Lajcin
DTI University, Dubnica nad Vahom, Slovakia

Lukasz Marecki
Warsaw School of Economics (SGH), College of Management and Finance,
Warsaw, Poland

Roxana Maria Stejerean
University 1 December 1918 Alba Iulia, Romania

Radu-Bogdan Matei
University 1 December 1918 Alba Iulia, Romania

Laila Mohebi
College of Education, Zayed University, Dubai, United Arab Emirates (UAE)

Dubravka Pekanov
Josip Juraj Strossmayer University of Osijek, Faculty of Economics in Osijek,
Croatia

Persefoni Polychronidou
Department of Economic Sciences, International Hellenic University, Greece

Jeļena Šalkovska
University of Latvia, Latvia

Nessrin Shaya
Ajman University, United Arab Emirates (UAE)

Daina Šķiltere
University of Latvia, Latvia

David Sommer
Institut Arbeit und Technik, Westfälische Hochschule, Germany,
Munscheidstraße 14, 45886 Gelsenkirchen, Germanysommer@iat.eu

Theoharis Spyropoulos
Department of Economic Sciences, International Hellenic University, Greece /
Department of International Business, Perrotis College, Thessaloniki, Greece

Alexandru Trifu
"Petre Andrei" University of Iasi, Romania

Agnieszka Wojcik-Czerniawska
Warsaw School of Economics (SGH), College of Management and Finance,
Warsaw, Poland

Titien Yusnita
Communication Science, Islamic Sahid Institute, Indonesia

Marijana Bubanić
University of Zagreb Faculty of Organization and Informatics, Varaždin,
Croatia

Dina Korent
University of Zagreb Faculty of Organization and Informatics, Varaždin,
Croatia

List of Figures and Graphs

List of Tables

Muna Mohamed Alhammadi and Zeina Hojeij
**Perceptions of College Students with Disabilities Regarding the
Accessibility of the UAE's E-Learning System**

Marijana Bubanić and Dina Korent
Clusters of the European Union's Countries Total Tax Burden

Lukasz Marecki and Agnieszka Wojcik-Czerniawska

Non-Bank Financial Services: Threat or Future?

1. Introduction

Nonbank financial businesses (NBFCs), also referred are nonbank financial institutions (NBFIs), are investment institutions that do not hold a banking relationship but offer a variety of financial services. Public client contributions, which have been instantly available assets, even those in the deposit account, are expressly forbidden by such banks. This limitation prevents them from falling within the jurisdiction of conventional provincial and national government regulators. The Dodd-Frank Wall Street Reform and Consumer Protection define nonbank financial firms as "primarily involved inside financial transactions" when enough than 85% of their combined yearly gross sales or combined assets are material to the financial statements (Liang & Reichert, 2012). Financial institutions, lending institutions, money market instruments, insurance businesses, and hedge funds are instances of NBFCs.

Foreign nonbank economic companies, U.S. nonbank financial businesses, and U.S. nonbank monetary companies regulated by the Fed Reserve Board of Governors are the three main types of nonbank financial companies defined by Dodd-Frank. Credits and credit amenities, currency trading, planning for retirement, financial marketplaces, insurance, and merging operations are all services that NBFCs can provide. Insurance companies, venture capital firms, cash transactions, certain microloan groups, and pawn shops are instances of nonbank banking firms.

Together with financial institutions, some other type of financial intermediary defined as 'non-bank financial institutions' plays an extremely important role in the process of financing from savers to borrowers even during the phase of economic reform and change (NBFIs). That since the introduction of something like the Annunzio Wylie Anti-Money Laundering Act in 1992, which also expanded the description of "financial institutions" as mentioned in the Bank Security Act (BSA) well beyond the boundaries of conventional establishments, the word "non-bank financial institution" has now become a widely used term. NBFIs were created with the aim to (1) provide a broader variety of financial services, (2) promote price competition with financial institutions, and provide clients with higher-quality and more diverse options; and (3) fulfill the potential needs of the individuals.

With both the rise of NBFIs and credit markets, which provide firms direct access to sensitive resources, the role of financial intermediaries in the industrialized nations has eroded slightly in new years. The financial subdivision has been started by financial institutions throughout the history of world economic development and has since become intimately tied with NBFIs. In comparison to whatever the institutions had previously accomplished, the NBFIs' contributions to general development appear to have increased since then. In actuality, the coexistence of banks and NBFIs looks to be essential, and competitiveness here between the two could assist boost economic growth and operational efficiency (Sakyi et al., 2014).

NBFIs have been proved to be a major connection in producing and communicating jeopardies, which leads to economic crises, in the latest days. Regulators have concentrated on clarifying the scope and purpose of NBFIs, and also the risks generated from their effect on the financial stability, in required to formulate measures to deal with banking meltdown. According to previous research, there are three involved in risk transmission channels:

Firstly, NBFIs create product-related risks by developing segment accounts, particularly securitized goods. Leading to a shortage of knowledge of the risks involved with securitized assets, a substantial number of banks and NBFIs held many risky investments than their initial assumptions, as seen by the recent recession (Shrestha, 2007).

Secondly, banks and NBFIs have a close relationship. As a result of this interconnectedness, financial stress experienced by a solitary NBFI may inexorably be passed to additional financial institutions (non-banks) via counterpart hazards, producing a massive economic system to collapse.

Thirdly, because some NBFIs operate on a big scale, whatever financial difficulties they have could swiftly spread to the rest of the finance industry.

The threat is among the most fascinating issues that most financial companies have faced in recent years. Numerous financial companies have gone bankrupt as a result of poorly handled risks. Non-Bank Financial Institutions (NBFIs) provide economic services to customers in Ghana, complementing the current mainstream financial firms (Rizwan & Semenoh, 2017). The increasing relevance of NBFIs, along with the recent global financial crisis, has necessitated determining the individual risk of all these organizations, and also the influence of hazard on their operation.

2. Non-Bank Financial Institutions and Their Influence on the Entire Industry

Whereas most people need financial assistance or advice, they just go to an institution immediately. Many customers, on the other hand, discover that the company's services fall short of their expectations, making them unsure about what to do next. NBFIs manually uninstall such offerings and customize their services to match the needs of the unique client, whereas banks tend to offer a range of banking products as part of a combo pack. As a result, many individuals who are unable to obtain assistance from a bank can do so through an NBFI. NBFIs provide a wide range of banking services, including:

• Loans
• Availability of credit
• Preparing for retirement
• Funding for education
• Stocks and share reinsurance
• Transactions on the stock exchange
• TFCs (Term Finance Certificates)
• Maintenance of one's wealth
• Administration of a stock and share investment
• Service is being discounted

3. Cybercrime: One of the Most Serious Threats to Non-Bank Financial Services

In regard to data loss, fear of criminals was a common response in our research. It's not surprising, considering that attacks like distributed denial of service (DDoS) assaults are getting more widespread by the year. These hacks can wreak havoc on a company's broadband network, pulling subdomains and web-based services offline for hours at a time and denying access permission. For something like a non-bank, cybersecurity can have huge financial consequences in a number of ways, such increasing cost efficiency and the expense of fighting against attacks, or simply diminishing customer confidence as a result of a data leak or failure to complete services as promised

Regardless matter where it is located for news, there seems to be chatter about something like a worldwide economic stalemate. When focusing on Europe, China, Japanese, or the United States, the belief in a synchronised global slowdown seems to be the only constant.

In modern banking theory, the sensitivity of non-bank financial services to broader market risk is known to as "beta." Financial institutions' service businesses have a low beta coefficient in compared with other industries, but they are still positively correlated, meaning that they will be negatively impacted if the wider market declines. From outside the biggest banks, few non-banking institutions can anticipate to have any influence over fiscal and monetary policy, making indicators of an impending global slowdown frightening for financial professionals who would be powerless in the face of a downturn. With all this in mind, a company might prepared for a wide economic downturn in a variety of ways (Worthington, 2001). Entertain the probability of a terrible economy in advance, maintain a long-term viewpoint despite the terrible short-term results, and make predictions associated with future growth and reducing costs are all useful strategies. Through preparing ahead of schedule and creating economic buffers, the effects of something like a coordinated economic slump can be reduced.

4. Changes in the Regulatory and Legislative Environment

In 2019, a huge number of financial researchers think legal and statutory improvements will pose a risk to their businesses, similar to projections of a global economic downturn. Plenty already been said about just the banking industry's extraordinarily high regulation expenses, with overall rules appearing to rise every several decades while paying institutions upwards of a hundred billion dollars each year. Look no farther than the Dodd-Frank Wall Street Reform and Consumer Protection Act for an instance of legislation that has a big effect on accounting organization company activities. The legislation, which was adopted in 2010 whilst also reeling from the economic meltdown and was phased in over several years, imposed restrictions on how banks may participate in investing and market speculation (Ofoeda et al., 2012).

But even though the legislation's declared purpose was to reduce financial system vulnerabilities and safeguard clients, it also put a strain on small community banks' profits, forcing them out of business completely, with the United States losing 14 % of these businesses between 2010 and 2014. The Dodd-Frank Act was largely overturned in 2018, which would exclude smaller institutions from most of these loan reporting regulations due to a better understanding of the consequences.

Non-bank financial institutions that have been effective inside a competitive economy, financial companies cannot relax on their laurels; an inventive industry upstart could develop and woo customers away using high-quality goods or reduced pricing. The finance system is nothing like that, with the introduction of finance approaches and creative ways to spend and save coinciding with the development of smartphones and other transportable World Wide Web items. Non-Banking institutions have been battling mobile share trading apps including Robinhood, along with internet loan and investment fund services, in recent times (Islam & Osman, 2011). Nevertheless, tech behemoths like Google and Amazon are always posing a threat to practically any business, especially finance. Consider Contactless Payments, which enables smartphone users to perform basic financial tasks like as tapping a credit or debit card and sending the money to family and friends. All of this is to mention nothing at all about the possibility that cryptocurrencies will acquire greater popularity in the future and create a paradigm role in the way financial institutions work. Anyone that has followed the cryptocurrency over the last few months can witness the industry's high volatility.

PayPal, formerly known as Concinnity, was launched in 1998, went public in 2002, and was subsequently purchased by eBay for $1.6 billion (Saal et al., 2017). EBay has made PayPal its current preferred option, making it a success tale from the dot com boom. On a web filled with fraudsters, the PayPal logo had become a hallmark of trustworthiness, accepted by a public not yet aware enough even to recognize a hoax. Economic circumstances improved, revenue soared, and PayPal undertook a wave of purchases as a consequence of this optimism. And if it wasn't a division of eBay until 2014, it may have been much higher. Ever since, the danger of a company employing technologies to deliver a similar result has persisted. Consumers have been drawn away from banking' primary services, such as international transactions and trading strategies, by a slew of competitors. This is notably true inside the UK where a slew of new banking organizations have cropped up as a response to new competition-friendly regulations. They promised service, flexibility, and functionality that the previous administration could not match. They mostly focused on the internet and had no real sites.

In 2014, Apple Pay was released, allowing users to use their iPhones in the same manner they would a squeeze bankcard. A year ago, Samsung released a comparable technology. This innovation irritated Australian banks, and then in 2016, the Financial Institution, Westpac, Standard Chartered Bank, and the Bendigo and Adelaide Banks petitioned the Australian Competition and Consumer Commission (ACCC) to enable banks to join unions with iPhone. The banks were specifically interested in gaining entry to the Near Field Communications antennas in iPhones to construct their respective competitive mobile wallet. The claims were vigorously contested by Apple. Apple's response to the ACCC stated, "Authorization of a cartel among the applicant banks, who hold access to the following of all cardholder in Australia, would results in considerable customer harm and prolong the oligopoly financial sector circumstances." The ACCC sided with Apple in March 2017, ordering each bank to engage with Apple independently (Ofoeda et al., 2016).

Amazon has indeed been pondering a move into the financial services industry. Top Up, a program that enables visitors to deposit money immediately to their

Amazon account using PayPoint stores, was officially launched somewhere at end of August this year. It had already introduced Amazon Cash, a comparable service in the United States, in July. Such services enable the company to reach out to a limited percentage of customers who have not had debit cards. Although money deposited into Top Up and Money cannot be retrieved, the programs are a precursor to a typical bank account.

The danger of new technology drawing consumers away from traditional processes will always be present in such a fast-paced industry as banking. For an organization to be successful and grow for a long time, such alterations should either be anticipated or adjusted to the best of one's capacity. Apple Card, for example, is expected to tempt current Apple users with its ease of use and lack of additional costs, leading other major credit card companies to refine and improve their solutions to the customers.

As the phrase goes, "time is money," and nowhere is this truer than in the financial world. Business interruptions result in decreased productivity, lower profits, and, in some cases, even brand damage. As already stated, these interruptions could be caused by attackers or simply by extreme weather.

Increased insurance coverage is purchased by some firms to mitigate a real risk, but such plans only cover damage or injury to actual objects, not lost revenue. In any case, there's no arguing that business disruptions should be avoided at all costs (Haque, 2021).

Price variations round out the list of the 12 most popular questionnaire surveys. "Price unpredictability that has a negative influence on the financial outcomes of people who both use and generate products" is how commodities prices risk is described. Commodities such as oil, corn, cotton, aluminium, and steel provide a price volatility to both businesses and consumers. Companies that are exposed to significant commodity price risk typically diversify by employing futures and options on global markets such as the Chicago Mercantile Exchange.

Tariffs on steel and aluminium in the United States highlight how price discrepancies can arise and severely hurt businesses. Since the tariffs were introduced, market capitalization factory owners have suffered with stock values and general corporate health due to greater expenses, lower output, and lower revenue.

According to Islam (1999), Bangladesh's legal structure stifles the expansion of leasing enterprises. NBFIs encounter challenges in collecting leased assets in the event of a default, even though the default mentality has not yet contaminated them to a significant degree. Another lawful issue that leasing firms face is the accurate of devaluation for leased property, which is common around the world (Schandlbauer et al., 2017).

5. Misalignment of Assets and Liabilities

According to Madura (2009), it is a common occurrence for all types of depository institutions for assets to have a longer average maturity than liabilities, which exposes banking institutions to interest rate changes. When it comes to managing the asset-to-liability mismatch, NBFIs are in a pickle.

The majority of NBFI officials polled agreed that, in comparison to banks, they engage in higher-risk initiatives. The explanation for this is that because their fund's cost of capital is high, they want a bigger return than usual. As a result, they select projects that have been rejected by banks due to their high risk. It may result in an unfavorable balance sheet for certain NBFIs.

NBFIs cater to the section of the market that is left intact by banks. In our country, there are 3 commercial banks with a total of forty-seven branches, with another 9 on the verge of opening. As a result, selling credit products is extremely competitive. When commercial banks participate in non-bank activities, the situation gets more difficult (Sytnik et al., 2017).

6. Suggested Alternatives

To alleviate the financial crisis and lower the cost of funds, NBFIs must make the first move to investigate other sources of funding, such as the issue of corporate debt and discount or sales of lease debtors. The financialization of property could be another new and attractive source of capital. As an alternate source of funding, IPDC released the first asset-backed bonds in 2004. In this sense, the organization should give the appropriate policy assistance.

We all know that asset-liability mismatches are one of the most serious problems that any lending institution faces. The problem can be solved if NBFIs can match the term of their asset items with their lending products. However, it is nearly impossible. As a result, NBFIs can use floating interest rates throughout their loans.

Increasing interest rates hurt financial firms with more interest-rate-sensitive liabilities than assets. Financial firms with long-term fixed-rate funding that use the money largely for floating-rate loans, on the other hand, are negatively affected by falling interest rates. Interest rate swaps can be used successfully by these financial organizations to mitigate interest rate risk.

As a result, NBFIs should invest in assets with a typical risk profile. They might adopt the BASEL-II rules in this respect. Delta-Brac housing has regularly kept a strong score across the nation for a few years.

7. Conclusion

Banks and non-bank financial firms are both important components of a healthy and secure monetary scheme. Most nations' financial systems are dominated by banks since companies, individuals, and the government all depend on the funding scheme for a variety of financial materials to satisfy their financial needs. NBFIs, on the other hand, have a large following in both industrialized and developing economies since they provide additional and alternative financial services. On the one hand, these organizations support ease long-term availability of funds, which can be difficult for banks to do, and on the other side, the development of NBFIs broadens the range of goods accessible to institutions and individuals with monetary backing.

Through their activities and venture funding, NBFIs can rally long-term funding for the growth of justice and due to the financial markets, lease, and folding. NBFIs also serve as a barrier in the market, which is especially important during period of recession instability. A well-functioning NBFI sector also contributes to the country's economic overall purpose of financial sustainability by reducing perverse incentives.

Because of the expanding prevalence of NBFIs, which help corporations to easily access savings and investments, banks' function as financial institutions in industrialized nations has dwindled. Financial development began with financial institutions and then grew to include non-bank financial entities, according to world economic history. NBFIs' role in Vietnam has increased as a result of this influx, although there are still worries about hazards and the financial system's fragility.

According to the study's quantitative findings, the synergistic impacts of NBFI development on the stability of Vietnam's financial system show some indicators of improvement rather than deterioration, as we had anticipated. The asset size of securities, finance, and financial services leasing enterprises is positively connected with stock market volatility, according to our analysis based on the segmentation of impacts by the NBFI group (Yao et al., 2018).

Simultaneously, the growth of insurance companies is accompanied by reduced levels of market volatility and decreased rates of non-performing credit at banks. This seems plausible, given that an expanding insurance market might produce more efficient inventory market hedging tools and also credit insurance products to help banks avoid bad loans.

On the other hand, while the current operational status of several NBFI categories may present possible hazards at different times, these do not appear to be significant to have an impact on Vietnam's banking system and overall financial stability. We planned to include the "financial stability index" as a predictor variable for our econometric approach earlier on in the research procedure, to create an accurate and appropriate analysis of the relationship between NBFI development and financial stability. However, because the data series for Vietnam's financial system appears to be insufficient, the authors created a composite index for the years 2010 to 2018 to combat such issues.

For NBFCs, the future appears to be very important, and only those that can meet the challenges will be likely to survive in the long run. NBFCs, on the other hand, must concentrate on their fundamental advantages while working on their deficiencies to stay alive and flourish.

References

Haque, M. G. (2021). Micro Financial Sharia Non-Bank Strategic Analysis: A Study at BMT Beringharjo, Yogyakarta. *Budapest International Research and Critics Institute (BIRCI-Journal): Humanities and Social Sciences, 4*(2), 1677–1686.

Islam, M. A., & Osman, J. B. (2011). Development Impact of Non-Bank Financial Intermediaries on Economic Growth in Malaysia: An Empirical Investigation. *International Journal of Business and Social Science, 2*(14).

Liang, H. Y., & Reichert, A. K. (2012). The Impact of Banks and Non-Bank Financial Institutions on Economic Growth. *The Service Industries Journal, 32*(5), 699–717.

Ofoeda, I., Abor, J., & Adjasi, C. K. (2012). Non-Bank Financial Institutions Regulation and Risk-Taking. *Journal of Financial Regulation and Compliance.*

Ofoeda, I., Gariba, P., & Amoah, L. (2016). Regulation and Performance of Non-Bank Financial Institutions in Ghana. *International Journal of Law and Management.*

Rizwan, C. A., & Semenoh, A. Y. (2017). *Non-Bank Financial Institutions Activity in the Context of Economic Growth: Cross-Country Comparisons.*

Saal, M., Starnes, S., & Rehermann, T. (2017). *Digital Financial Services.*

Sakyi, P. A., Ofoeda, I., Kyereboah-Coleman, A., & Abor, J. Y. (2014). Risk and Performance of Non-Bank Financial Institutions. *International Journal of Financial Services Management, 7*(1), 19–35.

Schandlbauer, A. (2017). How Do Financial Institutions React to a Tax Increase? *Journal of Financial Intermediation, 30,* 86–106.

Shrestha, M. B. (2007). Role of Non-Bank Financial Intermediation: Challenges for Central Banks in the SEACEN Countries. *Research Studies.*

Sytnik, M. M., & Miroshnichenko, O. S. (2017). *Current State and Possibilities of Development of Long-Term Bank Lending to Non-Financial Institutions in Russia.*

Worthington, A. C. (2001). Efficiency in Pre-Merger and Post-Merger Non-Bank Financial Institutions. *Managerial and Decision Economics, 22*(8), 439–452.

Yao, H., Haris, M., & Tariq, G. (2018). Profitability Determinants of Financial Institutions: Evidence from Banks in Pakistan. *International Journal of Financial Studies, 6*(2), 53.

Lukasz Marecki and Agnieszka Wojcik-Czerniawska

How Has the COVID-19 Affected the Stock Market

1. Introduction

Humankind has been plagued by uncountable scourges and pandemics since the dawn of time. The SARS CoV-2 infection was the most recent fatal disease to be eradicated by human progress. Because of its large number of symptoms and consistent transmission rate, this disease has turned into a tyrant. Unlike previous financial crises, such as those triggered by the Great Depression and the Great Recession of 2007–2009, this one is unique in that it encompasses a broad range of shady social relationships.

2. An Econometric Model for BET Document Growth

The findings indicate that further study is required to determine the effect of the COVID-19 epidemic on the securities exchange and other macroeconomic activities (Ashley & Patterson, 2010). A few research have centered on states that have been relentlessly struck by the COVID-19 disease, even though the mainstream of experiments have centered on states that were not touched by the pandemic (e.g., Europe, North America, and South Africa). The vast majority of examinations that have been discovered have used board data methods appropriately. Focusing on monetary differences across countries will likely lead to a better understanding of the pandemic's global impact. The evaluation follows a similar request method as previous time-series-based inspection approaches (Ashraf, 2020).

According to the findings, which are consistent with other surrounding research, BET's development has been influenced by development imperatives and cash-related methodological advance charge decreases, as well as the financial atmosphere in Europe, the United States, and China.

3. The Significant Threat of COVID-19 to the Worldwide Financial Areas

The COVID-19 epidemic posed a significant danger to the global financial and monetary sectors. This has resulted in the largest one-day declines in the history of major monetary trading transactions all over the world, with no place protected. The stock market in the United States had dropped by less than 30 % from its peak in March 2020. It looked at the monetary trade outcomes of other major nations and discovered that they were much more depressing than the US figures. In the United Kingdom, monetary trade decreased by 37 %, 33 %, and 48 %, respectively.

Covid cases along with passing were shown to have a substantial effect on the stock marketplace in a few experiments. New cases of COVID-19 have got a greater impact on the stock marketplace in China, France, Germany, and Spain from March 1 to April 10, 2020, than mortality deaths had before (Bai & Perron, 1998). Others have examined that the Covid incident has wreaked havoc on financial markets all across the globe.

It is investigated the reaction of monetary trade records in East Asian countries to the COVID-19 epidemic. The experts used first referred to the frequency of COVID-19 as a starting point for the investigation, which lasted from January 2 to September 30, 2020. The pandemic harmed the securities markets studied, according to quantile backslide models. Between 10 January and 16 March 2020, aboard information method was used to scrutinize the influence of the COVID-19 epidemic on two of China's most important monetary trade documents, and the results revealed that the daily increase in innovative events and the overall amount of demises caused by the corona were essentially inversely related. In Nigeria, GARCH models discover that pandemic factors harmed monetary trade between January 2nd and April 16th, 2020.

4. Actions Are Taken by General Health Experts

When people were encouraged to stay at home, it had an impact on a variety of businesses (such as transportation, housing, travel, and sports), as well as several aspects of the economy (like cash, the environment, prosperity, and preparing). Using evident monetary trade impulses from the UK, USA, and South Africa, a boarding technique to investigate the protections trade impact of social evacuation courses of action. The evaluation to include a handful of European nations in a comparative board approach (e.g., Italy, Germany, and Spain). Most experts concur that the number of lockdown periods, the amount of newly founded Covid patients, limitations on the inner turn of events, along general tour limitations all had an impact on cash trade esteem (Bogousslavsky, 2016).

The stock returns of West African monetary trade organizations during the COVID-19 eruption (Benin, Burkina Faso, Ivory Coast, Guinea-Bissau, Mali, and Niger). They hoped to learn about the consequences of authorities' opposition to COVID-19 initiatives for organizations in general, as well as the districts that make up the majority of public corporations in the US (i.e., industry, cash, and scattering). In general, the market reacted well to social avoidance and authoritative actions, but improvement constraints and lockup conjectures dragged down the stock price. According to the findings, moving restrictions harmed stock returns in all three domains, with lockout measures having a greater impact on modern and cash companies than flow enterprises (Brown & Evans, 1975). Furthermore, it focused on the protections market in Indonesia, focusing on clear links at both the national and provincial levels. Despite the additional incidents and passing, the lockout measures had a substantial influence on the securities market as seen by the fixed-impacts board backslide. Further investigation revealed that some endeavors (for example, fundamental industry; customer items; excavating and occupation, organization, in addition to theory) remained additional adversely exaggerated than others (for example, fundamental industry; purchaser stock); and that some endeavors (for example, fundamental industry; customer items; mining and trade, organization, and theory) were more decidedly affected than others (for example, fundamental industry; purchaser stock); and that a few endeavors (for example, fundamental industry; purchaser stock) were more adversely affected than others for example, fundamental (e.g., agriculture and establishment) (Campbell, 1987).

The Purchasing Managers' Index (PMI) is economic indicator that may be used in conjunction with crude oil prices to assess the economy's overall health (PMI). According to scholarly research, the PMI and the monetary trade have a strong relationship. To demonstrate this, the PMI's explanations had an influence on protections markets in Germany, France, Italy, and Spain, particularly amid money and financial crises. Shareholders may rebalance their collections by purchasing (or trading) bonds in response to data concerning an increase (or decrease) in the PMI, which is a similar process. The originators discovered that strong PMI news, when compared to extra money-related situations, has a significant impact on stock transaction outcomes between January 2005 and March 2008.

5. The Methodology Adopted for Investigating the Impact of COVID-19

From March 11, 2020, when the Romanian government started its fundamental steps to combat another strain of Coronavirus, until April 30, 2021, the most current information available for the broken down variables, a total of 416 days passed. To examine the impact of COVID-19 on the financial exchange, it uses the BET file, Romania's standard capital market file.

With the onset of the health emergency and, starting September 21, 2020, the presence of Romanian investment business sectors in the list of emerging business sectors, as defined by FTSE Russell, the evaluation of this list is vitally significant for Romania's economy as a whole.

The following trial survey approach will be used to achieve the above-indicated objectives: Identifying such linkages between parts, challenging for the unit origin exclusive of and with critical disruptions for the designated components, establishing interactions between the pieces, and determining the model's adequacy Data preparation in the form of charts and unambiguous measure marks is the first step in a quantifiable or economic evaluation that provides a wealth of information for the approval and purging of the informational index, as well as identifiable evidence of needed data changes (Fama & French, 1988).

The ARDL method, on the other hand, prohibits the fusion of second-solicitation or other factors. The first step in guiding a precise evaluation is to determine if the objects being evaluated are fixed. It estimates the use of the Bounds test to determine if a long point of contact between the components is conceivable. There are a few key points to remember about it. These critical elements are induced under a variety of conditions and define a stretch for which the lower limit is treated under the hypothesis, and the upper bound is handled under the hypothesis that all elements. Using critical potential gains provides several advantages. The invalid hypothesis of no cointegration is excused, and the variables are cointegrated, if the estimation is better than or equivalent to the higher bound; if it isn't, the invalid theory of no cointegration cannot be excused, and thus no extended associations can occur; if it is somewhere in the middle, the cointegration test is dubious (Geanakoplos, 2003).

6. COVID-19 Study under BET Index and Influence Variables

The development of the BET rundown from January 1, 2020, to April 30, 2021, matched these changes in Romania's monetary market. Following the crucial COVID-19 shock, the Romanian stock market steadily recovered, as shown by many industrial sectors. In the first seven months of 2020, monetary transactions in the United States and China recovered much more than those in Europe (Hong et al., 2018).

In Romania, ITC estimates included a ban on all development or a complete line suspension in April-May 2020; in July-September 2020, all persons arriving from high-risk zones were restricted; and in October 2020–April 2021, the blacklist was merely applied to appearances from certain locations. For the most part, internal progression barriers were lifted, except from June to October 2020, when no restrictions were imposed. Another aspect that supported business activity was the monetary procedure advance charge change (IR). It also depicts the cost of Brent's rough gasoline over time. The cost of crude oil has a substantial effect on the global economy's overall health (Inclan & Tiao, 1994). The COVID-19 illness slowed money-related development, resulting in lower oil income. WTI (West Texas Intermediate) and Brent Crude oil, two important benchmarks for oil estimation, experienced their lowest prices on April 20 and 21, 2020, respectively, due to lesser interest. Crude gasoline prices had only returned to pre-pandemic levels in February 2021, as financial supporters predicted that the economy would recover much faster with the introduction of the vaccine.

The Purchasing Managers' Index (PMI) in Europe hit a new low in April; in the United States, the PMI fell below 50 in March and hit a new low of 36.1 in April; and in China, the breakdown of the assembling area was not as clear as in Europe or the United States. Except for April, when there was a little decline that had no long-term impact, the PMI in Europe and the United States was over 50 by July 2020 (Ioannidis & Kontonikas, 2008).

It's important to remember that PMI values below 50 indicate a decrease in development, whilst values over 50 indicate an increase in development. The collecting region's result declined dramatically over the months due to the steps needed to prevent the smooth out of the Covid. According to the PMI report, efforts will begin on July 1, 2020, to complete another European and American gathering activity in April 2021, indicating an increase in monetary trade values. The most expressive factor proportions. Using standard deviation, it determined how much inconstancy there was in the audit series and how specialist the mean was. Marker for Purchasing Managers to guide their investigation, the engineers used EViews 10 programming.

7. PMI Use in Different Countries

The BET record has a significant impact on the National Bank of Romania's (NBR) cash-related plan (outstandingly oppositely correlated, but not unambiguously – 0.7), as well as the advance cost for monetary technique, as evidenced by the data. Additional research reveals that the BET record is clearly and definitively linked to monetary activities in Europe and the United States (PMI), but not to the PMI in China, as assessed by the purchasing managers' list (PMI) (Liu & Zidek, 1997). The monetary actions in Europe and the United States are quite encouraging, while the financial activities in China are very quiet (under 0.5). The global monetary situation, which is influenced by the price of oil, has a significant impact on the BET record. To summarize, the implications of simultaneous changes in European internal and international monetary circumstances should be obvious in the new BET document creation.

A 5 % significance edge was expected to detect cointegration links between the elements in each of the models studied. It uses a slip-up change model to handle the very long associations, similar to the ARDL models (ECM). The ECTt1 and interesting test readings for each model. The long-run coefficient measurements are also shown (Liu & Lee, 2020).

8. The Negative Impact of Pandemic Factors on BET Mobility

A negative association between monetary methodology advance expenditures and the BET was also discovered, indicating that the National Bank of Romania's slowing down had a substantial effect on the BET. In terms of the global environment, raw petrol had a varied impact on BET in each subperiod: positive before Romania joined the assistant emerging monetary regions, and negative after that. For both sub-periods, the Purchasing Managers' Indices in Europe and China continued positive and negative, while the influence in the United States shifted from negative to positive.

These beliefs, are categorically negative and miss the target when it comes to what one should do in concrete terms. In Romania, there are four remedies for BET deviations from the set forth plan: 19.3%, 11.8%, 37.5%, and 10.5% (Mallikarjuna & Rao, 2019). A brief demonstration suggests that factors employed to address the global scene and government-initiated adjustments had a substantial impact on BET's current behavior. The entire influence of each mutable on the contingent mutable is calculated using the number of basic coefficients to the pants.

The link between the BET list and the cost of crude oil in two sub-time periods examined by professionals and experts confirms the contradictions found in the extensive investigation into this highly intricate topic. There are a variety of outcomes that may be derived from the data, ranging from whether or not there is a strong connection to whether or not there is none at all. The M1a model discovered a transient negative linked relationship between the BET record and crude oil costs when Romanian capital business areas went through modernization and change to become an appropriate hypothesis focus on. As raw petrol costs rise, stock valuations fall; as oil costs fall, stock valuations rise. According to the M2a model, the cost of natural oil influences the BET record, implying that growth in the cost of crude oil would result in a rise in the monetary trade (McMillan & Speight, 2004).

There is a strong link between general society or the general monetary foundation and protections markets. The majority of the time, the protective markets are seen to reflect the final consequences of monetary development. For each of the investigated historical periods, as well as for each country and region separately, PMI elements were discovered to have a changing method and relevance in the BET record. This means that, in terms of M1a model outcomes, the European PMI had a destructive effect on the BET record in the main sub-period, decisively affected in the US, and insignificantly impacted not China. Even though Europe's PMI continued destructive, China's PMI had a definite influence in the second sub-time frame, whereas the United States' PMI had a negative impact, as evidenced by the M2a model results.

9. Conclusion

The COVID-19 pandemic, which seems to be the most recent and severe outbreak, has influenced the financial and commercial sectors. To do so, the audit considers three types of variables: pandemic factors (the number of novel cases and demises as a result of Covid), public-area factors (internal improvement restrictions, international travel restrictions, and budgetary plan measures), and var factors (the BET document) to assess the pandemic's impact on Romania's protections trade.

Romania's entry into the category of fast-expanding financial industries was a watershed moment in the Romanian economy (i.e., the hour of 11 March 2020–28 October 2020 and 29 October 2020–30 April 2021). As a result, monetary allies have a higher level of trust in the capital market, making it easier for Romanian organizations to raise funds. Before the result of October 2020, a fundamental breakdown in the BET's trajectory was founded, after that, it began to increase with a rapid as well as well-defined trend. This stage depicted the BET record's ideal progress in terms of the BSE being a growing business sector. Furthermore, the data revealed that the European financial concept had an impact on the BET record. There are now EU initiatives in place to assist the Member States with pandemic crisis response and recovery efforts. These EU initiatives back up this valuable point of view.

According to the ARDL Bounds test findings, the analyzed variables have long stretch associations. The trial examination's findings supported the exploratory hypothesis. A negative impact of pandemic conditions on long-term outcomes has been confirmed for both sub-periods. H1 and H2 are two sub-hypotheses that support the likelihood that government arrangements influence the BET record. Transient effects of adaptation restrictions on BET have also been confirmed, but only because of the overall impact of these restrictions on the economy. The National Bank of Romania's decision to reduce the financing cost from 2.5%

in March 2020 to 1.25% in April 2021 was proven correct, confirming the H2b estimate on the effect of decreased loaning costs on the BET list. Furthermore, both the impact of crude oil esteem (sub-hypothesis H3a) and the Purchasing Managers' Index (sub-hypothesis H3b) were seen as clear applications of hypothesis H3 (sub-theory H3b). the findings are consistent with such disclosures, as shown by other studies. Pandemic causes and movability barriers hurt the Romanian protective trade, while the cash-linked methodological advance expenditure had a beneficial impact. ARDL Bound cointegration and the effects of the COVID-19 epidemic on the Romanian stock market over 15 months are two of our promises to the field's writing (i.e., the impact of the COVID-19 epidemic on the Romanian protections trade). The findings might also help public health officials manage COVID-19 disease prevention programmed more effectively. The audit's primary flaw is that it does not focus on Romanian setting research. The COVID-19 pandemic report should be expanded to involve more European states concerned by the outbreak as well as compared to see how each country dealt with this difficult test. Furthermore, a variety of verifiable and money-related systems, including those based on the needs of several countries, may be used (e.g., dynamic board showing). Another flaw in the analysis is that important monetary aspects (such as extension, system fragility, and monetary measures) were missed.

References

Ashley, R. A., & Patterson, D. M. (2010). A Test of the GARCH (1, 1) Specification for Daily Stock Returns. *Macroeconomic Dynamics*, *14*(S1), 137–144.

Ashraf, B. N. (2020). Stock Markets' Reaction to COVID-19: Cases or Fatalities?. *Research in International Business and Finance*, *54*, 101249.

Bai, J., & Perron, P. (1998). Estimating and Testing Linear Models with Multiple Structural Changes. *Econometrica*, 47–78.

Bogousslavsky, V. (2016). Infrequent Rebalancing, Return Autocorrelation, and Seasonality. *The Journal of Finance*, *71*(6), 2967–3006.

Brown, R. L., Durbin, J., & Evans, J. M. (1975). Techniques for Testing the Constancy of Regression Relationships Over Time. *Journal of the Royal Statistical Society: Series B (Methodological)*, *37*(2), 149–163.

Campbell, J. Y. (1987). Stock Returns and the Term Structure. *Journal of Financial Economics*, *18*(2), 373–399.

Fama, E. F., & French, K. R. (1988). Dividend Yields and Expected Stock Returns. *Journal of Financial Economics*, *22*(1), 3–25.

Geanakoplos, J. (2003). January. Liquidity, Default, and Crashes. In *Advances in Economics and Econometrics: Theory and Applications: Eighth World Congress*.

Hong, H., Chen, N., O'Brien, F., & Ryan, J. (2018). Stock Return Predictability and Model Instability: Evidence from Mainland China and Hong Kong. *The Quarterly Review of Economics and Finance, 68*, 132–142.

Inclan, C., & Tiao, G. C. (1994). Use of Cumulative Sums of Squares for Retrospective Detection of Changes of Variance. *Journal of the American Statistical Association, 89*(427), 913–923.

Ioannidis, C., & Kontonikas, A. (2008). The Impact of Monetary Policy on Stock Prices. *Journal of Policy Modeling, 30*(1), 33–53.

Liu, J., Wu, S., & Zidek, J. V. (1997). On Segmented Multivariate Regression. *Statistica Sinica*, 497–525.

Liu, M., Choo, W. C., & Lee, C. C. (2020). The Response of the Stock Market to the Announcement of Global Pandemic. *Emerging Markets Finance and Trade, 56*(15), 3562–3577.

Mallikarjuna, M., & Rao, R. P. (2019). Evaluation of Forecasting Methods from Selected Stock Market Returns. *Financial Innovation, 5*(1), 1–16.

McMillan, D. G., & Speight, A. E. (2004). Daily Volatility Forecasts: Reassessing the Performance of GARCH Models. *Journal of Forecasting, 23*(6), 449–460.

Constantinos Challoumis

Rewarding Taxes on the Cycle of Money

1. Introduction

This analyzes the case of the cycle of money with all and without all the impact factors of the rewarding taxes. Then, in this scrutiny in one case, the impact factor of the rest rewarding taxes is and in the other case is avoided. Thence, using the Q.E. method extracted conclusions about the importance of this impact factor in the economy (Baker et al., 2020; Castaño et al., 2016; Cruce & Quinn, 2019; de Vasconcelos et al., 2019; Jensen, 2020; Lal et al., 2018; Moreno-Jiménez et al., 2014; Olcina et al., 2020; Tvaronavičienė et al., 2018; Van de Vijver et al., 2020). Moreover, this impact factor is about the administration of the public sector to the private sector and the returns of taxes to the market.

Contracts and agreements between participants in control transactions determine the allocation of profits and losses. Contract changes should be mentioned in the agreements. This is why tax authorities should conduct periodic inspections (Deng & Li, 2011; Dollery & Worthington, 1996; Jia et al., 2020; Kananen, 2012; Ng, 2018; Saraiva et al., 2020; "The East Asian Miracle: Economic Growth and Public Policy," 1994; Turner, 2010). Contracts must be specified regularly to be comparable. The arm's length principle requires periodic inspections of companies that participate in controlled transactions (Abate et al., 2020; Gilens & Page, 2014; Lucchese & Pianta, 2020; Martin & Freeland, 2021; Schram, 2018; Syukur, 2020). The cost-sharing is then determined based on a periodic check of companies that are tested parties. The scope of controlled transaction companies is to face issues related to the taxation of their activities. As a result, the requirements for companies conducting controlled transactions with tax authorities should fall within the scope of the arm's length principle (Berg et al., 2020; Challoumis, 2020a; "Crisis, Institutional Innovation and Change Management: Thoughts from the Greek Case," 2019; Kominers et al., 2017; Olcina et al., 2020; Rashid et al., 2020; Siegmeier et al., 2018). As a result, the appropriate agreement for controlled transaction companies allows them to maximize profits in tax environments with low tax rates while minimizing costs in tax environments with high tax rates.

2. Literature Review

The tax revenues correspond to the savings that the companies could have if the taxes were avoided. The way that these savings are administrated is different from case to case. Then the benefits of the companies could be managed in a completely different way, as could be saved or could be taxed. The theory of the cycle of money shows when the savings robust the economy and when the taxes robust the economy but. It is crucial for this determination to be a separation of savings into the non-returned savings (or escaped savings) and the returned savings (or enforcement savings). For the scope of this analysis below are demonstrated the equations:

$$\alpha = \alpha_s + \alpha_t \ \text{ or } \ \frac{1}{v} + \alpha_t \tag{1}$$

$$x_m = m - a \tag{2}$$

$$m = \mu + \alpha_p \tag{3}$$

$$\mu = \sum_{t=0}^{n} \mu_t \tag{4}$$

$$\alpha_p = \sum_{j=0}^{m} \alpha_{pj} \tag{5}$$

$$c_m = \frac{dx_m}{dm} \tag{6}$$

$$c_\alpha = \frac{dx_m}{da} \tag{7}$$

$$c_y = c_m - c_\alpha \tag{8}$$

The variable of α symbolizes the case of the escaped savings. This means that there are savings that are not returned to the economy or come back after a long-term period (Challoumis, 2018c, 2020b, 2021e, 2022b, 2022c, 2023e, 2023c, 2023d, 2021d, 2021a, 2021c, 2021f, 2021i, 2021g, 2021b, 2021h, 2022b, 2022c, 2023c, 2023d, 2023e). The variable of α_s symbolizes the case that there are escaped savings which come from transfer pricing activities. The variable of α_t it symbolizes the case that there are escaped savings not from transfer pricing activities but from any other commercial activity. For instance, α_t could refer to the commercial activities that come from uncontrolled transactions. The variable of m symbolizes the financial liquidity in an economy. The variable of μ symbolizes the consumption in an economy. The variable of α_p symbolizes the enforcement savings, which come from the citizens and from small and medium sized enterprises. The variable of x_m symbolizes the condition of financial liquidity in an economy. The variable of c_m symbolizes the velocity of financial liquidity increases or decreases. The variable of c_α symbolizes the velocity of escaped savings. Therefore, the variable of c_y symbolizes the term of the cycle of money. Thereupon, the cycle of money shows the level of the dynamic of an economy and its robustness.

The rewarding taxes are the only taxes which have an immediate and important role in the market of any economy (Challoumis, 2018a, 2018b, 2019a, 2019b, 2020b, 2021i, 2021c, 2022a, 2023h, 2023g, 2023b, 2023a, 2023 f, 2023d). These factors are affiliated with education, with the health system of each society, and with the rest relevant structural economic factors of the prior two impact factors. This issue is illustrated in the next scheme:

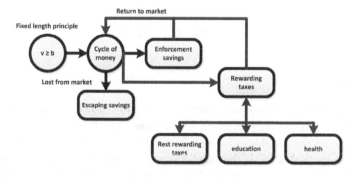

Figure 1. The cycle of money with rewarding taxes (Author's scheme)

In the previous figure, there is the case that the tax system includes all the tax factors and all the rewarding tax factors. In the next scheme there is an absence of one rewarding factor which is the impact factor of rest rewarding impact factors:

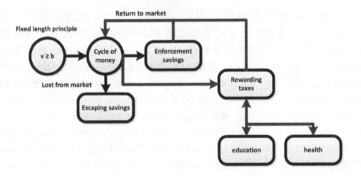

Figure 2. The cycle of money with rewarding taxes except from the impact factor of rest rewarding taxes (Author's scheme)

It is concluded from the previous scheme that in this case all rewarding impact factors are there except the impact factor of the rest rewarding taxes. Therefore, it can proceed to mathematical and quantity analysis of the cycle of money in the case of rewarding taxes.

3. The Cycle of Money with and Without the Impact Factor of the Rest Rewarding Taxes

For the mathematical approach to the cycle of money:

$$\alpha_p = \alpha_r + \alpha_n * h_n + \alpha_m * h_m \tag{9}$$

$$\alpha_r \geq \alpha_n * h_n \geq \alpha_m * h_m \tag{10}$$

In the prior two equations used some impact factors, which are the a_p which is also demonstrated in the previous equation, moreover the variables α_r, α_n, h_n, α_m and the h_m. The variable α_r symbolizes the impact factor of the rest rewarding taxes. The symbol of α_n is the impact factor of education and any technical knowledge. The symbol of α_m is about the impact factor of health anything relevant and supporting of this issue. The symbol of h_n, and of the h_m, are the coefficients of the education and the health impact factor accordingly:

Table 1. Compiling coefficients (Author's data)

Factors	Values	Values
α_s	0.6	0.6
α_t	0.7	0.7
μ	0.9	0.9
α_r	0.4	-
$\alpha_n.h_n$	0.3	0.3
$\alpha_m.h_m$	0.2	0.2

The generator of this procedure used the coefficients which appeared in the previous table. Therefore, the factors have an upper limit of 1, and a lower limit of 0, but s and $\tilde{s}$ are plausible to receive values greater than one as their mathematical structure allows this. After 461 iterations the following diagram:

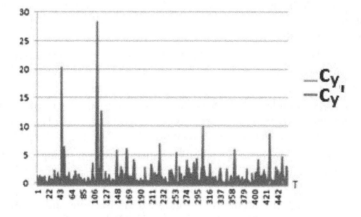

Figure 3. Comparison of the cycle of money with and without the impact factor of the rest rewarding taxes (Author's scheme)

In the previous scheme, it was revealed that the impact factor of rest rewarding taxes has an impact on the cycle of money. An economy with structural problems in the supporting settings of education and health diminishes its economic dynamic. This means that these taxes belong to the supportive taxes for the economy. Therefore the economy has low bureaucracy (supportive and

not extended) and the public administration effectively returns the taxes to the
market.

4. Conclusions

It is concluded that the supportive administration of the public sector to the
private sector enforces the economy as was expected. Then the impact factor
of the rest rewarding taxes describes this situation. The effective and low
bureaucracy public sector supports the market and the economic dynamic of
any economic environment.

References

Abate, M., Christidis, P., & Purwanto, A. J. (2020). Government Support to
Airlines in the Aftermath of the COVID-19 Pandemic. *Journal of Air Transport
Management*, 89. https://doi.org/10.1016/j.jairtraman.2020.101931

Baker, S. D., Hollifield, B., & Osambela, E. (2020). Preventing Controversial
Catastrophes. *Review of Asset Pricing Studies*, *10*(1). https://doi.org/10.1093/
RAPSTU/RAZ001

Berg, A., Markey-Towler, B., & Novak, M. (2020). Blockchains: Less Government,
More Market. *Journal of Private Enterprise*, *35*(2). https://doi.org/10.2139/
ssrn.3301714

Castaño, M. S., Méndez, M. T., & Galindo, M. Á. (2016). The Effect of Public
Policies on Entrepreneurial Activity and Economic Growth. *Journal of
Business Research*, *69*(11). https://doi.org/10.1016/j.jbusres.2016.04.125

Challoumis, C. (2018a). Analysis of the Velocities of Escaped Savings with that of
Financial Liquidity. *Ekonomski Signali*, *13*(2), 1–14. https://doi.org/10.5937/
ekonsig1802001c

Challoumis, C. (2018b). Methods of Controlled Transactions and the Behavior
of Companies According to the Public and Tax Policy. In *Economics* (Vol. 6,
Issue 1). https://doi.org/10.2478/eoik-2018-0003

Challoumis, C. (2018c). The Impact Factor of Health on the Economy Using the
Cycle of Money. *Bulletin of the Transilvania University of Brașov*, *11*(60), 125–
136. https://webbut.unitbv.ro/index.php/Series_V/article/view/2533/1979

Challoumis, C. (2019a). The Cycle of Money with and without the Escaped
Savings. *Ekonomski Signali*, *14*(1), 89–99. https://doi.org/336.76 336.741.236.5

Challoumis, C. (2019b). The R.B.Q. (Rational, Behavioral and Quantified)
Model. *Ekonomika*, *98*(1). https://doi.org/10.15388/ekon.2019.1.1

Challoumis, C. (2020a). Analysis of the Theory of Cycle of Money. *Acta Universitatis Bohemiae Meridionalis*, *23*(2), 13–29. https://doi.org/https://doi.org/10.2478/acta-2020-0004

Challoumis, C. (2020b). The Impact Factor of Costs to the Tax System. *Journal of Entrepreneurship, Business and Economics*, *8*(1), 1–14. http://scientificia.com/index.php/JEBE/article/view/126

Challoumis, C. (2021a). Index of the Cycle of Money – The Case of Belarus. *Economy and Banks*, *2*.

Challoumis, C. (2021b). Index of the Cycle of Money – The Case of Greece. *IJBESAR (International Journal of Business and Economic Sciences Applied Research)*, *14*(2), 58–67.

Challoumis, C. (2021c). Index of the Cycle of Money – The Case of Latvia. *Economics and Culture*, *17*(2), 5–12. https://doi.org/10.2478/jec-2020-0015

Challoumis, C. (2021d). Index of the Cycle of Money – The Case of Montenegro. *Montenegrin Journal for Social Sciences*, *5*(1–2), 41–57.

Challoumis, C. (2021e). Index of the Cycle of Money – The Case of Serbia. *Open Journal for Research in Economics (OJRE)*, *4*(1). https://centerprode.com/ojre.html

Challoumis, C. (2021f). Index of the Cycle of Money – The Case of Slovakia. *STUDIA COMMERCIALIA BRATISLAVENSIA Ekonomická Univerzita v Bratislave*, *14*(49), 176–188.

Challoumis, C. (2021g). Index of the Cycle of Money – The Case of Thailand. *Chiang Mai University Journal of Economics*, *25*(2), 1–14. https://so01.tci-thaijo.org/index.php/CMJE/article/view/247774/169340

Challoumis, C. (2021h). Index of the Cycle of Money – The Case of Ukraine. *Actual Problems of Economics*, *243*(9), 102–111. https://doi.org/10.32752/1993-6788-2021-1-243-244-102-111

Challoumis, C. (2021i). Index of the Cycle of Money – The Case of Bulgaria. *Economic Alternatives*, *27*(2), 225–234. https://www.unwe.bg/doi/eajournal/2021.2/EA.2021.2.04.pdf

Challoumis, C. (2022a). Conditions of the CM (Cycle of Money). In *Social and Economic Studies within the Framework of Emerging Global Developments, Volume -1*, V. Kaya (pp. 13–24).

Challoumis, C. (2022b). Index of the Cycle of Money – The Case of Moldova. *Eastern European Journal of Regional Economics*, *8*(1), 77–89.

Challoumis, C. (2022c). Index of the Cycle of Money – The Case of Poland. *Research Papers in Economics and Finance*, *6*(1), 72–86. https://journals.ue.poznan.pl/REF/article/view/126/83

Challoumis, C. (2023a). A Comparison of the Velocities of Minimum Escaped Savings and Financial Liquidity. In *Social and Economic Studies Within the Framework of Emerging Global Developments, Volume - 4, V. Kaya.*

Challoumis, C. (2023b). Impact Factor of Liability of Tax System According to the Theory of Cycle of Money. In *Social and Economic Studies within the Framework of Emerging Global Developments Volume 3, V. Kaya* (Vol. 3).

Challoumis, C. (2023c). Index of the Cycle of Money: The Case of Costa Rica. *Sapienza, 4*(3), 1–11. https://journals.sapienzaeditorial.com/index.php/SIJIS

Challoumis, C. (2023d). Index of the Cycle of Money – The Case of Canada. *Journal of Entrepreneurship, Business and Economics, 11*(1), 102–133. http://scientificia.com/index.php/JEBE/article/view/203

Challoumis, C. (2023e). Index of the Cycle of Money – The Case of England. *British Journal of Humanities and Social Sciences, 26*(1), 68–77.

Challoumis, C. (2023f). The Impact Factor of Tangibles and Intangibles of Controlled Transactions on Economic Performance. *Economic Alternatives, 29*(3).

Challoumis, C. (2023g). Utility of Cycle of Money with and without the Enforcement Savings. *Gospodarka i Innowacje, 36*(1), 269–277.

Challoumis, C. (2023h). Utility of Cycle of Money without the Escaping Savings (Protection of the Economy). In *Social and Economic Studies within the Framework of Emerging Global Developments Volume 2, V. Kaya.*

Crisis, Institutional Innovation and Change Management: Thoughts from the Greek Case. (2019). *Journal of Economics and Political Economy, 6*(1). https://doi.org/10.1453/jepe.v6i1.1854

Cruce, J. R., & Quinn, J. C. (2019). Economic Viability of Multiple Algal Biorefining Pathways and the Impact of Public Policies. *Applied Energy, 233–234.* https://doi.org/10.1016/j.apenergy.2018.10.046

de Vasconcelos, F. de A. G., Machado, M. L., de Medeiros, M. A. T., Neves, J. A., Recine, E., & Pasquim, E. M. (2019). Public Policies of Food and Nutrition in Brazil: From Lula to Temer. *Revista de Nutricao, 32.* https://doi.org/10.1590/1678-9865201932e180161

Deng, Y., & Li, H. (2011). Retracted Article: Measures of Public Economic Policy under the Financial Crisis in China. In *2011 International Conference on E-Business and E-Government, ICEE2011 – Proceedings.* https://doi.org/10.1109/ICEBEG.2011.5877027

Dollery, B. E., & Worthington, A. C. (1996). The Evaluation of Public Policy: Normative Economic Theories of Government Failure. *Journal of Interdisciplinary Economics, 7*(1). https://doi.org/10.1177/02601079x9600700103

Gilens, M., & Page, B. I. (2014). Testing Theories of American Politics: Elites, Interest Groups, and Average Citizens. *Perspectives on Politics, 12*(3). https://doi.org/10.1017/S1537592714001595

Jensen, P. H. (2020). Experiments and Evaluation of Public Policies: Methods, Implementation, and Challenges. *Australian Journal of Public Administration, 79*(2). https://doi.org/10.1111/1467-8500.12406

Jia, M., Liu, Y., Lieske, S. N., & Chen, T. (2020). Public Policy Change and Its Impact on Urban Expansion: An Evaluation of 265 Cities in China. *Land Use Policy, 97*. https://doi.org/10.1016/j.landusepol.2020.104754

Kananen, J. (2012). International Ideas Versus National Traditions: Nordic Economic and Public Policy as Proposed by the OECD. *Journal of Political Power, 5*(3). https://doi.org/10.1080/2158379X.2012.735118

Kominers, S. D., Teytelboym, A., & Crawford, V. P. (2017). An Invitation to Market Design. *Oxford Review of Economic Policy, 33*(4). https://doi.org/10.1093/oxrep/grx063

Lal, A., Moodie, M., Peeters, A., & Carter, R. (2018). Inclusion of Equity in Economic Analyses of Public Health Policies: Systematic Review and Future Directions. In *Australian and New Zealand Journal of Public Health* (Vol. 42, Issue 2). https://doi.org/10.1111/1753-6405.12709

Lucchese, M., & Pianta, M. (2020). The Coming Coronavirus Crisis: What Can We Learn? *Intereconomics, 55*(2). https://doi.org/10.1007/s10272-020-0878-0

Martin, A. S., & Freeland, S. (2021). The Advent of Artificial Intelligence in Space Activities: New Legal Challenges. *Space Policy, 55*. https://doi.org/10.1016/j.spacepol.2020.101408

Moreno-Jiménez, J. M., Pérez-Espés, C., & Velázquez, M. (2014). E-Cognocracy and the Design of Public Policies. *Government Information Quarterly, 31*(1). https://doi.org/10.1016/j.giq.2013.09.004

Ng, Y. K. (2018). Ten rules for Public Economic Policy. *Economic Analysis and Policy, 58*. https://doi.org/10.1016/j.eap. 2018.01.002

Olcina, G., Tur, E. M., & Escriche, L. (2020). Cultural Transmission and Persistence of Entrepreneurship. *Small Business Economics, 54*(1). https://doi.org/10.1007/s11187-018-0089-2

Rashid, H., Warsame, H., & Khan, S. (2020). The Differential Impact of Democracy on Tax Revenues in Developing and Developed Countries. *International Journal of Public Administration*. https://doi.org/10.1080/01900 692.2020.1741616

Saraiva, M. B., Ferreira, M. D. P., da Cunha, D. A., Daniel, L. P., Homma, A. K. O., & Pires, G. F. (2020). Forest Regeneration in the Brazilian Amazon: Public

Policies and Economic Conditions. *Journal of Cleaner Production, 269*. https:// doi.org/10.1016/j.jclepro.2020.122424

Schram, A. (2018). When Evidence Isn't Enough: Ideological, Institutional, and Interest-Based Constraints on Achieving Trade and Health Policy Coherence. *Global Social Policy, 18*(1). https://doi.org/10.1177/1468018117744153

Siegmeier, J., Mattauch, L., Franks, M., Klenert, D., Schultes, A., & Edenhofer, O. (2018). The Fiscal Benefits of Stringent Climate Change Mitigation: An Overview. *Climate Policy, 18*(3). https://doi.org/10.1080/ 14693062.2017.1400943

Syukur, M. (2020). Insentif Pajak terhadap Sumbangan Covid-19 dari Perspektif Relasi Hukum Pajak Indonesia dengan Hak Asasi Manusia. *Jurnal Suara Hukum, 2*(2). https://doi.org/10.26740/jsh.v2n2.p184-214

The East Asian Miracle: Economic Growth and Public Policy. (1994). *Choice Reviews Online, 32*(02). https://doi.org/10.5860/choice.32-1052

Turner, A. (2010). The Crisis, Conventional Economic Wisdom, and Public Policy. *Industrial and Corporate Change, 19*(5). https://doi.org/10.1093/icc/ dtq042

Tvaronavičienė, M., Tarkhanova, E., & Durglishvili, N. (2018). Sustainable Economic Growth and Innovative Development of Educational Systems. *Journal of International Studies, 11*(1). https://doi.org/10.14254/2071-8330.2018/11-1/19

Van de Vijver, A., Cassimon, D., & Engelen, P. J. (2020). A Real Option Approach to Sustainable Corporate Tax Behavior. *Sustainability (Switzerland), 12*(13). https://doi.org/10.3390/su12135406

Theoharis Spyropoulos, Christos Andras, Michalis Dritsas and
Persefoni Polychronidou

Founder's Perceptions Analysis Using Graph Theory and Mutual Information-A Comparison before and after COVID-19 in Greek Start-Ups

1. Introduction

Entrepreneurship studies based on quantitative analysis are dominated by statistical analysis and more specifically, dominated by correlation-based analysis. Correlation indeed identifies linear relationships between variables within a given dataset. However recent research suggests use of other mathematic tools in quantitative analysis, such as Mutual Information and Graph (Network) Theory. Mutual Information (a mathematical concept based on probabilistic analysis and Entropy Theory) can be used to reveal non-linear relationships between variables, by providing a degree of estimated value of one variable if another variable is known; Graph Theory enables the study of connections between variables and/or specific values.

Both concepts have been recently used in financial and economic studies, while recent studies (Spyropoulos et al., 2023 (in press); Spyropoulos et al., 2022, 2021) used these tools on entrepreneurial research, concluding that these mathematical tools provide additional insights.

Another interested approach of the present research is that it examines different groups within the same dataset, and more specifically the perceptions of Start-Up founders categorized according to their level of their perceived success; more specifically it examines whether a start-up founder who consider himself more successful behaves differently or makes different choices than a less successful one.

The present study attempts a comparison on the Perceptions of IT Start-Up founders in Greece between 2018 and 2023. There are many reasons for justifying the need to monitor and assess possible views of Start-Up founders during this period.

First of all, there is a time period of 5 years; during this time many of the Start-ups had the opportunity to grow as more mature business, or fail, or still struggle for survival, therefore key perceptions (challenges, competition, competitive advantage).

A second reason is the global effects of Covid-19 pandemic and its effects on business and the economy. During the pandemic tremendous changes took place on a global scale. These changes had a major impact on the economy since it created a new business environment – solutions for automation, touchless transactions, e-transactions and e-processes were introduced rapidly and both business and consumers responded very positive to such changes.

The new government formed in July 2019 made an attempt to reduce the gap between the "business friendly" economies within EU and Greece; this included an effort to create a much more friendly ecosystem for start-ups.

In addition, the global political and business environment changed drastically. "The war, the rise of interest rates, and the high inflation worldwide; the global public market's disappointing performance (at the time of writing, Nasdaq is at -30 % YTD); many socioeconomic indicators and data points suggest that we are experiencing a preamble of a new recession." (Start-Ups in Greece, Venture Financing Report 2022–2023, Foundation / EIT Digital, Foundation Innovation Reports 2022, p. 4)

Since 2018, The Equifund funding mechanism changed drastically the landscape of Greek Start-Up Ecosystem. More specifically, "more than 138 companies have been supported by the initiative in total, and have received their share of funding whether it is Pre-Seed, Seed, or Series A+. It is estimated that these companies as a whole employ more than 6.000 people in Greece and the total amount allocated to these companies has reached more than 350 million euros" (Start-Ups in Greece, Venture Financing Report 2022–2023, Foundation / EIT Digital, Foundation Innovation Reports 2022, p. 4). From this respect the Greek Start Up Ecosystem of 2023 is very much different from the one described in 2019 (Spyropoulos, 2019)

2. Literature Review

Extensive Literature review regarding the key factors that determine success and failure of start-ups has been examined in past studies as summarized by Spyropoulos et al. (2023), Yadav (2015), Santisteban et al. (2017), Roy (2019), Roberts et al. (2015), Gregori et al. (2019), Aulet (2013). In addition, the Scale Up Report 2023 (Start Up Genome 2023) examines the effect of several variables for entrepreneurial success, such as Founders Number, Age, Experience, Gender, Education, Business Model Innovation, International Sales and key Achievements, Competitive Advantage, Disruptive Innovation, Funding, Strategic Alliances.

Previous research also different types of factors that can be determining for new start-up success; these factors can be categorized to personal (Frank et al., 2007), organizational and environmental factors (Elia et al., 2020; Yadav, 2015).

The importance of studying IT start-ups is highlighted by further research; Roberts et al. (2015) highlights the fact that due to a number of technology changes; IT start-ups enable entrepreneurs to start their ventures at a lower cost (e.g., using APIs to connect with other existing systems), which also increases positive network effects and enables entrepreneurs to start their business ventures at a younger age and Nambisan (2017), who also refers to the easiness to create (and scale) digital start-ups, which may have a significant impact to the economic ecosystems. However, research also indicates from a strategic view the complexity and difficulty in order for newly established IT start-ups to integrate with other companies across their business ecosystems (Garcia et al., 2023)

Recent research (Bermana et al., 2023) reviewed a number of factors, both regarding the entrepreneur (personal) and the company (organizational) that play a critical role on success and/or failure of a business venture.

3. Methodology

In both 2018 and 2023 research projects the same questionnaire was used for data collection, and the questionnaires were distributed to the same population (Greek IT start-up Founders) which provided the data unanimously. Even though the population is the same, there are considerable changes – first of all there was a difference in the number of responders and of course many of the companies evolved during this period as mentioned above. The data collection used the same approach in both cases; questionnaires were distributed, to the founders of Start-Up companies. More specifically 94 responses were collected on 2018 research and 45 responses were collected on 2023 research, from Greek Start Up Founders of the I.T. sector.

The data were analyzed using Mutual Information Ratio (Entropy based) and Graph Theory with the use of R software. Both datasets (2018 and 2023) were analyzed as a whole and then split to 4 different categories, according to the perceived level of Success, where each of the 4 levels represent a different level of success (as perceived by the founders) with Level 1 representing the lower level of success (we are far from success), Level 2 (we will know within a year), Level 3 (we are on the right path) and Level 4 (definitely yes), representing the higher level of success.

For the Graph Theory analysis, the 4 networks were created in a tree format, with each tree representing one of the Success Levels (1–4) and knots were created corresponding to the values of the variables examined, while the edges represented the connections to the knots for each entrepreneur who stated the specific success Level.

4. Descriptive Statistics

The critical changes between the 2018 and the 2023 business environment for IT Start Up founder's perceptions and reality became evident from descriptive statistics. More specifically, descriptive results are presented on Table 1 below:

Table 1. Descriptive results

Variables	2018 Data				2023 Data			
Age	18–28 years old	29–35 years old	36–45 years old	46+	18–28 years old	29–35 years old	36–45 years old	46+
Age%	36 %	31 %	28 %	5 %	11 %	13 %	40 %	36 %
Education	Secondary	Bachelor	Master	Ph.D.	Secondary	Bachelor	Master	Ph.D.
Education%	5 %	47 %	36 %	12 %	9 %	31 %	42 %	18 %
Founders	1	2	3	4+	1	2	3	4+
Founders%	35 %	32 %	34 %	9 %	24 %	40 %	18 %	18 %
Success	1	2	3	4	1	2	3	4
Success%	16 %	25 %	46 %	13 %	11 %	18 %	53 %	18 %
Employee Experience	Up to 1 year	Up to 2 years	Up to 5 years	6 years or more	Up to 1 year	Up to 2 years	Up to 5 years	6 years or more
Employee Experience%	17 %	14 %	27 %	42 %	27 %	4 %	13 %	56 %
Entrepreneurial Experience	0 companies	1 company	2 companies	3+ companies	0 companies	1 company	2 companies	3+ companies
Entrepreneurial Experience%	66 %	27 %	2 %	5 %	67 %	22 %	7 %	4 %
Reasons	Business Opportunity	Technology Breakthrough	Business Model Innovation	Process Innovation	Business Opportunity	Technology Breakthrough	Business Model Innovation	Process Innovation
Reasons%	37 %	24 %	20 %	19 %	49 %	24 %	16 %	11 %

Just by comparing the descriptive data, we observe that founders are, in general, of older age, better educated, larger founding teams, more successful, having more experience as employees before starting their start-ups, depend to a larger degree on the identification of business opportunities and have a similar relationship to serial entrepreneurship (with a small increase from 7 % to 11 % for serial entrepreneurs)

5. Mutual Information Analysis

Recent Research (Spyropoulos et al., 2022) used the Mutual Information to study non-linear relationships within the entrepreneurial framework, in an attempt to identify non-linear relationships between entrepreneurial variables. According to related studies, (Batina et al.., 2011, pp. 272–273): "The mutual information is a general measure of the dependence between two random variables. It expresses the quantity of information one has obtained on X by observing Y."

Table 2 below compares the top pairs of variables in terms of Mutual Information values between 2018 and 2023 datasets; as such it provides useful insights regarding which variables are mostly associated with Success in 2018 and 2023 datasets. The first variable is always success, while the second variable are the corresponding variables.

52   Theoharis Spyropoulos et al.

Table 2. Success and top variables of mutual information values – A comparison between 2018 and 2023

	2018 Dataset		2023 Dataset	
Variable 1 – Success	Variable 2	Mutual Information	Variable 2	Mutual Information Value
Success	Operation Years	0.387	Value to end customer	0.58
Success	Pr. Surviving	0.157	No Disruptive	0.5
Success	Previous SU	0.136	Minor Value	0.487
Success	Funding	0.127	Comp. Ad. Other	0.482
Success	Strategic	0.124	Years of Operations	0.479
Success	Age	0.116	Value Not Clear	0.464
Success	Experience	0.115	Competition	0.43
Success	Founders	0.115	No Strategic Partners	0.408
Success	Previous Reasons	0.112	Strategic SpinOff	0.407
Success	Funds 100k	0.097	Full Time Employees	0.377
Success	Unclear	0.076	Comp,Ad, Technology	0.371
Success	Prototype	0.076	No Competition	0.369
Success	Openness	0.062	New Approach Value	0.363
Success	Traditional	0.061	International sales	0.359
Success	Education	0.054	Look for Funding – No	0.358
Success	B2B	0.05	Yes Disruptive	0.322
Success	Sales 100k	0.05	Not Sure If Disruptive	0.32

It becomes clear that in 2023 reveals a very different reality than 2018. The top factors associated to success in 2003 are Value to Customer, No Disruptive Innovation, Minor Value offered to customer, different basis for Competitive Advantage and Years of Operation. This represents a far more mature environment than 2018, where Years of operations and personal achievements (number of companies founded) were associated to success. Furthermore, funding and Strategic Alliances are top ranked for 2018, and while Years of operations is an important factor in 2023, companies do not appear so dependent on further funding on 2023.

As a general comment success in 2023 lays in offering specific value and forming new bases for competitive advantage, offering values in areas than do not represent a critical value for the customer (more focus on niche markets, since basic needs are already served).

Furthermore, by creating the 4 groups based on the level of perceived success, it becomes clear that different variables are associated with a different level of success. E.g., for the most successful companies (Level 4), Competitive Advantage (other: not based Technology, Management, Intellectual Property or Business Model) is mostly associated with (higher) success, while Success Level 3 is strongly associated with value offered to customer. Success Level 2 is closely associated primarily with Years of Operations and for less successful companies their success level (1) is associated with international sales.

Table 3. Mutual information and success levels, 2023 data

Success Level 4		Success level 3		Success Level 2		Success Level 1	
Variable	Mutual Information Values	Variable	Mutual Information Values	Variable	Mutual Information Values	Variable	Mutual Information Values
Comp. Ad. Other	0.508	Value to end customer	0.335	Years of Operations	0.366	International sales	0.408
Minor Value	0.487	Competition	0.293	Work Experience	0.225	Value to end customer	0.316
No Disruptive	0.363	Full Time Employees	0.283	Work Experience as Employee	0.526	Comp.Ad., Technology	0.3
Value to end customer	0.292	Comp. Ad. IP	0.264	Reason Previous Process	0.487	Value Not Clear	0.298
Look for Funding – No	0.205	International sales	0.236	Reason Previous Business Model	0.037	Not Sure If Disruptive	0.2
Look for Funding – Yes	0.188	Success L4	0.191	Previous Start Ups	0.194	Look for Funding – Yes	0.184
Competition	0.163	Strategic Angels	0.183	Pr. Surviving	0.038	Full Time Employees	0.169
International sales	0.145	No Disruptive	0.18	Main Challenge Secure Funding	0.123	Yes Disruptive	0.14
Innov. Improved Product	0.127	New Approach Value	0.157	Main Challenge Other	0.032	Yes Disruptive	0.14

Not Sure If Disruptive	0.115	Yes Disruptive	0.148	Gender	0.106	Competition	0.124
Achievement POC	0.093	Innovation New Approach	0.136	Founders	0.237	Look for Funding – No	0.079
No Strategic Partners	0.086	Success L3	No Competition	Entrepreneurial Education	0,261	Achievement Sales 100k	0.054
Traditional Companies Competition	0.082	Success L3	Value Not Clear	Education	0.116	Yes Disruptive	0.14
Traditional StartUps and disruptive StartUps Competition	0.072	Success L3	Minor Value	Current Reason Technology	0.005	Competition	0.124
Full Time Employees	0.068	Success L3	Comp. Ad. Other	Current Reason Business Opportunity	0.015	Look for Funding – No	0.079

It becomes clear by reviewing the results of Tables 3 that different variables appear to have higher Mutual Information values; therefore, the different levels of success (as perceived by founders and presented to different tables) are associated with different variables as examined within the entrepreneurial process. Based on this analysis we can have some insights on the views and perceptions of the founders of different success perceptions levels.

6. Graph Theory Analysis

Previous research on the fields of Graph / Network Theory (Biggs, 1986; Kenett et al. 2015) highlighted the applications this theory in economic and financial fields. More recent research used Graph / Network Theory in order to examine relationships between the options (variables) available to entrepreneurs (Spyropoulos et al., 2021). Using the 2018 dataset the study examined the four levels of success and the graphs of each group.

Table 4. Key network values for the 2018 dataset

Key Rations	Network Level 1	Network Level 2	Network Level 3	Network Level 4
No of Founders	15	24	43	12
Density	0.4577	0.5446	0.641	0.3884
Number of Connections	1760	2085	2454	1487

The study based on 2018 dataset concluded that the lower density of successful entrepreneurs (Level 4) and lower number of connections indicated that the most successful entrepreneurs tend to have less options available, or tend to have a similar behavior on a number of choices (e.g., education, competitive advantage, number of companies established, basis of competitive advantage, number of members of the founding team), and therefore less diversification and more limited, specific choices was a behavior more common and associated with high success.

Table 5. Key Network values for the 2018 dataset

Key Rations	Network Level 1	Network Level 2	Network Level 3	Network Level 4
No of Founders	5	8	24	8
Density	0.2991	0.4194	0.5198	0.3950
Number of Connections	808	1133	1404	1067

However, Graph Theory reveals a different trend for 2023 dataset; in this case lower density and lower number of connections is associated with founders who are at the lowest success level. The fact remains that high success is associated with the 2nd lower values of density and connections.

One way to interpret this is a significant change in the percentage of each group; while in the 2018 dataset Level 1 founders were 15 against just 12 Level 4 founders, in 2023 dataset the balanced shifted: just 5 Level 1 founders and 8 Level 4 founders, and despite the weighted analysis the fact remains that successful founders may followed more flexible paths on the way to success.

However, in both datasets (2018 and 2023) the middle levels of success (Levels 2 and 3) were associated larger density values, therefore with wider networks of choices (more flexible options and variable values) while the lower density values were characterized with either the highest (Level 4) or the lower (Level 1) levels of success.

7. Conclusions

Our findings reveal a drastic change in the ecosystem between 2018 and 2023, with elements of these changes becoming visible during descriptive statistics. However Mutual Information Analysis provides the ground for additional evidence of the changing conditions. The key variables associated with perceived success changed drastically, and the new top factors address mainly to variables associated with the company (and less with the entrepreneur), been closely associated with the value offered, the nature of the competitive advantage and less associated with attributes of the individual entrepreneur. From this point of view a paradigm shift is noticeable, which can be interpreted as a more mature ecosystem.

Furthermore, by examining different groups of entrepreneurs based on their perception of success, Mutual Information highlights the fact that different Levels of Success are associated with different entrepreneurial variables.

Currently Graph / Network analysis confirm that more flexible strategies and higher differentiations to the values of entrepreneurial variables tend to lead to medium results (Levels 2 and 3) in both cases (2018 and 2023); however more structured behaviors with similar choices and less differentiation may lead to more extreme results (Levels 1 and 4). To this respect there is non conclusive conclusion but rather an indication for further research.

7.1. Limitations and Further Research Recommendation

There are several limitations to the present research, which highlight promising areas for further research. First of all, the sample is rather small, and further data collection may provide more solid insights. Second, the study examines exclusively the I.T. sector, which alongside with healthcare is one of the most financed sectors of Greek Start-Ups (Start-Ups in Greece, 2023 Venture Financing Report). Third, some of the same companies have greatly evolved; between 2018–2023 more than 300 companies received funds of 2.4 billion euros. As a result, a number of 2018 Start-Ups had become successful companies by 2023, and as a result they now face much more different challenges, operate in different ways and have different perceptions regarding their markets and future opportunities.

Furthermore, the results of the Graph/Network analysis offer a great opportunity for further research, by identifying the variables where specific values may have a much stronger association with success or failure, and combing such findings with the findings which associate Mutual Information Values with Success Levels may provide further insights on the importance on each factor for entrepreneurial success.

References

Aulet B. (2013). *Disciplined Entrepreneurship, 24 Steps to a Successful Start Up.* John Wiley & Sons, Inc.

Batina, L., Gierlichs, B., Prouff, E., Rivain, M., Standaert, F. X., & Veyrat-Charvillon, N. (2011). Mutual Information Analysis: A Comprehensive Study. *Journal of Cryptology, 24*(2), 269–291.

Bermana, T., Stucklerb, D., Schallmoc, D., & Sascha, K. (2023). Drivers and Success Factors of Digital Entrepreneurship: A Systematic Literature Review and Future Research Agenda. *Journal of Small Business Management.* https://doi.org/10.1080/00472778.2023.2238791

Biggs, Norman, E. Keith Lloyd, & Robin J. Wilson. (1986). *Graph Theory, 1736–1936.* Oxford University Press.

Elia, G., Margherita, A., & Passiante, G. (2020). Digital Entrepreneurship Ecosystem: How Digital Technologies and Collective Intelligence Are Reshaping the Entrepreneurial Process. *Technological Forecasting and Social Change, 150,* 119791. https://doi.org/10.1016/j.techfore.2019.119791

Frank, H., Lueger, M., & Korunka, C. (2007). The Significance of Personality in Business Start-Up Intentions, Start-up Realization and Business Success. *Entrepreneurship & Regional Development, 19*(3), 227–251. https://doi.org/10.1080/08985620701218387

Garcia Martin, P. C., Sjödin, D., Nair, S., & Parida, V. (2023). Managing Start-Up – Incumbent Digital Solution Co-Creation: A Four-Phase Process for Intermediation in Innovative Contexts. *Industry and Innovation,* 1–27. https://doi.org/10.1080/13662716.2023.2189091

Gregori, P., Wdowiak, M. A., Schwarz, E. J., & Holzmann, P. (2019). Exploring Value Creation in Sustainable Entrepreneurship: Insights from the Institutional Logics Perspective and the Business Model Lens. *Sustainability, 11*(9), 2505. https://doi.org/10.3390u11092505

Kenett, Dror Y., & Shlomo Havlin. (2015). Network Science: A Useful Tool in Economics and Finance. *Mind & Society, 14*(2): 155–167.

Nambisan, S. (2017). Digital Entrepreneurship: Toward a Digital Technology Perspective of Entrepreneurship. *Entrepreneurship Theory and Practice, 41*(6), 1029–1055. https://doi.org/10.1111/etap.12254

Roberts, E. B., Murray, F., & Kim, J. D. (2015). *Entrepreneurship and Innovation at MIT, Continuing Global Growth and Impact.* Martin Trust Center for MIT Entrepreneurship, MIT.

Roy, R. (2019). For Innovations That Have no Precedent in Human History It's Time to Ask Disruptive Questions. *Performance Improvement, 58*(6). https://doi.org/10.1002/pfi.21879

Santisteban, J., & Mauricio, D. (2017). Systematic Literature Review of Critical Success Factors of Information Technology Startups. *Academy of Entrepreneurial Journal, 23*(2), Scale Up Report 2023, Start Up Genome.

Spyropoulos, T. S. (2019). "Start-Up Ecosystems Comparison: MIT and Greece Experiences". Research Papers Collection, *The Małopolska School of Economics in Tarnów Research Papers Collection,* Volume 42, Issue 2, Special Issue: Entrepreneurship Theory & Practice Current Trends and Future Directions, June 2019. https://doi.org/10.25944/znmwse.2019.02.4358. http://zn.mwse.edu.pl/en/wp-content/uploads/2019/11/Zeszyty-Naukowe-Vol.-42-4-2019_EN-druk.pdf

Spyropoulos, T. S. (2020). *Digital Greek Start-Ups – An Analysis of Founder's Perceptions, Advances in Management and Informatics*, Issue 5, 5th Edition, August 2020. Available at: https://figshare.cardiffmet.ac.uk/articles/journal_contribution/Advances_in_Management_and_Informatics_Issue_5_Working_Papers_Journal_/13027697

Spyropoulos, T. S., Andras, C., & Dimkou, A. (2021). Application of Graph Theory on Entrepreneurship Research, EBEEC 2021, The Economies of the Balcan and the Easter European Countries, Pafos, Cyprus May 14–16, 2021, KnE Social Sciences Publications, *The 13th International Research Conference Economies of the Balkan and Eastern European Countries (EBEEC)* held online on the 14th–16th of May 2021.

Spyropoulos, T. S., Andras, C., & Polychronidou, P. (2022). An Analysis of Start-Up Founders Perceptions based on Entropy Ratios – Evidence from the Greek IT Market. *European Research Studies Journal, XXV*(3), 500–516.

Spyropoulos, T. S., Andras, C., Dimkou, A., & Polychronidou, P. (2023). *Using Mutual Information and Information Gain Ratios on Entrepreneurial Research: An Empirical Case for Greek I.T. Start-Ups* (in press)

Start-Ups in Greece, Venture Financing Report 2022–2023. (2022). *Foundation / EIT Digital, Foundation Innovation Reports 2023*, p. 4

Yadav, M. P. (2015). Model of Entrepreneurial Success: A Review and Research Agenda. *Journal of Advanced Academic Research, 2*(1).

Ileana Hamburg and David Sommer

AI and Cyber Security Awarness Training

1. Introduction

Cybersecurity became a significant topic also due to the number and complexity of cyber-attacks on organizations and private persons increased in the last years. Particularly small and medium sized companies (SME) are often the targets of attacks because cybersecurity aware training for both employers and employees as well as security measures are missing. Therefore, SMEs will have to quickly adopt Artificial Intelligence (AI) methods in their infrastructure and improve competencies of their managers and employees to defend themselves effectively and efficiently. Including knowledge about AI into cybersecurity training could help to detect cyber threats like phishing. Phishing attacks are done very often, involves social engineering methods where the attacker sends messages convincing the victim to provide some important information and data. providing his credentials. So it is important that social engineering is a topic of awareness training.

AI is important also for cybersecurity professionals helping them to prepare direct incident response and identify malware attacks like phishing before it is not too late.

AI methods have advantages for company business i.e. to improve operational efficiency, organizational performance, to increase sales volume, minimize the cost, support customer management methods. Collection of advanced data and processing of data can be done more quickly and so time can be saved.

In this paper, first advantages but also requirements of using AI in cybersecurity are explained. Then it is exemplified how AI and Interdisciplinary training could be used for the development and assessment of cybersecurity training particularly for employers and employees from SMEs. Some Training modules like Malware and Attacks, Data Encryption, Social Engineering, Social Networks which have been developed and tested within the European project Interdisciplinary Cyber Training (www.incytproiect.eu) will be redesigned. The prevention of phishing attacks using AI methods will be a new training topic within Social Engineering training module. An introductory training Module about AI is in the development.

2. Cybersecurity Frameworks and Training Strategies

Some Applications of AI Are:

1. Assisted Intelligence, helps to process large amounts of data.
2. Augmented Intelligence, a more sophisticated form of AI enhances human intelligence rather than replacing it. Augmented intelligence can integrate new data with existing information to develop innovative solutions.
3. Autonomous Intelligence is an advanced form of AI that enables systems, computers to operate independently without human intervention.

One of the key benefits for companies by using artificial intelligence in cybersecurity is its procedures to analyse vast amounts of data and to detect patterns that humans can not do. AI systems can be used to monitor networks, detect malicious activities and give an answer in real-time; it reduces the time for detecting threats and finding a response.

The use of Artificial Intelligence (AI) in cybersecurity has been discussed some years ago. It is known that due to human errors, being big risks to a business, some threats are done but not detected. The number and complexity of cyber-attacks increased in the last years and the use of AI can help to identify such threats before it's too late. Hackers and scammers use different types of attacks to attack computer systems (Daengsi et al., 2021). Most of them use a specific set of software that completely takes over a user's system (Chatchalermpun & Daengsi, 2021). An example are phishing attacks.

Cisco (2022) defines phishing as, " the practice of sending fraudulent communications that appear to come from a reputable source. It is usually done through email". Phishing attacks have as a goal to know sensitive information such as login and credit card information (Back & Guerette, 2021). Phishing attacks can also install malware on users' machines. 36 % of all breaching cases involves phishing attacks (Aljeaid et al., 2020). The use of phishing attacks increased in last years (Alamri et al., 2022). The use of the internet, particularly due to pandemic, digitalization and unprepared devices and users support hackers attacks also in phishing. So phishing and other forms of social engineering are a continued danger in the community today. These forms are supported also by AI technology. Attackers use AI and machine learning in their attacks (Purkait, 2015). Advanced technologies in AI have developed and adopted by phishing attackers (Purkait, 2015) to achieve their objective.

3. Improving Cybersecurity Awareness Training through AI Knowledge

Small and medium sized companies (SME) are one of the biggest targets for cyber-attacks in the last years. This is also because most of them think only big companies will be attacked, do not have cybersecurity strategies and adequate security measures. Both employers and employees are not aware about cybersecurity, this is not the main topic in company, resources and competences are missing. During the pandemic time managers, employees were unaware of the risks that working from home requires cybersecurity defences – and neither their business systems nor their staff's home networks were set up for the situation. Remote working and hybrid working continue to be the norm businesses and cybersecurity measures are neglected. Cyber criminals know this so that attempted and successful cyber-attacks increased exponentially. They take advantage i.e., by using malware to infect IT systems through emails, downloaded attachments and malicious software. So, including approaches to detecting and preventing cyber threats, malware, fraud into cybersecurity aware training of employees and employees based on AI is a necessity. AI is important also for cybersecurity professionals' knowledge providing analysis and threat identification that help them to minimize breach risk, prioritize risks, prepare direct incident response, and identify malware attacks before they occur.

Some methods for using AI in cybersecurity are:

- Detection and Identification of Cyber threats in real-time. By using Machine learning algorithms large amounts of data can be analysed, standard behaviour patterns learned, and deviations indicating an attack identified.
- Assessment of Vulnerabilities: AI can help identify software and detect potential security issues.
- Detection of Malware and other malicious software by analysing their behaviour, characteristics, and signatures. Predictive models could be used to identify new and unknown threats.
- Fraudulent activities such as financial fraud or identity theft can be detected by analysing patterns of behaviour and transactions.
- AI can help to assess organization's overall security risks and recommend strategies to mitigate those risks.
- Automation of security operations, such as incident response can be done, by analysing and prioritizing alerts and initiating responses based on predefined rules. So security professionals can better understand attack surface and adapt

their response to potential risks. AI can also help to automate routine tasks so that security professionals can fulfil other tasks requiring human intervention. As a result, the efficiency and effectiveness of cybersecurity operations can be improved by reducing human errors (https://www.computer.org/publicati ons/tech-news/trends/the-use-of-artificial-intelligence-in-cybersecurity).

Some key factors should be considered when developing AI solution within cybersecurity, like Data Quality, Model Selection, Scalability, Ethical Implications.

- Used Data Quality has a critical role in the performance of the solution, so it is important to have a clean and sure dataset to train the model.
- Right Model Selection for the problem with a corresponding architecture is crucial. This depends on the problem to solve, the amount of available and the desired level of accuracy.
- Computational requirements of desired AI solution have been considered and necessary hardware resources to support it should be assured.
- Explain ability of the model because the AI models become more complex and it's harder to understand how certain decisions is done. It is particularly important especially in sensitive fields like healthcare or finance.
- Security and Privacy of the data used to train and deploy the model, as well as the security of the system itself should be considered.
- Scalability of the developed AI solution should be considered as the volume of data, or the number of users increases.
- Ethical Implications of AI solutions, such as bias and fairness are to be researched.
- Integration of the AI solution with existing systems and processes should be planned.
- Maintenance of AI systems and updates should be considered keeping the system updated and running smoothly over time.
- Monitoring Methods for the performance of the AI solution are important.

AI methods can be used to improve cybersecurity activities, but these should be combined with other techniques, with human expertise and best practices. One problem to be considered in using AI methods is that cybercriminals can manipulate algorithms used by AI to execute incorrect actions. One example is in the cryptocurrency sector where hackers have modified trading algorithms. So, knowledge in this context is necessary about these dangers.

4. Application

NIST's National Initiative for Cybersecurity Education (NICE) underlines that shortage of "people with the knowledge, skills, and abilities to perform the tasks required for cybersecurity work", should be solved, i.e., technical and nontechnical staff.

NICE concentrates on the US and identifies that through cooperation with international organizations, associations who established norms, and education and training institutions, useful outcomes can be developed. It is important that international educational society produces results worldwide applicable (Paulsen et al., 2012). In order o develop a practical cybersecurity framework, organizations must consider AI-based cybersecurity awareness competencies and corresponding awareness training. Amazon presents viCyber (https://vicyber.com), an intelligent system capable to propose a rapid cybersecurity curriculum and training development by using AI and visual mappings. Organizations can use viCyber service to protect their infrastructure from cyber-attacks. The viCyber model design is based on the NICE framework with feedback from organisations.

Within the Erasmus+ project Interdisciplinary Cyber Training (InCyT -https://www.incytproject.eu) with partners from University, Research, VET, Industry from 7 European countries, analysis of cybersecurity measures and training in partner countries has been done, a digitally supported interdisciplinary training program supported by mentoring and a collaborative digital platform (https://www.incytproject.eu/elearning/) particularly oriented to SMEs employers and employees have been developed and tested. Within InCyT, first by using the NICE, a Cybersecurity Competence Framework that vocational training and companies can use to improve competencies and skills of employees and employers in order to avoid cyber-attacks has been developed and tested. The Cybersecurity Competence Framework developed within the Erasmus+ project InCyT will be improved using the AI-based model viCyber to support development of a training strategy. Human-computer dealings will be included and the experience of the user achieved via the training with real-time feedback done during the test phase. The training modules for SMEs managers and employees will be completed by including AI approaches. One example is the training module developed within InCyT Social Engineering including topics like Importance of Social Engineering Training, How to Protect from Phishing Attacks and Social engineering from an interdisciplinary view. The participants learned that it is difficult to protect against social engineering because the tactics that attackers use are based on individuals' behaviour and if employees do not have corresponding training to recognize social engineering attacks, the risk of falling victim is great. It was important to include social engineering training in security awareness programs giving employees the knowledge and tools they need to recognize these types of attacks and protect both themselves and their organization (Weßelmann, 2008). Training participants learn the Lifecycle of social engineering attacks. Figure 1 explains the Lifecycle of an attack.

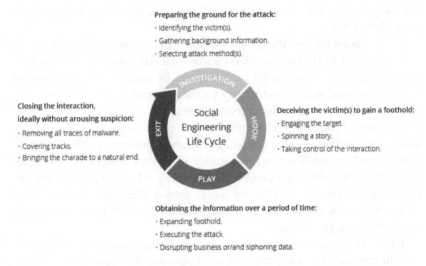

Preparing the ground for the attack:
· Identifying the victim(s).
· Gathering background information.
· Selecting attack method(s).

Closing the interaction,
ideally without arousing suspicion:
· Removing all traces of malware.
· Covering tracks.
· Bringing the charade to a natural end.

Social
Engineering
Life Cycle

Deceiving the victim(s) to gain a foothold:
· Engaging the target.
· Spinning a story.
· Taking control of the interaction.

Obtaining the information over a period of time:
· Expanding foothold.
· Executing the attack.
· Disrupting business or/and siphoning data.

Figure 1. Attack lifecycle (https://www.iacpcybercenter.org/resource-center/what-is -cyber-crime/cyber-attack-lifecycle/)

Different Social engineering attack techniques like Baiting, Scareware, Pretexting and particularly Phishing as one of the most popular social engineering attack types are explained. Spear phishing is a special form of the phishing attack because an attacker chooses specific individuals or enterprises. Phishing emails and text messages can be similar with ones coming from a known company or a trust person. They could look like they're from a bank, a credit card company, a social networking site, an online payment website or app, or an online store. Real examples of phishing which appear in SMEs have been included into the training; training participants learn how to protect against phishing. System protections are helpful to mitigate some social engineering attacks, but it is not enough. The Federal Bureau of Investigation's internet crime underlined the increased use of social engineering and business email fraud schemes resulted in billions of dollars in losses over the past several years (Abbate, 2020). Again methods of hackers, it is necessary to use an interdisciplinary approach to understand these and especially how these attacks affect businesses. Literature reviews highlight perspectives of cybersecurity from different disciplines: information technology, psychology, business, and ethics. Figure 2 illustrates this view (Washo, 2021). The literature review from different disciplines explains the need for an integrated approach to study the complex subject of social engineering and cyber-attacks.

Each discipline provides information to protect against various types of attacks and understand the impact of social engineering from both a human and organizational standpoint. But this information is useful when considered in the context of the other disciplines.

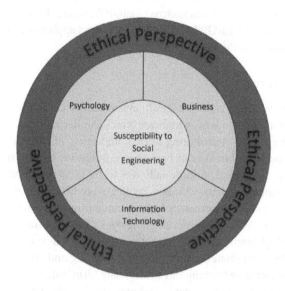

Figure 2. Relationships between fields in SNA

The learners have to understand that one of the key reasons phishing is always effective is a lack of awareness from users (Daengsi et al., 2021). Most of them do not understand the potential risks associated with internet use (Back & Guerette, 2021) and this should be one topic of the training.

The InCyT training modules will be improved to support cybersecurity awareness, to provide people with the information they need to understand AI-based cybersecurity and how they can use it to protect themselves (Ansari, 2022). Training on AI-based cybersecurity ensures that individuals have protected themselves from the risk of providing secrets about the company (Chatchalermpun & Daengsi, 2021). Users should learn how they can implement the same levels of security on their systems.

Individual roles, responsibilities, and required skills for managers and employees to understand AI will be better considered in this context.

Approaches, derived from the experience within the first training within InCyT as well as concrete situations and human errors done will be included into training. One of the test results of InCyT training shows that the training should be more personalized, and a new and specific set of skills should be developed to understand and use AI tools. Employee training on AI tools should help them to navigate specific tools such as ChatGPT. So, an introductory AI module including the use of ChatGPT will be developed and applications i.e., to respond at different attacks included.

4. Conclusions

Artificial intelligence has advantages in cybersecurity i.e. by improving analysis of vast amount of data, identify malware attacks, understanding, and prevention of cybercrime and so contributing to trust and safety of companies, employees and private persons. But AI can be resource intensive, require special training and not always practical. Additionally has to be known that attackers use AI methods to improve their attacks. Possibilities of prediction, personalization, and customization make AI necessary to be included into cybersecurity awareness training also for SMEs employers and employees. But such training should meet their individual learning needs directly. So long-form videos, training with characters they can relate to, on task-based learning and simulations could be used. AI cybersecurity training can strategically "drip" information to employees giving them most relevant, valuable, and memorable information at the moment. It is necessary to adapt the amount of information delivered in training with employee attention spans, retention, their interests and time. Due to few SME resources employees are busy. This makes it difficult to get employees engaged and focused on training. It is important that employers, employees know from the beginning benefits of AI based cybersecurity awareness training i.e. individualized learning, focus on their needs.

References

Abbate, P. (2020). *Internet Crime Report 2020*. https://www.ic3.gov/Media/PDF/AnnualReport/2020_IC3Report.pdf

Alamri, E., Alnajim A., & Alsuhibany, S. (2022). Investigation of Using Captcha Keystroke Dynamics to Enhance the Prevention of Phishing Attacks. *Future Internet, 14*(3), 82. https://doi.org/10.3390/fi14030082.

Aljeaid, D., Alzhrani, A., Alrougi, M., & Almalki, O. (2020). Assessment of End-User Susceptibility to Cyber Security Threats in Saudi Arabia by Simulating Phishing Attacks. *Information, 11*(12), 547.

Ansari, M. (2022). A Quantitative Study of Risk Scores and the Effectiveness of AI-Based Cybersecurity Awareness Training Programs. *International Journal of Smart Sensor and Adhoc Network* (2022), 1–8. https://doi.org/10.47893/ijs san.2022.1212.

Back, S., & Guerette, R. (2021). Cyber Place Management and Crime Prevention: Effectiveness of Cyber security Awareness Training Against Phishing Attacks. *Journal of Contemporary Criminal Justice.*

Chatchalermpun, S., & Daengsi, T. (2021). Improving Cyber Security Awareness Using Phishing Attack Simulation. *IOP Conference Series: Materials Science and Engineering, 1088*(1).

Cisco. (2022). *What Is Phishing?* https://www.cisco.com/c/en_ae/products/secur ity/email-security/what-is-phishing.html

Daengsi, T., Pornpongtechavanich P., & Wuttidittachotti, P. (2021). Cyber Security Awareness Enhancement: A Study of the Effects of Age and Gender of Thai Employees Associated with Phishing Attacks. *Education and Information Technologies, 27*(4), 4729–4752.

Paulsen, C., McDuffie, E., Newhouse W., & Toth, P. (2012, May–June). NICE: Creating a Cyber Security. Workforce and Aware Public. *IEEE Security & Privacy, 10*(3), 76–79. https://doi.org/10.1109/MSP.2012.73.

Purkait, S. (2015). Examining the Effectiveness of Phishing Filters against DNS Based Phishing Attacks. *Information & Computer Security, 23*(3), 333–346. Available: https://doi.org/10.1108/ics-02-2013-0009.

Washo, A. (2021). *An Interdisciplinary View of Social Engineering: A Call to Action for Research.* https://www.researchgate.net/publication/353448049 _An_interdisciplinary_view_of_social_engineering_A_call_to_action_for _research

Weßelmann, B. (2008). Maßnahmen gegen Social Engineering: Training muss Awareness-Maßnahmen ergänzen. *Datenschutz und Datensicherheit* DuD, 601–604.

Dubravka Pekanov

Evaluating the Economic Viability of Forest Biomass Energy Production

1. Introduction

To achieve the target of limiting global warming "significantly below 2°C" by the end of the 21st century (UN, 2015), there is an imperative to substantially reduce CO_2 emissions. As energy consumption is projected to rise, and fossil fuel reserves decline (IEA, 2022), renewable energy sources are becoming increasingly significant in energy generation.

Biomass is the primary source of renewable energy in the EU, accounting almost 60 % of all renewables (EC, 2019). Moreover, biomass plays a crucial role in electricity production, representing a balancing mechanism for variable renewable energy sources (EC, 2023). The largest end-user of this energy source in the heating and cooling sector, accounting for about 75 % of all bioenergy[1] consumption. At the same time, bioelectricity accounts for 13 %, and transport biofuels account for 12 % (EC, 2019).

The significance of bioenergy in enhancing the EU's energy security is undeniable, primarily due to its reliance on domestically produced biomass, which accounted for approximately 96 % of the demand in 2016, according to the European Commission (EC, 2019). Forestry stands as the principal supplier, providing over 60 % of the total biomass supply within the EU (EC, 2019). This strong emphasis on utilizing locally sourced biomass not only strengthens the region's energy independence but also fosters sustainable energy practices and reduces dependence on external energy sources.

Biomass for energy generation yields substantial benefits, enabling significant reductions in greenhouse gas emissions and actively mitigating the impact of climate change. Its availability and capability to provide a consistent and controllable energy supply make biomass a critical component in supporting energy security and sustainability within the EU.

To qualify for EU renewables targets and subsidies, biomass-based renewable energy must meet sustainability criteria. The revised Renewable Energy Directive 2018/2001 (EU, 2018) expands these criteria to cover large-scale biomass for heat

---

1   Bioenergy is the type of energy obtained from biomass.

and power, alongside biofuels and bioliquids for transport. It introduces new requirements for forest biomass, demanding evidence of sustainable harvesting laws and emissions accounting from the country of origin. If evidence is lacking, bioenergy generators must demonstrate sustainability compliance at the biomass sourcing area level. This ensures responsible and sustainable biomass usage within the EU.

In Croatia, the importance of bioenergy becomes evident as it represents 18 % to the overall renewable energy mix, contributing to 28 % of the final energy consumption from renewables, according to IEA (2021). While hydropower remains dominant in energy generation, encompassing 25–50 % of electricity consumption in past decades, a transformation is observed as fossil fuel-based power has decreased from 30 % to 23 % in the previous decade (IEA, 2021). This decline is accompanied by growth in non-hydro renewable electricity, which accounted for 13 % in 2019, with notable growth in bioelectricity and wind energy, according to the same source. Solid biofuel use is still relatively modest despite abundant forest land.

Forest biomass offers efficient generation of electricity and heat through cogeneration technologies that improve overall energy conversion efficiency. Wood chips are particularly notable for their accessibility, ease of processing and drying, as well as their reliable combustion or gasification behavior (Gonzalez et al., 2015). However, before making any investment decisions regarding a biomass-based power plant, it is crucial to assess the economic viability of such a venture.

In that sense, this paper presents an evaluation of producing energy from biomass, focusing on the utilization of forest biomass combined heat and power (CHP) systems. Key financial indicators, namely Net Present Value (NPV), Internal Rate of Return (IRR), and Payback Period (PBP), for a 5 MWe biomass CHP system in Croatia were estimated. The findings from this study will provide valuable insights for making informed investment decisions in forest biomass systems, and at the same time ensure insights into economic feasibility and sustainable energy practices.

The remainder of this paper is organized in the following way. After the introductory part, a literature review with contextual background on the economic viability of investing in biomass-based energy production is given. Chapter 3 provides a detailed explanation of the applied methodology, while Chapter 4 is dedicated to presenting the research findings. Finally, the paper concludes in Chapter 5, providing an assessment of the overall economic viability of producing electricity and heat from forest biomass.

2. Literature Review with Contextual Background

Research on biomass-based energy production has gained significant attention both within and outside Europe. Outside Europe, researchers have explored various aspects of biomass-based electricity and heat production. In Mississippi, Nandimandalam and Gude (2022) identified the potential of utilizing local waste biomass to replace electricity suppliers, indicating economic feasibility and emissions reduction. Similarly, De Deus Ribeiro et al. (2021) investigated the economic feasibility of a 10 MW eucalyptus woodchip-based power plant in Brazil, emphasizing cost-determining factors and feasible energy trading scenarios. Marchenko et al. (2020) assessed biomass gasification in Russia's Irkutsk region, demonstrating the cost-effectiveness of wood fuel. Nzotcha and Kenfack (2019) focused on cogeneration with wood residues in Sub-Saharan Africa, highlighting economic viability with increasing capacity. Pighinelli et al. (2018) compared single biomass to bio-oil production to distributed processing for electricity in Brazil, finding better economic benefits for the single facility scenario, with potential competitiveness in the future considering auxiliary benefits and market trends. In Malaysia, Malek et al. (2017) studied biomass power, revealing emissions reductions and positive environmental impact. Perez et al. (2015) analyzed biomass CHP in Cuba and demonstrated the viability of the project under certain electricity sales price conditions, while Moon, Lee, and Lee (2011) assessed the economic viability of biomass power generation in Korea, comparing alternatives for small-scale distributed energy production.

Within Europe, extensive research has been dedicated to examining the economic viability and potential of biomass technologies as a sustainable and viable solution for energy generation. Rey, Pio and Tarelho (2021) undertook a study in the Aveiro region, Portugal, comparing the economic viability of integrating biomass gasification for electricity generation and replacing natural gas in lime kilns. They analyzed three scenarios: electricity generation from residual forest biomass (RFB) using a gasification combined cycle system, RFB gasification to replace natural gas in lime kiln burners, and combined electricity and heat production. Their economic model yielded positive indicators, including NPV, IRR, and a short PBP, indicating favorable investment outcomes. Malaťáková et al. (2021) examined the feasibility of small gasification units for CHP generation in the Czech Republic. The study focused primarily on utilizing wood from salvage logging and involved the analysis of 21 gasification units. Economic profitability under various operating conditions for three investment variants (10 kWel, 100 kWel, and 200 kWel) was assessed. Interestingly, the findings indicated that while the 200 kWel alternative proved to be economically viable, the smaller alternatives resulted in economic losses. These results highlight the importance of scale when it comes to the economic feasibility of small gasification units. It seems that larger capacities are better positioned to generate positive cash flow and net present value, making them more financially attractive.

Similarly, Cardoso et al. (2020) conducted a techno-economic analysis to evaluate the potential of utilizing forest biomass blends for energy valorization in the Azores. The study employed numerical simulation of biomass gasification and analyzed two unit sizes. The research indicated that the 100 kW unit was not economically feasible, while the 1000 kW unit showed positive economic indicators, such as an NPV of 486 k€, an IRR of 17.44 %, and a payback period of 7.4 years. Nonetheless, the study's sensitivity analysis identified potential risks related to electricity sales tariffs and production, emphasizing the need for careful consideration and strategic planning when venturing into biomass gasification projects. Understanding and mitigating these risks is crucial to ensure long-term economic viability and investor attractiveness.

Safarian, Unnthorsson and Richter (2020) conducted a techno-economic analysis of electricity generation through timber and wood waste gasification in Iceland. They concluded that total costs increased with higher implemented power, but NPV remained positive for all subgroups and grew with gasifier scale. Discounted payback period was inversely proportional to the installed capacity. These findings are in line with those of Maľáťáková et al. (2021) and Cardoso et al. (2020), suggesting that larger capacities can offer more favorable economic outcomes and returns on investment. Moreover, Cardoso, Silva, and Eusebio (2019) conducted a detailed techno-economic analysis of a gasification power plant with an 11 MW capacity in Portugal, utilizing forest biomass blends. They developed a comprehensive economic model that demonstrated feasibility with an NPV of 2.367MV, an IRR of 8.66 %, and a PBP of 23.1 years. Sensitivity analysis indicated reasonable levels of risk for potential investors, emphasizing the significant impact of electricity sales price and production on the NPV.

In Italy, Porcu et al. (2019) presented a techno-economic analysis of small-scale (2 MWe) power generation from biomass using gasification technologies. Their study focused on a pilot-scale air-blown bubbling fluidized-bed (BFB) gasification plant with a capacity of 500 kWth. The findings indicated that this kind of power generation can be financially viable for applications using low-cost biomass, such as agricultural waste. However, it became apparent that the technology was less competitive when applied to high-quality biomass.

Regarding policy implications, Moiseyev, Solberg and Kallio (2014) examined the impact of subsidies on wood-fired CHP plants and wood with coal co-fired power plants in the EU from 2020 to 2030. They found that subsidies can increase wood consumption for energy, promoting the displacement of traditional fossil-fuel-based power sources. Without subsidies, wood-fired electricity has a minimal market share because of the restricted availability of affordable wood resources.

The literature review has emphasized the need for comprehensive techno-economic analyses, and risk assessment when considering biomass-based energy projects. The research findings within Europe suggest that large-scale gasification projects, with careful consideration of biomass type, gasifier scale, and financial risk factors, have the greatest potential for economic success.

3. Methodology

3.1. Techno-Economic Assumptions

The analysis is based on a real case study of investment in a co-generation plant in Croatia using forest biomass, primarily aimed at supplying industrial consumers with process steam, while generating electricity as a by-product. The primary fuel used is forest biomass in the form of wood chips. The plant consists of a boiler fuelled by forest biomass, a steam turbine, a main transformer for electricity delivery to the grid, an internal consumption transformer, a system for thermal preparation of feedwater, a closed-loop water-cooled condenser, a dry cooling tower for water cooling, a fuel and ash handling system, and a chemical feedwater treatment.

The maximum net power output of the plant is 5 MWe. It generates an annual production of 32,090 MWh of electricity and 119,790 tons of steam. The plant operates continuously for 8,000–8,300 hours per year, running both in summer and winter modes. To ensure smooth operation, the plant receives an annual delivery of approximately 65,000 tons of wood chips.

The economic viability assessment involved certain assumptions. The investment implies a 30-year operating lifespan, with an 18-month construction period. The investment cost includes 70 % allocated to equipment, 25 % to construction works, and 5 % for other expenses. The financing is structured with 70 % from credit funds and 30 % from the investor's resources. Prices for electricity are determined according to the status of a privileged producer, while prices for thermal energy, forest biomass and demineralised water are estimated based on market conditions. The operational and maintenance cost is projected to be 2 % of the investment value.

3.2. Methods

Based on the above-mentioned assumptions, three methods were used to assess the economic viability of investing in a co-generation plant using forest biomass: NPV, IRR, and PBP.

The **Net Present Value (NPV)** is a key criterion used to assess the economic viability of an investment. It is calculated by computing the difference between the present value of all cash inflows and outflows throughout the lifetime of the project, using the following formula (IFC, 2017):

Equation 1. Net present value calculation

$$NPV(i,N) = \sum_{t=0}^{N} C_t * \frac{1}{(1+i)^t}$$

where:

C_t represents the net cash flow at time t,
i is the financial discount rate,
t is for the time periods,
N stands for the total number of time periods.

The NPV evaluates the profitability of an investment project; when NPV positive, it is an indication that the project or investment is profitable, and vice versa.

The **Internal rate of return (IRR)** is commonly used together with NPV as an indicator of a project feasibility. The IRR indicates the discount rate that results in the NPV of all cash flows of the project being equal to zero. In that sense, it presents the minimum rate of return to make the project economically viable. Equation 2 presents the formula for calculating the IRR.

Equation 2. Internal rate of return calculation

$$0 = \sum_{t=0}^{N} C_t * \frac{1}{(1+i)^t}$$

Project is found to be feasible if the IRR is higher than the discount rate, and vice versa.

The **Payback period (PBP)** represents the duration required to recover the initial capital investments. The formula for calculating PBP is presented in Equation 3 (IFC, 2017).

Equation 3. Payback period calculation

$$PBP = \frac{net\ operating\ income}{total\ debt\ service}$$

The shorter PBP indicates that the project is more financially feasible.

4. Results

During the construction period of the CHP plant, the cash outflows exceed the cash inflows of the project. With the commissioning of the CHP plant, however, the project proves its economic viability, as the cash inflows exceed the cash outflows. This is partly due to the guaranteed electricity price and the privileged producer status.

In that sense, Figure 1 illustrates the economic viability of the project as evaluated through its cash flow analysis (Figure 1).

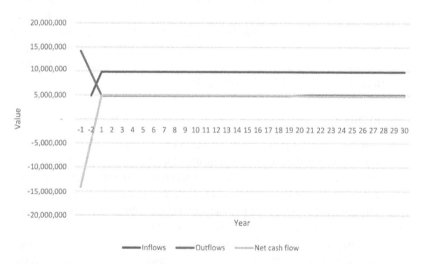

Figure 1. CHP project's cash flows (in EUR)

The incremental cash flow from revenues increases positively over the years, underlining the importance of the benefits from electricity sales prices for the profitability of the project. Furthermore, the net cash flow increases after the loan repayment period. Based on these project's cash flows, the NPV, IRR and PBP of the project were determined.

The NPV is calculated for a given discount rate, which is used to discount the net cash flows of the project. In this case, the discount rate represents the cost of using financing sources and stands at 7 %. At a given discount rate, the NPV amounts to €36,5 million. In addition, the NPV of the project is positive up to a discount rate of 22.56 %, which is the project's internal rate of return (IRR).

The payback period is the year when, according to the Figure 1, the cumulative net cash flows become positive. The total investment value is recovered in the 5th year of operation. Assuming that the equity investment (investor's own funds) is 30 % and the loan portion is 70 % (with an interest rate of 7 % and a repayment period of 7 years), one can observe that the equity investment (own funds) is recovered in the 4th year of operation.

Comparing the above results with similar plants (e.g., the study by Cardoso et al., 2019), the plant in Croatia achieves better economic results. This can be attributed to the privileged electricity purchase price, as mentioned earlier in this paper. It is important to note that similar studies in their project's sensitivity analysis have identified electricity price as an important risk factor in biomass energy investments, which is partially mitigated in this project (see Cardoso et al., 2020; Cardoso et al., 2019). The results obtained in this study regarding the size of the plant are consistent with the findings of Maľaťáková et al. (2021) Safarian et al., (2020), and Cardoso et al. (2020).

5. Conclusion

Biomass has significant potential as an adaptable energy producer, capable of effectively balancing the energy system and facilitating the incorporation of variable renewable energy sources like solar and wind into the power grid. These integrated systems could provide flexible solutions for energy supply (both heat and electricity) and enable the grid to absorb a higher share of renewable energy while ensuring the adaptability and resilience of the energy sector.

With an emphasis on forest biomass energy production and CHP technology, this paper contributes to the growing body of research on sustainable energy solutions. The focus on a 5 MWe capacity enables the economic viability evaluation of a larger-scale biomass CHP system, providing valuable insights into the potential benefits and challenges associated with such installations. Additionally, the financial assessment of this specific capacity helps to identify the scale at which the technology becomes more economically competitive and financially attractive.

Biomass-based energy production through CHP technologies holds significant potential in the EU. Large-scale projects utilizing the right biomass feedstock can yield positive economic indicators. Policymakers should consider providing targeted support and incentives to encourage investment in such projects while considering sensitivity analysis to assess potential risks. Additionally, research should continue to explore advanced gasification technologies, sustainable biomass supply chains, and environmental impacts to ensure a sustainable transition to renewable energy in the EU.

The findings are relevant for government officials, investors, and stakeholders, offering essential information to support informed decision-making in adopting forest biomass-based energy projects. Furthermore, the study highlights the significance of sustainable energy generation and waste utilization as key pillars of a greener and more environmentally conscious future.

References

Cardoso, J., Silva, V., & Eusebio, D. (2019). Techno-Economic Analysis of a Biomass Gasification Power Plant Dealing with Forestry Residues Blends for Electricity Production in Portugal. *Journal of Cleaner Production, 212*, 741–753.

Cardoso, J. S., Silva, V., Eusébio, D., Azevedo, I. L., & Tarelho, L. A. (2020). Techno-Economic Analysis of Forest Biomass Blends Gasification for Small-Scale Power Production Facilities in the Azores. *Fuel, 279*, 118552.

de Deus Ribeiro, G. B., Batista, F. R. S., de Magalhães, M. A., Valverde, S. R., Carneiro, A. D. C. O., & Amaral, D. H. (2021). Techno-economic Feasibility Analysis of a Eucalyptus-Based Power Plant Using Woodchips. *Biomass and Bioenergy, 153*, 106218.

EC. (2019). European Commission, Joint Research Centre. *Brief on Biomass for Energy in the European Union*, Publications Office, 2019. https://data.europa.eu/doi/10.2760/546943 [July 22 2023]

EC. (2023). European Commission (2023). *Biomass*. Available at: https://energy.ec.europa.eu/topics/renewable-energy/bioenergy/biomass_en [July 22 2023]

EU. (2018). Directive (Eu) 2018/2001 of the European Parliament and of the Council of 11 December 2018 on the Promotion of the Use of Energy from Renewable Sources (Recast). Available at: https://eur-lex.europa.eu/legal-content/EN/TXT/PDF/?uri=CELEX:32018L2001

González, A., Riba, J. R., Puig, R., & Navarro, P. (2015). Review of Micro-And Small-Scale Technologies to Produce Electricity and Heat from Mediterranean Forests' Wood Chips. *Renewable and Sustainable Energy Reviews, 43*, 143–155.

IEA. (2022). *World Energy Outlook 2022.* Paris: IEA. https://www.iea.org/repo
rts/world-energy-outlook-2022, License: CC BY 4.0 (report); CC BY NC SA
4.0 (Annex A).

IEA Bioenergy. (2021). *Implementation of Bioenergy in Croatia – 2021 Update.*
https://www.ieabioenergy.com/wp-content/uploads/2021/11/CountryRepor
t2021_Croatia_final.pdf [July 22 2023]

International Finance Corporation. (2017). *Converting Biomass to Energy: A
Guide for Developers and Investors.* World Bank.

Malaťáková, J., Jankovský, M., Malaťák, J., Velebil, J., Tamelová, B., Gendek, A.,
& Aniszewska, M. (2021). Evaluation of Small-Scale Gasification for CHP for
Wood from Salvage Logging in the Czech Republic. *Forests, 12*(11), 1448.

Malek, A. A., Hasanuzzaman, M., Abd Rahim, N., & Al Turki, Y. A. (2017).
Techno-Economic Analysis and Environmental Impact Assessment of a 10 Mw
Biomass-Based Power Plant in Malaysia. *Journal of Cleaner Production, 141,*
502–513.

Marchenko, O., Solomin, S., Kozlov, A., Shamanskiy, V., & Donskoy, I. (2020).
Economic Efficiency Assessment of Using Wood Waste in Cogeneration
Plants with Multi-Stage Gasification. *Applied Sciences, 10*(21), 7600.

Moiseyev, A., Solberg, B., & Kallio, A. M. I. (2014). The Impact of Subsidies and
Carbon Pricing on the Wood Biomass Use for Energy in the EU. *Energy, 76,*
161–167.

Moon, J. H., Lee, J. W., & Lee, U. D. (2011). Economic Analysis of Biomass Power
Generation Schemes under Renewable Energy Initiative with Renewable
Portfolio Standards (RPS) in Korea. *Bioresource Technology, 102*(20),
9550–9557.

Nandimandalam, H., & Gude, V. G. (2022). Renewable Wood Residue Sources
as Potential Alternative for Fossil Fuel Dominated Electricity Mix for Regions
in Mississippi: A Techno-Economic Analysis. *Renewable Energy, 200,*
1105–1119.

Nzotcha, U., & Kenfack, J. (2019). Contribution of the Wood-Processing Industry
for Sustainable Power Generation: Viability of Biomass-Fuelled Cogeneration
in Sub-Saharan Africa. *Biomass and Bioenergy, 120,* 324–331.

Pérez, N. P., Machin, E. B., Pedroso, D. T., Roberts, J. J., Antunes, J. S., & Silveira,
J. L. (2015). Biomass Gasification for Combined Heat and Power Generation
in the Cuban Context: Energetic and Economic Analysis. *Applied Thermal
Engineering, 90,* 1–12.

Pighinelli, A. L., Schaffer, M. A., & Boateng, A. A. (2018). Utilization of
Eucalyptus for Electricity Production in Brazil Via Fast Pyrolysis: A Techno-
Economic Analysis. *Renewable Energy, 119,* 590–597.

Porcu, A., Sollai, S., Marotto, D., Mureddu, M., Ferrara, F., & Pettinau, A. (2019). Techno-Economic Analysis of a Small-Scale Biomass-to-Energy BFB Gasification-Based System. *Energies, 12*(3), 494.

Rey, J. R. C., Pio, D. T., & Tarelho, L. A. C. (2021). Biomass Direct Gasification for Electricity Generation and Natural Gas Replacement in the Lime Kilns of the Pulp and Paper Industry: A Techno-Economic Analysis. *Energy, 237*, 121562.

Safarian, S., Unnthorsson, R., & Richter, C. (2020). Techno-Economic Analysis of Power Production by Using Waste Biomass Gasification. *Journal of Power and Energy Engineering, 8*(06), 1.

United Nations: Paris Agreement, Paris (2015). https://unfccc.int/sites/default/files/english_paris_agreement.pdf, last accessed 2022/2/25.

Konrad Gunesch

Cultural and Art Economics, and State Subsidies for Inspired Individuals: Pervading Paradoxes from Historical, Economic, Sociopolitical and Psychological Perspectives

1. Introduction and Overview

1.1. Recent Research Interest in, and Increasing Relevance of Cultural and Art Economics

The literature highlights a recent "expansion in the [...] interest in the economics of art and culture [with] promising lines of future research [and more] expansion in the future" (Throsby, 2006, p. 21). Concurrently, basic questions about art and cultural economics keep being asked, exemplified by Blaug's 2019 book *The Economics of the Arts*, whose sixteen chapters are all reprints of publications between 1956 and 1974. Several of them are cited in this research, their thoughts still valid in a complex and globalized economic, cultural and artistic landscape.

Challenging the analysis of "economics" together with "arts" and "culture" is economics' reputation as "the dismal science" (see just the book titles of Levy, 2002; Marglin, 2008, and Rodrik, 2015), whereas culture and art, even when analyzed through economic glasses, are still considered "sublime" human experiences (see just the book and the chapter titles of Amariglio et al., 2009a, 2009b), characterized by "the creative genius in literature, music, and the visual arts" (as spells out the chapter title of Simonton 2014), where the professed value of the "aesthetic experience" (see the chapter headings of Locher, 2014) contribute to "art's economic exceptionalism" (as spells out the book title of Beech, 2015).

Also challenging is the field's state of flux even in its basic elements, starting with its name. As Ginsburgh and Throsby maintain in the second volume of their *Handbook of the Economics of Arts and Culture* (2014), the "historical evolution" within the decade since the publication of the first volume (2006) allowed "cultural economics [to be] more appropriately referred to as the economics of art and culture" (2014, p. 1; similarly Frey, 2019, p. 3). This research uses the shorter expressions of "art economics" and "cultural economics" for euphony and concision.

The field is divided into numerous economic inquiries of art aspects and products, ranging from paintings (Throsby & Zednik, 2014, pp. 81–100), music (Levinson, 2014, pp. 101–117) and concerts (Courty & Pagliero, 2014, pp. 299–356) over festivals and cultural awards (English, 2014, pp. 119–143; Frey, 2019, pp. 63–70) to cultural heritage and museums (Frey, 2019; pp. 77–88, 97–114; Willis, 2014, pp. 145–182), movies and books (Walls, 2014, pp. 185–214), or from technical and organizational aspects such as progressive technologies (Potts, 2014, pp. 215–232) over investment, property and labor (Whitaker, 2021, pp. 177–243) to global trade and transactions (Bisin & Verdier, 2014, pp. 439–484; Mandel, 2014, pp. 233–260; Platteau & Wahhaj, 2014, pp. 633–678) including cultural institutions (Castañer, 2014, pp. 263–276), or from legal, copyright and digitization aspects (Waldfogel, 2014, pp. 277–298) over media ownership (Doyle, 2014, pp. 357–378) to cultural trading systems (Iapadre, 2014, pp. 381–410; Macmillan, 2014, pp. 411–438), or finally from considerations of cultural values and diversity to conflict scenarios (Aldashev & Platteau, 2014, pp. 587–632; Ginsburgh & Weber, 2014, pp. 507–544; Montalvo & Reynal-Querol, 2014, pp. 485–506; Schwartz, 2014, pp. 547–586).

Against the background of these many viewpoints, and by integrating the most relevant recent literature, this research combines historical, sociopolitical and macroeconomic perspectives in a differentiated evaluation of public support and state subsidies for the cultural and creative industries. The focus of this differentiation will be on pervading paradoxes, whose analysis and discussion contributes to the field by clarifying concepts and connections, to improve public awareness, transparency, and decision-making.

1.2. Origin, Terms and Relationship of Cultural and Art Economics

The field of Cultural Economics is based on Baumol and Bowen's 1966 book *Performing Arts – The Economic Dilemma: A Study of Problems Common to Theater, Opera, Music and Dance*. Its authors use "economic analysis [to] illuminate [...] the role of the arts sector in the economy" (Throsby, 2006, p. 4). Yet only the book's last part, "Sources of Financial Support", and its two last chapters, deals with "Government Support in Practice" or the "Rationale of Public Support" (Baumol & Bowen, 1966, pp. 347 ff., 369 ff.).

While the field's first journal, *Journal of Cultural Economics*, was founded in 1977, only as of the 1990s had it accumulated enough material to warrant an overview (Throsby, 2006, pp. 4–5). It established "cultural economics" as a wide area that embraced the fields and sub-fields of art, heritage and media studies, and that included many more disciplines including art history and philosophy, law and sociology, and economics and management (Throsby, 2006, p. 5).

Only in the first decade of the 21st century did scholarly confidence claim "a sufficiently cohesive body of work [...] to identify a field labeled 'cultural economics' or 'the economics of the arts and culture' [...] even though the outer boundaries [...] remain somewhat fuzzy", which allowed "assembling a purposeful collection of essays commissioned from researchers working at the theoretical and empirical frontiers of the field" (Throsby, 2006, p. 6).

A basic concern immediately pointed out was that of "defining whether and how cultural goods and services differ from other goods and services in the economy", recognizing that "whilst it is the mysterious and possible unfathomable nature of art in all its forms that ultimately must underlie much of the behavior of individuals, firms and markets in the arts, economics requires a more systematic basis on which its analysis can rest" (Throsby, 2006, p. 6).

1.3. Terminology and Differentiation

Even broad terms as "cultural economics" and "art economics" require more basic definitions, namely of "art" and of "culture". For simplicity and inclusivity, this research follows Throsby's description of culture as "comprising or being defined as a set of attitudes, beliefs or values common to a group that somehow identifies and binds the group together", which allows us "to speak of a national culture, a religious culture, a corporate culture and so on" (2006, p. 6).

"Culture" can furthermore be demarcated functionally as "the practices and products of cultural activity, including especially the arts", and as "sometimes divided into the performing arts (acting, dancing, singing, playing a musical instrument, etc.) and the initial creative arts (visual art, sculpture, craft, creative writing, musical composition, etc.) though there are obvious overlaps between these categories", all of which make "the arts comprise a subset of culture more broadly defined" (Throsby, 2006, pp. 6–7).

Consequently, in the below mentioned concept of "cultural goods", elements of cultural, art and creative economics overlap, in that "cultural goods have some public-good properties; in aggregate they yield positive externalities or diffused benefits that may be demanded in their own right" (Throsby, 2006, p. 7). As for the term "cultural industries", this research follows literature that defines them "as those industries producing those goods" (Throsby, 2006, p. 11).

2. Literature Review

2.1. Intersection of Economic and Cultural Policy

The literature reveals "four specific areas where cultural and economic policy intersect: support for the arts; trade in cultural goods, heritage; and urban and regional development issues" (Throsby, 2006, p. 19), and five cultural policy areas especially suited to economic analysis: "support for the creative arts; cultural goods in international trade; the management of cultural assets; industry and innovation; and foreign policy" (Throsby, 2012, p. 106). The first area, "support for the creative arts", is the focus of this chapter.

Relatedly to note is that "the intersections between cultural policy and economic policy are extensive, including [...] the appropriate level for government support for the arts and culture, and the balance between direct (grant-related) and indirect (tax-related) means of support", as well as "the role of the arts and culture in employment creation and income generation in towns and cities; especially those affected by industrial decline" (Throsby, 2006, p. 18).

2.2. Discussion of State Support for the Arts

Baumol and Bowen hesitated about "the long-run prospect for government support in the arts", while for the United States they merely stated that it "seems favorable" (1966, p. 405), or that "future professional performance may well survive and prosper" (1966, p. 407). Recent literature highlights the connection between state support and the arts as yet conceptually and empirically unresolved, concurrently calling for more research, all while rooting governmental support and related regulations in economic and political liberalism (Throsby, 2006, p. 19):

> The rationale for state support for the arts has been one of the longest-running issues [...] in the literature of cultural economics over the last 40 years. [...] Empirical evidence is by no means extensive, and positive theories of assistance may be [...] explaining levels and patterns of support actually observed in various democratic countries around the world [...] Why, at a time when the trend is towards privatization in many sectors of the economy, the provision of government grants, tax relief and regulatory protection continues in the arts and heritage industries. The answer [...] lies in government skepticism that consumers know what is best for them; in these circumstances producer interests can exert a strong influence on government policy, with consequent effects on both allocative and productive efficiency.

2.3. Reaches of Cultural Policies

The literature differentiates between "the broad reach of cultural policy" and the fact that "its coverage and its level of importance in national policy agendas vary considerably between countries" (Throsby, 2006, p. 18). European cross-continental comparisons only hint at an unspecified "central government level":

> In Europe [...] there are substantial differences between countries in the volume of public resources they devote to the arts and culture in the ways those resources are

deployed. Administrative structures also vary [...] from arm-lengths arts councils to full-scale Ministries of Culture. There are also sub-regional and supra-regional interests in cultural policy in Europe [with] sub-national regions with distinctive cultural identities [that] promote their own artistic and cultural endeavors [while] the European Union and the Council of Europe have interests in developing pan-European cultural policies (Throsby 2006, p. 18; similarly Baumol & Bowen, 1966, pp. 360–365).

Throsby (2006, pp. 18–19) contrasts this with America:

> In the United States [...] there has never been a great deal of interest in the formulation of specific cultural policies at the central government level; rather the major players in the formation and execution of direct public expenditure programs in the arts and culture are located at sub-national levels of government [...] provided indirectly, via tax concessions for gifts to not-for-profit arts organizations and also via tax concessions to private owners of cultural heritage buildings and sites. The role of tax incentives in stimulating cultural donations and the significance of philanthropy as a characteristic of American life are [part of] the peculiarly American tradition of individual and corporate giving that has sustained the growth of the arts in the United States for more than a century. [An] 'American model' for cultural support [...] may be difficult to replicate it in other countries where institutional structures, income levels and tax-price responsiveness may differ markedly from the US situation.

We thus constate (as do Ekelund et al., 2017) a European preference for more centralized governmental subsidies for the arts, contrasting with a more individualistic, indirect and administrative hands-off American understanding of national artistic and cultural support.

3. Research Methodology: Transdisciplinary Framework of Analysis

The literature highlights the need for multidisciplinary frameworks in cultural economics, in that "a broad definition of cultural goods that embraced popular cultural forms such as sports, television programs, magazines [...] would open up an enormous field of interest in mass cultural consumption and production [...] explored within sociology, contemporary cultural studies, and media economics" (Throsby, 2006, p. 7).

This gathering of disciplines for investigating the intersection of economics, art and culture is supported by recent publications that describe the field as having turned "from a sub-discipline of economics into a sub-discipline of anthropology" (Ginsburgh & Throsby, 2014, p. 1).

Therefore, this research uses a comprehensive approach that unites social and political scopes with a macroeconomic analytical focus. Furthering disciplinary integration and methodological benefits, and beyond a mere coexistence of approaches often labeled as "multidisciplinary", it explicitly proposes a "transdisciplinary enquiry" (see Martin, 2017, p. 130) to share and to advance frameworks, and to produce fresh methodological, conceptual and practical insights.

4. Analysis and Discussion: Economic, Sociopolitical and Psychological Paradoxes

The literature points to several pervading paradoxes in art and cultural economics, and in that context, highlights several contentious issues of state subsidies for artists and culturally creative and inspired individuals. As Adams (2019, p. 28) summarizes:

> The arts is [sic] a paradoxical economy because for a very long period (at least a century, probably 150 years) the majority of artists have had tiny incomes from art; according to economic theory this commonly known information should cause a contraction in the number of people entering the profession [...] thereby raising the medium income. Yet [...] the reverse [has happened]: there are ever more art graduates at a time when the average income of artists is low [...]. Apparently, the social cachet, personal satisfaction and tiny possibility of great wealth outweigh the stark financial figures and probability statistics.

Below, the six related main paradoxes are analyzed and discussed from historical, economic, political, social, psychological and philosophical perspectives. The literature argues those perspectives under these six lines or labels: (1) art as a social marker, (2) self-deception of the art economy, (3) winners take all, (4) artists as ill-informed gamblers, (5) subsidies create poverty, and (6) states encourage artistic oversupply.

Importantly, those argumentative lines can be interpreted as either favoring or as rejecting state subsidies for the arts and for artists. As Adams (2019, pp. 35–36) states, "there are many legitimate reasons why the arts are subsidized, [while] many common justifications for art subsidies are spurious". Without taking sides a priori, this research however aligns with voices that stipulate "greater honesty and clarity about why we fund art and what we expect to get in return" (Adams, 2019, p. 36).

The ambiguity of either favoring or rejecting state support will be pointed out for each analyzed paradox. It might lead to equally paradoxical conclusions in that final recommendations about supporting or rejecting state subsidies and public funding of art and artist are also ambiguous. That, then, would in itself be a valuable insight and worthy contribution to this complex area.

4.1. Paradox 1: Art as a Socioeconomic and Demographic Marker

Adams (2019, p. 23) and Abbing (2002, pp. 22–23) point out in unison to the first paradox, namely art as a socioeconomic and demographic marker. Rather than clearly stratifying people as consumers or spectators, it creates additional social and psychological upwards pressures:

> People higher on the ladder look down on the art of people lower than them, while the latter do not look down, but look up to the art of the former.

Adams (2019, p. 23) finely differentiates internationally, claiming an independence of class from economic considerations in favor of personal conviction and social convention:

> Those ascending the social ladder will wish to consume high art, while those descending will cling to high art despite straitened circumstances. (This, incidentally, undermines the American definition of class as primarily income defined. It isn't. Class is primarily the adoption of distinctions in taste, education, occupational and social conventions generally facilitated by wealth.) This explains why a carpet tycoon in China buys an Andy Warhol as a symbol of his improved social status and great wealth, while an unemployed professor will still love Mondrian and Mahler even without his former position.

This highlights both the paradox of art as a socioeconomic and demographic marker as well as the ambiguity of whether state subsidies benefit artists or the public: the abyss between "high" and "low" art only gets exacerbated, and the public will orient their tastes "upwards" anyway.

4.2. Paradox 2: Self-Deception of the Art Economy

Abbing (2002, p. 55) points out that "aesthetic value and market value differ in definition", and that unlike in traditional economics, "price" is only a partially appropriate indicator, namely for unique artworks, whereas for quantifiable or serialized items (such as books or music discs) it gets confused with "revenue streams". While he maintains that economic and aesthetic values can coincide (2002, p. 58), he acknowledges that they often contradict each other (2002, pp 62–65), even if in the end they might converge (2002, pp. 73–75). Abbing sees this as "the fight between two different forms of power", where "the power to tell what is good and what is bad in the arts competes with purchasing power" (2002, p. 77).

Adams (2019, pp. 23–24) spins this paradox further, claiming "the sensitivity, self-deceit and hypocrisy about the connection between aesthetic appreciation and financial value" as "distinctive to the arts", due to "the peculiarities of the special economy of high-status luxuries and the quasi-sacred status of items which are also commodities", specifically in that:

> We love and value art because it seems to stand apart from monetary considerations; the more we love particular examples of art, the more valuable they become as commodities. Knowledge about the value of items makes us suspicious about the quality of the art.

Yet when thought to its logical conclusion, this means that state subsidies or public funding could never be connected to a reliable monetary indicator (such as price), either for the value of the produced art, or for the creative process that enabled it. One solution would be simply to wait, with Abbing, until a time when aesthetic and economic appreciation converge. But since artists usually need funding short-term, this solution seems more philosophical than political.

4.3. Paradox 3: Winners Take All

Adams (2019, p. 26) maintains that both Pareto (the 80/20 rule) and Zipf distributions (sharp declines in occurrence for each next-ranked item) apply to artists' public recognition and personal income, meaning large shares of both goods benefitting only very few fortunate artists, while leaving the great majority with little to nothing. He formulates this paradox as follows:

> Multiple instances of winner-takes-all conditions provide opportunity for great fame and income in contrast to the poverty of most practitioners, which in turn adds to the excitement and appeal of being an artist. Artists […] are risk-takers [and] will conclude that they are talented and lucky enough to benefit from a big-win economy rather than a share-small one.

Consequently, even if most artists would indeed require state subsidies, their inclination would let them bet on personal success rather than shared social benefits. This paradox seems directly connected to the next, that of artists being ill-informed gamblers.

4.4. Paradox 4: Artists as Ill-Informed Gamblers

Both Adams (2019, pp. 26–27) and Abbing (2002, p. 114) point out that "more than other professionals, the average artist is inclined to overestimate his or her skills", and that "the average artist is less well informed [about his or her profession] than other professionals". That lack of appropriate assessment of self and society paradoxically leads to a career choice not despite, but precisely because of lower economic rewards (Adams, 2019, p. 27):

> [Aspiring artists] cleave to a life in the arts not despite […] but partly because of the poverty [seen as] authenticity and unwillingness to compromise. The lack of reward in a

perverse way validates the career choice by emphasising how uncommercial their art is and how determined they have been [...] Artists think they are more in control of their careers than they actually are. Changing taste, external market conditions and luck are all beyond an individual's control.

Thus here, state support would meet two paradoxical hurdles: first, artists' willingness to forge their career without that support, and second, their illusion of control over their own career.

4.5. Paradox 5: Subsidies Create Poverty

Adams (2019, p. 28) states this paradox in terms of "exceptionality": "In terms of income from gifts/subsidies compared to income from the market, for artists the former dominates the latter to degree [sic] unparalleled in any other profession. [...] Thus the exceptionality of the art economy is again apparent". Both Adams (2019, p. 28) and Abbing (2002, pp. 143, 184, 198) also stress the informal but highly influential supporting role of "families" and "friends".

Hence, private donations, gifts and subsidies would potentially undermine the real or perceived economic value of state subsidies, or weaken the psychological benefits of public support systems and sources.

4.6. Paradox 6: The State Encourages an Oversupply of Artists

Both Adams (2019, pp. 29–30) and Abbing (2002, pp. 147–149) argue that the state actively encourages an oversupply of artists, even in socioeconomically advanced countries of the West:

Financial assistance for artists has no effect on artists' incomes. [...] Irrespective of [...] donations, subsidies and social benefits, the incomes of artists have remained relatively low throughout the West for more than a century [...] If there is a trend in the second half of the twentieth century, it is a downward one. [...] where there is an extensive subsidization of the arts, the artist's average income is the same or lower than of artists in countries like the US or in England, where subsidization levels are lower.

Adams (2019, p. 30) directly points to the paradox by admitting that "the conclusion is [...] chilling [...] and contradicts most common wisdom", and then unites with Abbing (2002, p. 139) in the conclusion that "if the sole aim is to reduce poverty in the arts then then the best policy is to reduce overall subsidisation of the arts".

Yet Adams explicitly concedes that "common wisdom" deems differently. Also, his conclusion presumes that the sole aim of subsidies is to reduce poverty, while other motives are commonly known, such as allowing some art forms or artists to exist at all, poor or not.

5. Conclusions and Recommendations

It is the characteristic definition of a paradox that it cannot be easily or evidently solved to all-round satisfaction. Adams makes clear that his and Abbing's "findings go against many of our common cultural assumptions, vested interests and current socio-economic structures", so that "logic, evidence and intuition suggest that most of the economic observations are correct – but that we simply refuse to accept them or act upon them", while they are not "pushing a political agenda in favor of free-market capitalism or abandonment of artistic subsidy" (2019, p. 35).

Adams' final reflections are this research's beginnings of recommendations: "One wonders if it will ever be possible to speak honestly about why we fund art and what we expect to get in return" (2019, p. 36). As mentioned at the beginning of the analysis and discussion part, the highlighted paradoxes of the cultural and art world, and the resulting ambiguities about either favoring or rejecting state support might finally force, or rather, permit us to admit that research recommendations, just as policy actions, will equally reflect and manifest those ambiguities. That insight and result could however be a distinct academic advantage and practical relief: forced to reveal our intellectual uncertainties, our international research and our institutional policies can finally be professionally and publicly transparent about our underlying motives, employed methods, economic measures, social meanings, and political intentions.

References

Abbing, H. (2002). *Why Are Artists Poor? The Exceptional Economy of the Arts.* Amsterdam: Amsterdam University Press.

Adams, A. (2019). *Culture War: Art, Identity Politics and Cultural Entryism.* Exeter: Imprint Academic.

Aldashev, G., & Platteau, J. P. (2014). Religion, Culture, and Development. In V. A. Ginsburgh & D. Throsby (Eds.), *Handbook of the Economics of Art and Culture, Volume 2* (pp. 587–632). Amsterdam, Boston and Oxford: Elsevier.

Amariglio, J., Childers, J. W. & Cullenberg, S. E. (Eds.) (2009a). *Sublime Economy: On the Intersection of Art and Economics.* London and New York: Routledge.

Amariglio, J., Childers, J. W., & Cullenberg, S. E. (2009b). Introduction: Sublime Economy: On the Intersection of Art and Economics. In J. Amariglio, J. W. Childers & S. E. Cullenberg (Eds.), *Sublime Economy: On the Intersection of Art and Economics* (pp. 1–26). London and New York: Routledge.

Baumol, W. J., & Bowen, W. G. (1966). *Performing Arts - The Economic Dilemma: A Study of Problems Common to Theater, Opera, Music and Dance*. New York: Kraus Reprint.

Beech, D. (2015). *Art and Value: Art's Economic Exceptionalism in Classical, Neoclassical and Marxist Economies*. Leiden and Boston: Brill.

Bisin, A., & Verdier, T. (2014). Trade and Cultural Diversity. In V. A. Ginsburgh & D. Throsby (Eds.), *Handbook of the Economics of Art and Culture, Volume 2* (pp. 439–484). Amsterdam, Boston and Oxford: Elsevier.

Blaug, M. (2019). *The Economics of the Arts*. New York and Oxon: Routledge.

Castañer, X. (2014). Cultural Innovation by Cultural Organizations. In V. A. Ginsburgh & D. Throsby (Eds.), *Handbook of the Economics of Art and Culture, Volume 2* (pp. 263–276). Amsterdam, Boston and Oxford: Elsevier.

Courty, P., & Pagliero, M. (2014). The Pricing of Art and the Art of Pricing: Pricing Styles in the Concert Industry. In V. A. Ginsburgh & D. Throsby (Eds.), *Handbook of the Economics of Art and Culture, Volume 2* (pp. 299–356). Amsterdam, Boston and Oxford: Elsevier.

Doyle, G. (2014). Media Ownership: Diversity Versus Efficiency in a Changing Technological Environment. In V. A. Ginsburgh & D. Throsby (Eds.), *Handbook of the Economics of Art and Culture, Volume 2* (pp. 357–378). Amsterdam, Boston and Oxford: Elsevier.

Ekelund, R. B., Jackson, J. D., & Tollison, R. D. (2017). *The Economics of American Art: Issues, Artists and Market Institutions*. Oxford and New York: Oxford University Press.

English, J. F. (2014). The Economics of Cultural Awards. In V. A. Ginsburgh & D. Throsby (Eds.), *Handbook of the Economics of Art and Culture, Volume 2* (pp. 119–143). Amsterdam, Boston and Oxford: Elsevier.

Frey, B. S. (2019). *Economics of Art and Culture*. Cham: Springer.

Ginsburgh, V., & Throsby, D. (2014). Introduction and Overview. In V. A. Ginsburgh & D. Throsby (Eds.), *Handbook of the Economics of Art and Culture, Volume 2* (pp. 1–12). Amsterdam, Boston and Oxford: Elsevier.

Ginsburgh, V., & Weber, S. (2014). Culture, Linguistic Diversity, and Economics. In V. A. Ginsburgh & D. Throsby (Eds.), *Handbook of the Economics of Art and Culture, Volume 2* (pp. 507–544). Amsterdam, Boston and Oxford: Elsevier.

Iapadre, P. L. (2014). Cultural Products in the International Trading System. In V. A. Ginsburgh & D. Throsby (Eds.), *Handbook of the Economics of Art and Culture, Volume 2* (pp. 381–410). Amsterdam, Boston and Oxford: Elsevier.

Levinson, J. (2014). Values of Music. In V. A. Ginsburgh & D. Throsby (Eds.), *Handbook of the Economics of Art and Culture, Volume 2* (pp. 101–117). Amsterdam, Boston and Oxford: Elsevier.

Levy, D. M. (2002). *How the Dismal Science Got Its Name: Classical Economics and the Ur-Text of Racial Politics*. Ann Arbor: The University of Michigan Press.

Locher, P. J. (2014). Contemporary Experimental Aesthetics: Procedures and Findings. In V. A. Ginsburgh & D. Throsby (Eds.), *Handbook of the Economics of Art and Culture, Volume 2* (pp. 49–80). Amsterdam, Boston and Oxford: Elsevier.

Macmillan, F. (2014). Cultural Diversity, Copyright, and International Trade. In V. A. Ginsburgh & D. Throsby (Eds.), *Handbook of the Economics of Art and Culture, Volume 2* (pp. 411–438). Amsterdam, Boston and Oxford: Elsevier.

Mandel, B. R. (2014). Investment in Visual Art: Evidence from International Transactions. In V. A. Ginsburgh & D. Throsby (Eds.), *Handbook of the Economics of Art and Culture, Volume 2* (pp. 233–260). Amsterdam, Boston and Oxford: Elsevier.

Marglin, S. A. (2008). *The Dismal Science: How Thinking Like an Economist Undermines Community*. Cambridge, Massachusetts and London, England: Harvard University Press.

Martin, V. (2017). *Transdisciplinarity Revealed: What Librarians Need to Know*. Santa Barbara and Denver: Libraries Unlimited and ABC-CLIO.

Montalvo, J. G., & Reynal-Querol, M. (2014). Cultural Diversity, Conflict, and Economic Development. In V. A. Ginsburgh & D. Throsby (Eds.), *Handbook of the Economics of Art and Culture, Volume 2* (pp. 485–506). Amsterdam, Boston and Oxford: Elsevier.

Platteau, J. P., & Wahhaj, Z. (2014). Strategic Interactions Between Modern Law and Custom. In V. A. Ginsburgh & D. Throsby (Eds.), *Handbook of the Economics of Art and Culture, Volume 2* (pp. 633–678). Amsterdam, Boston and Oxford: Elsevier.

Potts, J. (2014). New Technologies and Cultural Consumption. In V. A. Ginsburgh & D. Throsby (Eds.), *Handbook of the Economics of Art and Culture, Volume 2* (pp. 215–232). Amsterdam, Boston and Oxford: Elsevier.

Rodrik, D. (2015). *Economics Rules: The Rights and Wrongs of the Dismal Science*. New York and London: W. W. Norton.

Schwartz, S. H. (2014). National Culture as Value Orientations: Consequences of Value Differences and Cultural Distance. In V. A. Ginsburgh & D. Throsby (Eds.), *Handbook of the Economics of Art and Culture, Volume 2* (pp. 547–586). Amsterdam, Boston and Oxford: Elsevier.

Simonton, D. K. (2014). Creative Genius in Literature, Music, and the Visual Arts. In V. A. Ginsburgh & D. Throsby (Eds.), *Handbook of the Economics of Art and Culture, Volume 2* (pp. 15–48). Amsterdam, Boston and Oxford: Elsevier.

Throsby, D. (2006). Introduction and Overview. In V. A. Ginsburgh & D. Throsby (Eds.), *Handbook of the Economics of Art and Culture, Volume 1* (pp. 3–22). Amsterdam, Boston and Oxford: Elsevier.

Throsby, D. (2012). Why Should Economists Be Interested in Cultural Policy? *Economic Record, 88*(1), 106–109.

Throsby, D., & Zednik, A. (2014). The Economic and Cultural Value of Paintings: Some Empirical Evidence. In V. A. Ginsburgh & D. Throsby (Eds.), *Handbook of the Economics of Art and Culture, Volume 2* (pp. 81–100). Amsterdam, Boston and Oxford: Elsevier.

Waldfogel, J. (2014). Digitization, Copyright, and the Flow of New Music Products. In V. A. Ginsburgh & D. Throsby (Eds.), *Handbook of the Economics of Art and Culture, Volume 2* (pp. 277–298). Amsterdam, Boston and Oxford: Elsevier.

Walls, W. D. (2014). Bestsellers and Blockbusters: Movies, Music, and Books. In V. A. Ginsburgh & D. Throsby (Eds.), *Handbook of the Economics of Art and Culture, Volume 2* (pp. 185–214). Amsterdam, Boston and Oxford: Elsevier.

Whitaker, A. (2021). *Economics of Visual Art: Market Practice and Market Resistance.* Cambridge and New York: Cambridge University Press.

Willis, K. G. (2014). The Use of Stated Preference Methods to Value Cultural Heritage. In V. A. Ginsburgh & D. Throsby (Eds.), *Handbook of the Economics of Art and Culture, Volume 2* (pp. 145–182). Amsterdam, Boston and Oxford: Elsevier.

Alexandru Trifu

The Knowledge of Generational Particularities: Essential for the Profitability of Companies/Organizations

1. The Generational Theory in Support of the Company Management

Mannheim (1952) provided the definition of generations, considering that they were formed based on two elements:

a. A temporally common location so that there are common events and experiences;
b. An awareness of that common location, reinforced over time.

The ascendancy of the concept today also reflects the speed of social change. A key example is the growing imbalance between older and younger populations in Western societies, which raises issues of generational justice, especially at times when many governments have cut public spending and social benefits.

The supposed clash of generations in the workplace starts from the belief, even the reality, that the generations differ related to their values, the attitudes towards leadership and the behavior at the workplace and outside of it, and that the lack of understanding between the generations about these differences leads to intergenerational conflicts and negative effects upon communication and work (Gabrielova & Buchko, 2021).

The company's inner contradictions can become a threat to the company more than the external economic challenges. The CEO entrepreneur can restore the peace and the mutual understanding among the employees of various ages within the company/organization, in order for it to achieve its existential goals, i.e. primarily its profitability and its sustainability.

The fact that in this day and age people with various life experiences, various values and work motivations have to work side by side often becomes the terrain of deep disagreements and conflicts. The causes of conflicts can be multiple. For instance, when managers who are considered to have outdated, more conservative ideas in the eyes of young employees lead processes that they do not understand and, therefore, they cannot properly motivate the younger employees. Also, it is the case when the older generation manager higher education graduates who are too zealous by the standards of conservative adults to innovate or to find ways to provide effective tools for the collective work. The problem of intergenerational communication is becoming one of the most painful and topical. And here the theory of generations comes to the aid of businesses. This theory attempts to clearly highlight the characteristics of each generation to help leaders bring the report back to the office (Trends, 2022).

Let us also make a reference to the main reference within *the Generational Theory*, namely the Theory of William Strauss and Neil Howe based on the real facts of the labor market and the operation of firms/companies in the United States (Strauss & Howe, 1997). The second part of the book's title also gives the specificity of its content.

They believe that the latest 80 years studied indicate a division into cycles (specific economic-social aspect) and each cycle is divided into periods, defined from each of the generations presented below:

- **The baby boomers (born between 1943–60)**

The post-war period, the birth boom and the global economic growth have endowed this generation with optimism, confidence in progress and a desire for teamwork.

- **Generation X (born between 1961–81)**

This generation is characterized by a deep involvement in social networks, by a slow process to becoming adults, by civic engagement and they show high moral principles with which they seek to change the world for the better.

- **Generation Y, Millennials (born between 1982–2004)**

This is a generation of individualists who didn't want to work in offices which values freedom and pragmatism. This generation was mainly impacted by the global economic recession caused by the oil crisis of the 1970s.

- **Generation Z, Zers (born between 2005–2010/12)**

Little is known about this generation. They are assumed to be more pragmatic and flexible and that the moral rigidity and civic activism of their parents will not impact them so much, but the digital technologies are expected to be very present in their daily life and work.

Each of the stages highlighted by the two American researchers characterizes a generation at a given time and each stage is associated with a certain societal role. Most importantly, in each human life cycle, the society goes through four major events of change as each generation moves from one stage to the next.

So, the 4 (four) stages considered as the skeleton of the Generational Theory are:

a. *The Awakening,*which is considered to be the summertime of the cycle;
b. *The Crisis*is the wintertime;
c. + d. *The Unraveling + the High* represent seasons, periods of transition, i.e. the autumn and the spring.

Neil Howe is the author who thought through and stated these phases, which are very similar to economic cycles, guided by the seasons of the year and considering that the society goes through major events of change as each generation moves from one stage to the next in its development.

The modern history moves in cycles, each lasting roughly the length of a long human lifetime; each cycle is composed of four twenty-year eras – or "turnings" – that comprise the history's seasonal rhythm of growth, maturation, entropy and rebirth.

In fact, if we make the comparison with the business/development cycle, the correct order is as follows:

a. *The High* – this is a post-crisis, optimistic age during which the institutions and the communities are strengthened while the individualism weakens;
b. *The Awakening* is a period of spiritual turmoil, with the current value system attacked by a new value regime;
c. *The Unraveling*, i.e. a less optimistic era of the strengthening of individualism and weak institutions, with the emergence of a new value system;
d. *The Crisis*, i.e. the culmination and turning point and which disrupts the normal course of existence or development. The value regime results in the replacement of the old civic order with another. It is considered that the last "turning point" is represented by the events in America since 9/11 (2001).

Certainly, these theoretical, general problems must be known especially by the people working in the HR departments or who have duties regarding the personnel. But neither the owners nor the CEOs (especially when the quality of the owner overlaps with that of the CEO, as is the case of the famous and controversial Elon Musk) must know these elements, especially the characteristics of the generations that dominate or will dominate the labor market: the Millennials and Generation Z (Zers).

Another sensitive but important aspect is the understanding of the HR: the obtaining of information and the constant connection to everything that is communicated and published in the field of the workforce, whether already existing or potential. For the second situation, we come up with a recent situation, relevant to the American youth: the use of the label "rizz", which in slang means someone's ability to flirt, to be pleasant (charming) but, for the present topic, the characteristic of charisma in communication (Munson, 2023). It is believed that this term comes from the word "charisma", a very important aspect for a certain person.

This can also be considered an additional method of getting to know young people, of the future employees, alongside the already existing method of monitoring valuable pupils during high school (especially in the "cutting edge" fields of IT, or the research using new technologies), meaning *the head hunter* method, rather than *scouting*.

2. Methodology

In this paper we sought to combine a survey on the opinions related to the activity of departments or HR specialists, presented in papers or information appearing in the media, with the experiences of some managers, entrepreneurs and even our own experiences, related to how they should be brought to the common denominator of the company/organization, the characteristics, the skills, the specific knowledge of the workers, so as to achieve the company goals, but also the satisfaction of the employees for the work performed.

We have, therefore, a qualitative research that, taking into account the general characteristics of the generation to which each employee belongs and also the specific individual traits, synthesizes possible management approaches to obtain what can also be called here a *modus in rebus*.

Therefore, it is a matter of suggesting an approach to the issue under discussion, an approach that is predominantly subjective, but useful, we say, both for the management of the companies and also for the employees.

3. Pattern or Managerial Art

We are back to highlighting what needs to be done to work effectively with Gen Z (www.workplace.com/blog/ 2023):

a. The focus on diversity and inclusion;
b. The flexibility in work;
c. Encouraging communication;
d. Ensuring autonomy in action (to the extent possible);
e. Creating a favorable working climate within the organizational culture;
f. Ensuring financial stability and wellness benefits.

Gen Z has the most numerous members at the moment, with a share of 32 % of the world's population.

We were saying that we need to highlight the characteristics of the Millennials and the Gen Z members which are the generations that will soon become the majority in the labor market.

To this end, let's present, among the many informative sources on the net of well-known HR consulting firms, which are the *common traits* of the Millennials and of Gen Z in the workplace, bearing in mind that the Millennial Generation is currently the most numerous on the labor market and that there is a need to harmonize these requirements/characteristics (www.deskbird.com/blog/ 2023):

1. *The work flexibility.* The work flexibility is very high on the list of demands of the Millennials and Generation Z members. For any office job, these two generations members expect to have the choice of working from home, on-site or in another workplace (part-time);
2. *The skills development and the career growth* are common goals for both Millennials and the Gen Z members as they want to continue to expand their soft and hard skills;
3. *Achieving a better work-life balance* is also a top priority for them. According to certain studies in this regard, in 2022 for example, when applying for a job the work-personal life balance was at the top of priorities, for both generations;
4. **Creating purpose** *is* **fundamental** when working with the two generations. Pursuing a meaningful career is a solid reason for both generations to change jobs quite often. Both generations use the phenomenon of "job-hopping", changing jobs until they find their purpose in professional life and they fit into the values of that particular job.

But there are also differences between the members of these generations at the level of their professional activity. Thus, the Millennial members are open to collaborations, group work, while the Gen Z members are loners, that is, they and the modern search and communication technologies. This near-total dependence on the digital technologies makes Gen Z members more concerned with the privacy and the rejection of the interaction with other people. They are followers of privacy and they seek to pay very close attention to what they say or to what they do.

Then, both generations aspire to earn good salaries, to obtain higher incomes. But while the Millennials rely on their flair for success and they take out loans, which they can then repay, the Gen Z members rely on their own strength to thrive in the convenient environment and earn a decent income.

Let us also talk about the corporate management, the one called to ensure the training of all resources to achieve the goals set for the entity, with the profitability as the first goal, but with the appropriate use of the workforce.

In the corporate management, there is first of all, the figure and personality of the CEO who, as we have shown, in many cases identifies with the entrepreneur/owner. On the one hand, there is the image, based on examples from the surrounding reality, can be of a mature person, at the height of his or her managerialknowledge and practice. On the other hand, there are young people of 25–30 years old, who start successful start-ups.

But, because we claim that the management and the business are both science and art, we believe the CEO to be somewhere around 40–45 years old. For example, from the analysis and the list presented by Fortune 500 for the year 2023, 267 of the people listed belong to Generation X, that is, between the ages of 43 and 58 (www.day1strategic.com/post/2023). While every CEO is different, there is one archetype that emerges with a different set of skills and challenges than that of the last generation. The archetype is created for each generation, based upon the characteristics of that particular generation by taking into account the specific commandments of the leadership of a business and which, of course, also takes over common and valuable elements from the previous generation.

From our own experience and also from the discussions we had with the key factors of the management or from the stated experiences, we identified the situation in which it is better to work with Millennials (34 % of the respondents), for productivity and technical skills. The Millennials also stand out for their honesty (Berger, 2023).

Creating the special environment required by the Zers is not only beneficial to them, but it also has other advantages. It's about completely transforming the workplace into an attractive organization that continues to grow, as they value the potential of each employee, if the employer focuses on retaining talent and if it is willing to help all employees develop and perform in a safe environment.

All this indicates to us that the labor productivity, the newly created value at the level of the company/organization will increase and therefore the profitability of the business is ensured, i.e. obtaining profit.

For the owner, the CEO and the other managers, this means knowing these general, but also individual, generational traits, for the substantiation of a viable strategy in the medium term and also a know-how, an entrepreneurial art for the fruition of opportunities arising at the level of the entire functional mechanism of the company.

So, the owner/CEO himself must have the necessary knowledge of the field in which he or she operates, but also of interpersonal relations, of the intervention, if necessary, if threats occur in his business activity.

Actually, from practice and the surrounding reality, there can be a situation where the owner is also the CEO, or he/she is the majority shareholder and he/she uses the medium-term strategy with the very purpose of achieving his/her financial goals. Even if we witness a phenomenon like "The Great Resignation", or simple resignations/dismissals, the management intends to quickly find efficient professional replacements, or they are willing to learn in a short amount of time. The permanent training and the proper motivation are arguments for employees to remain loyal and stable for a longer period of time and all this for profitability and sustainability in that peculiar market.

Another practical situation coming from the General Management of the company: for companies that for several years have spent significant amounts of money hiring top people, the reassigning of employees to new roles can be a way to fill jobs vital to future plans, by reducing at the same time the costs associated with old strategies, HR executives say. The employees might decide to quit if they feel stuck in a job they don't want, but as the job market loses momentum, many believe the best option is to stay put and hunt internally for a better matching.

This is called "quiet cutting" – when employees are reassigned to new roles within their current organizations. They are told that the jobs they had are now being cut, but they can move to another job as part of an organizational restructuring (Mensik, 2023). Analysts and employees who have gone through years of practice in the field, can say that this method is not something new, but it can be successfully implemented given the current situation.

The second situation describes an owner/CEO which has that flair we were talking about related to people, to bring out everything that is good and valuable, in the service of the company, but also of the respective employees. We can therefore speak, in this case, of *an art of management*, as stated by Henry Mintzbeg, among others, because we cannot present recipes, universally valid patterns for solving difficult situations in a company, or any external threats, but the most suitable decisions must be made, in conditions most diverse and of various complexity (such as those 4–5 years back) (www.edukyu.com 2023).

But, there are more unusual situations (from the multitude of actions and situations that occur in this period regarding the HR) where the employer utilizes certain employment techniques, which can be classified as subliminal (really, unrelated to the generational characteristics).

This is the case of Trent Innes, development director at SiteMinder (former CEO of Xero Australia), who uses a peculiar but controversial technique: *the hiring is only done if the candidate takes his cup of coffee to the kitchen after the interview is over* (www.digi24.ro/stiri/externe/ 2023).

The justification, which is based on the analyzed topic, attitudes are developed thereby(emphasis added), apart from the development of skills, the acquisition of knowledge and experience, which can be achieved through other HR methods and tactics. The criticisms relates to the fact that Trent Innes manipulates the minds of candidates, but the reality has shown that most candidates have taken this "walk" to the kitchen, showing that they are also willing to do activities to help themselves and the company.

4. Conclusions

What must be done regarding a company's personnel? We must seek to identify areas of generational understanding and collaboration and the areas of potential conflict. While the Millennials and the Generation Z members share many professional values, such as the work-life balance and achievements, as we have seen, this still requires managers and CEOs to be members of the Millennials, of the Generation X or even of the Baby Boomers generations.

Within an entity, the productivity and accountability are pursued, which can also be achieved through the appropriate training and motivation of the staff. A "modus vivendi" must be reached on the part of the participants.

The effective communication is essential in any workplace and understanding the somewhat contrasting communication styles of the Millennials and the Gen X members can spark something valuable.

References

Berger, Chloe. (2023). *Gen Z Is at the Top of Bosses' Firing List because.. They're the Most Difficult Generation to Work With.* www.fortune.com/2023/. Retrieved September 12, 2023.

Gabrielova, K., & Buchko, A. A.(2021) *Here comes Generation Z: Millennials as Managers*, Business Horizons, Elsevier. www.science.direct.com/science/arti cle/. Retrieved September 8, 2023.

Mannheim, Karl. (1952, republished 1972). *The Problem of Generations, Essays.* In Paul Kecskemeti (Ed.), chapter VII, Routledge. www.marcuse.faculty.hist ory.ucsb.edu/classes/. Retrieved September 11, 2023.

Mensik, Hailey. (2023). *WTF Is Quiet Cutting?* www.worklife.news/talent/. Retrieved September 15, 2023.

Munson, Olivia. (2023). What Does 'Rizz' Mean? Here's the Definition of Social Media Slang Term and How to Usr It. *USA Today*. www.eu.usatoday.com/ story/tech/. Retrived September 10, 2023.

Strauss, W., & Howe, Neil. (1997). *The Fourth Turning: What the Cycles of History Tells Us about America's Next Rendevouz with Destiny*. New York: Three Rivers Press.

———. (2023b). *Millennials and Gen Z in the Workplace: Same But Different?* www.deskbird.com/blog/. Retrieved September 3, 2023.

———. (2023c). *Gen Z in the Workplace: How to Keep Them Happy*. Meta. www. workplace.com/blog/. Retrieved September 2, 2023.

———. (2023d). Management as an Art. *EduKyu*. www.edukyu.com. Retrieved August 31, 2023.

———. (2023e). *Testul ceştii de cafea° prin care se aleg candidaţii*. www.digi24.ro/ stiri/externe/ Retrieved September 8, 2023.

——— Trends. (2022). *Teoria generaţională la locul de muncă: cum să rezolvi conflictele de vârstă într-o echipă*. www.ro.healthy.food-near-me.com. Retrieved September 5, 2023.

Daniel Lajcin

Managerial Personality

1. Introduction

The concept of personality has one important common characteristic in scientific research. While in ordinary life this term is used to denote important people from various areas of social life (politics, economy, culture, sports, art, science, etc.), in the scientific context every manager is also a unique personality. Human personality and its manifestations represent a complicated issue. It is difficult to give a single definition of personality, because the understanding of the concept of personality is influenced by the theoretical starting points and the school that the author of the given definition represents. Despite several differences in the conceptualization of the term personality, the recurring characteristics in individual definitions are the individual unity of biological, psychological and social influences, the unity of psychological processes, states and properties as determinants of experience and behavior, the constant development of personality, but also the relative stability of personality, its manifestations in time and space. To these recurring characteristics in the definitions of the personality category, it is possible to add the attributes system, organization and self-regulation, structured-ness, integrity, and integration. Personality develops and forms with the participation of the processes of socialization and individualization of a person and processes that are under the influence of genetic factors, respectively. under the influence of the environment. These processes accompany the entire life journey of people. They are not independent processes, but on the contrary, processes that work together on a person from birth.

The construct of the manager's personality examined in the presented chapter is based on the definition of Smékal (2004), who views personality from the point of view of a systemic approach as an individualized system of psychological processes, states and properties that arise on the one hand through socialization (effect of education and environment), on the other hand by reshaping the innate internal conditions of a person's being, and they determine and control the subject activities of the individual, their social relations and spiritual relations. Therefore, the investigation of a person's personality is oriented towards the analysis of the whole as well as the analysis of individuality (Cloninger, 2008).

2. General View of Personality Traits

Trait, disposition is a relatively constant characteristic of an individual, which manifests itself in their experience and behavior. Different authors define them differently. For some, traits are the core of personality, for others they are just a cognitive construct, created by the observers themselves. There is still a debate about what features contain and whether it is expedient to examine features using psychometric approaches (Hřebíčková et al., 2002). Mikšík (2007) understands personality traits as the so-called core of personality and considers them as the building blocks of an individual's inner integrity. He divides these character traits into three substructures by model: temperament, personality motivational system, abilities and prerequisites for effective interactions with life's reality. According to the author, these substructures work in connection with each other and are inseparable in their activity.

In accordance with Praško et al. (2003), the concept of personality is divided into temperament, which is considered innate, and character, which develops in interaction with the world. Each individual completes their character with their goals and focus. On the one hand, our personality structure is relatively stable in adulthood, but on the other hand, we develop and change throughout our lives by how we react to the environment. Cloninger (2008) considers character and temperament as measurable quantities, thanks to which it is possible to assess differences between individual people. Character is also related to the higher cognitive functions of our mind, which includes executive functions (Cloninger & Svrakic, 2009).

People differ from each other in how they perceive themselves, other people, and objects, which reflects what their values and goals are. Individual components of character mature depending on social learning throughout life (Cloninger & Svrakic, 1997). Character is shaped by environment and is not correlated with temperament. Adequate development of individual dimensions of character is a prerequisite for a harmonious and mature personality of an individual (Cloninger & Svrakic, 2009).

Eysenck (1960) created an interpretation of the theory of personality structure, in which he assumes that the structure of temperament is formed by two mutually independent dimensions: neuroticism and introversion/extraversion. By combining them, it is possible to arrive at classical temperament types, which the author confirmed by examining these dimensions using evaluation scales, objective tests and questionnaires. Neuroticism as a personality characteristic is marked as a dimension of emotional stability and lability. According to Eysenck and Eysenck (1993), a low neuroticism score means that the individual's personality is well integrated, the individual is emotionally stable, quickly regains balance after a strong emotional experience. He takes reality as it is, he does not think about the different possibilities of the given situation. A high score, on the other hand, indicates emotional lability, instability and poor personality integration. According to Eysenck and Eysenck (1970) such individuals are anxious and have many unnecessary fears. They are restless, hypersensitive and irritable, sometimes react inappropriately even to little things. They lack self-confidence and suffer from feelings of inferiority.

3. Personality Traits of Managers

The personnel and social processes that take place in the company can be understood as the activities of managers who directly and indirectly affect individual workers through their activities, stimulating their willingness to work and their ability to perform at their best (Bedrnová & Nový, 2002). The effectiveness of their work depends, among other things, on professional and personal prerequisites for managerial work. Studies by Lukeš and Nový (2005) focused on managerial work confirmed that personality traits have an impact on the success of managers. They concluded that personality influences the goals and strategies a manager chooses, and these then directly influence success. Personality traits have an impact on organizational skills, motivation, vision and strategy. In this context, it should be noted that there are also research results by Procházka and Smutný (2010), which did not demonstrate a direct influence of personality traits on the performance of the group leader. However, the research authors examined job performance as a whole. A manager influences many people, therefore, desirable qualities and characteristics of a manager should be as follows (Bedrnová & Nový, 2002):

1. Accept the actions of employees, understand them, tolerate them and guide them.
2. Act in accordance with your conscience, be consistent, honest and responsible.
3. Be able to clearly express your wishes, instructions, suggestions.
4. Be able to make decisions even in demanding situations.
5. Be able to navigate even in difficult problems.
6. Be able to react flexibly in new situations.
7. Cope with demanding situations and mental stress.
8. Know how to formulate your thoughts and communicate them to employees in a comprehensible, clear and matter-of-fact manner.
9. Know how to organize and control the work of employees well.
10. Know how to specifically define goals for employees.

11. Provide feedback to employees, as well as receive it from them.

The authors add that attempts to determine the specific characteristics required for managerial work encounter many obstacles such as uniqueness, individuality of the individual, differences in the demands of individual functions and social conditions of organizations. Therefore, it is necessary to take into account the point of view of social conditions and the development of the situation in the organization.

Research studies on personality traits important for the performance of managerial work and work activities deal with conscientiousness, emotional stability, cognitive abilities, psychological abilities, psychomotor abilities, motivation, social behavior, social intelligence, self-confidence of individuals and the like (Hametová, 2004). The practical use of the results of the investigation of the personality of managers in work activities, as well as the determination of the personality profile of managers and the analysis of characteristics that are important in the given work area, are essential for the quality performance of managerial work (Hametová, 2004).

In this context, Van Den Berg and Feij (1993) found through a quantitative analysis that there is a statistically significant relationship between personality traits, the nature of the work performed and the experience of job satisfaction. They conducted the research through four personality traits – neuroticism, extraversion, openness to experience and ambition. The already mentioned research by Lukeš and Nový (2005) was focused on the question of whether managers differ in some personality traits from employees. The authors concluded that managers differ from employees in a higher degree of extraversion (important for gaining contacts, dealing with other people) and openness to experience (necessary for discovering new opportunities). Similarly, the results of other research confirmed a higher level of dimensions of extraversion, friendliness, emotional stability, openness to experience and conscientiousness in people in managerial positions (Lukeš & Stephan, 2004). In the context of specifying the personality traits of managers, Porvazník et al. (2013) describe the characteristics that a good manager should possess. In addition to professional knowledge, they should have well-developed application skills, specifically communication and motivational skills, and the skills necessary for effective teamwork. It also emphasizes their creativity, will, character, emotionality and physical, mental qualities. Porvazník et al. (2007) also emphasize the moral personality traits of managers formed primarily by their character.

Durdová (2002) draws attention to the importance of temperament, intelligence, sound judgment, empathy, understanding of others, imagination, and complements them with innate qualities of the manager's personality, in addition to those already mentioned. He recommends adding a good mental and physical state to the acquired qualities of a manager. Gajdoš (2007) adds to the varied palette of mentioned and investigated characteristics of managers with characteristics related to versatility in knowledge, abilities, personal profile, emphasizing empathy, resilience, trustworthiness, complexity, communicativeness. On a more general level, Šuleř (2002) draws attention to the importance of biological, social and cultural factors that participate in the formation of a manager's personality. As part of the manager's personality, he emphasizes knowledge, skills and practical habits, attitudes in relation to other people and facts, skills for performing the work, experience and values that the manager considers important. The concept of self-development and the art of collaboration come to the fore in the approach of Covey (2014). Bělohlávek, Košťan and Šuleř (2006) in turn emphasized good management and planning of one's time and the art of delegating tasks to subordinates. Vodák and Kucharčíková (2011) similarly characterize personality prerequisites for managerial work. The authors describe the personality traits needed to perform managerial work, such as effective conflict resolution, delegation, planning, and employee evaluation. Mesárosová et al. (2008) complements them with stress management, conflict, decision-making, leadership, planning, creativity, delegation, learning through action and interpersonal skills. Kubeš, Spillerová and Kurnický (2004) claim that for highly effective behavior a manager needs abilities, skills, experience, as well as knowledge that he can use correctly in a given environment, and is willing to expend the necessary energy for this.

Cejthamr and Dědina (2010) generalize individual specifications of managerial characteristics and distinguish:

1 Conceptual assumptions (ability to make decisions).
2. Social prerequisites (ability to communicate and lead people, effective use of human resources).
3. Professional, technical skills (specific knowledge, procedures and skills).

When evaluating a manager, it is important to observe their personality traits, the ability of self-education, decision-making, as well as flexibility, innovativeness in solving tasks (Lojda, 2011). Therefore, a well-rounded personality who wants to constantly work on themselves and use their potential is important for the effective performance of managerial work. According to Bělohlávek (2000), all specific managerial characteristics create the personal potential of the manager, which is a prerequisite for achieving managerial skills. The potential allows the manager to focus on such activities, activities and decisions in which he can excel as much as possible and achieve the set goals. Mikuláštík (2007) emphasizes that through self-knowledge we can know ourselves better, which increases the level of knowing other people. Trying to improve relationships with others without the manager working on themselves is ineffective, according to Covey (2014). In this understanding, the developed social intelligence of the manager is very important. In the theoretical part, the knowledge presented from the problems of the manager's personality, social intelligence in managerial work and coping with demanding situations in the work of managers confirm the fact that these areas are not outside the interest of scientific research.

4. How to Measure Personality Traits

Cattell (1957) considers personality traits as determinants of behavior that have predictive value. Using factor analysis, he specified sixteen personality factors: warmth, deduction, emotional stability, dominance, liveliness, principledness, social boldness, sensitivity, vigilance, dreaminess, closedness, fearfulness, openness to changes, self-sufficiency, perfectionism, tension. The psychometric tool for determining Cattell's factors is the 16PFQ methodology (Pervin & John, 1999). Another of the general theories of personality traits is the Big Five concept, which describes an individual's personality in five dimensions. Authorship of the Big Five theory is attributed to the couple McCrae and Costa (1986). Their theory is based on the aforementioned Cattell concept of 16 PF. By factor analysis of the second order of Cattell's questionnaire scales, Costa and McCrae identified the first three factors: Neuroticism, Extraversion and Openness to experience. The other two factors were created on the basis of lexical studies (Říčan, 2010), which were based on the lexical analysis of a dictionary of adjectives that related to personality traits. Factor analysis revealed two additional factors: Conscientiousness and Agreeableness. The five-factor model of personality is not a theory of personality as such, but nevertheless contains the basic principles of trait theories, according to which an individual can be characterized on the basis of relatively permanent ways of thinking, experiencing and acting. Thanks to the methods derived from this model, we can quantitatively determine personality traits. Research confirms a certain degree of coherence of traits in different situations (Hřebíčková, 2000). The Big Five model does not mean that we can reduce personality differences to just five traits. These five traits only try to describe personality at a general level of abstraction, where each of the dimensions includes a large number of differences in specific personality traits (Pervin & John, 1999).

The entire system consists of five postulates and dynamic processes that determine the mutual interactions of individual elements (Hřebíčková, 2000; Hřebíčková & Urbánek, 2001):

1. Basal tendencies are biologically conditioned abilities and dispositions that are not objectively observed, including individuality, origin, development, and structure.
2. The characteristics of adaptation are a concrete manifestation of basal tendencies, they contain e.g. values, personal goals, habits and the like.
3. Objective biography includes the life path of an individual who creates their plans in accordance with their personality traits.
4. Self-concept represents a schema of oneself and gives the individual a sense of coherence.
5. External influences are, for example, development and the influence of the environment.

Meyer (1998; according to Hřebíčková, 2000) claims that personality must be viewed as a system that needs to be defined, its components must be distinguished, and the mutual links and development of the entire system must be described. The five-factor theory tries to take into account these requirements, to include all levels explaining the individual. According to the Czech version by the authors Hřebíčková and Urbánek (2001), personality factors are: neuroticism, extraversion, openness to new experiences, friendliness and conscientiousness. Each factor manifests itself through specific manifestations, whether for individuals with high or low levels of the observed personality trait.

The extraversion factor partially corresponds to Eysenck's (1960) interpretation. A distinctive feature of extraversion is sociability, activity and assertiveness. High-scoring individuals are described as sociable, confident, dominant, active, talkative, energetic, passionate, cheerful, and optimistic. People with a low score are described as closed, quieter, restrained, passive, independent and independent (Hřebíčková & Urbánek, 2001).

Friendliness as a personality dimension is primarily related to the area of interpersonal behavior. One side of this dimension is characterized by altruism, warmth, caring for others, understanding others, tendency to trust, preference for cooperation and emotional support. On the opposite side, there is hostility, egocentrism, indifference, animosity, jealousy, ruthlessness, inviolability, a tendency to disregard other people's intentions and competition instead of cooperation (Hřebíčková & Urbánek, 2001).

Conscientiousness refers to the ability to actively plan, organize and complete tasks. Research cited by Cloninger (2008) shows that conscientious people receive more rewards for their work, which contributes to their generally higher self-esteem (Costa et al., et al., 1991). Conscientious individuals set higher goals and are less often late with work results (Judge et al., 1997). Buss and Shackelford (1997) noted a connection with family relationships, where people scoring high on the Conscientiousness factor are happier in marriage. Orientation of the manager's personality in the direction of conscientiousness, similar to the characterization of extraversion and friendliness, can be considered as a predictor of the effectiveness of managerial work.

The neuroticism personality dimension involves the contrast between coping with the environment, emotional stability, or emotional lability. Individuals who are emotionally unstable are easily embarrassed, often feel ashamed, are more vulnerable, insecure, nervous, anxious. They also experience fear, worry or sadness more often. Emotionally stable individuals are calm, balanced, resilient, carefree, and stressful situations rarely upset them (Hřebíčková & Urbánek, 2001). Ruisel (2008) understands neuroticism as a tendency to experience negative emotions, such as fear, anxiety, sadness, threat or distress. Individuals who score low on the neuroticism scale are happier and more satisfied with life. They do not suffer from low self-esteem and self-confidence (DeNeve, Cooper, 1998; Schmutte, Ryff, 1997; according to Cloninger, 2008).

The effectiveness of managerial work is clearly related to emotional stability, which is a significant predictor of this effectiveness. Costa and McCrae (according to Hřebíčková & Urbanek, 2001) understand the personality dimension of openness to experience as flexibility of thinking, openness to new stimuli, thoughts and ideas. Other authors understand this dimension more like aesthetics, culture or even general intelligence. Openness to experience expresses active imagination, preference for diversity, intellectual curiosity, independent judgment (Ruisel, 2008).

There are different opinions on the use of personality tests, for example, in the selection of job applicants and people for managerial positions. Some argue that personality test scores are not sufficient predictors of job performance (Arnold et al., 2007). Other authors claim that personality traits are good predictors of behavior, especially in interpersonal situations (Fleeson & Gallagher, 2009).

5. Conclusion

Due to the huge number of concepts, the need to construct a general concept of the issue of personality traits began to appear. The problem is that knowledge is rather similar to a certain pluralism, which not only carries with it a diversity of concepts, but there are also many agreements and similar positions (Kolaříková,

2005). An attempt to integrate different systems of personality traits at a high level of generalization is represented, for example, by the five-factor personality model – Big Five (Pervin & John, 1999).

Management is not a static discipline, but a process of systematic planning, organizing, leading people and controlling towards the achievement of organizational goals. In this sense, the presented chapter point to the necessity of taking into account not only generally accepted managerial competences, but also the specific requirements of a particular managerial position in terms of managerial personality when selecting people for managerial positions.

References

Arnold, J. et al. (2007). *Psychologie práce pro manažery a personalisty*. Brno: Computer Press.

Bedrnová, E., & Nový, I. (2002). *Psychologie a sociologie řízení*. Praha: Management Press.

Bělohlávek, F. (2000). *Jak řídit a vést lidi*. Praha: Computer Press.

Bělohlávek, F., Košťan, P., & Šuleř, O. (2006). *Management*. Brno: Computer Press.

Buss, D. M., & Shackelford, T. K. (1997). From Vigilance to Violence: Mate Retention Tactics in Married Couples. *Journal of Personality and Social Psychology, 72*, 346–361.

Cattell, R. B. (1957). *Personality and Motivation Structure and Measurement*. New York: World Book.

Cejthamr V., & Dědina, J. (2010). *Management a organizační chování*. Praha: Grada Publishing.

Cloninger, C. R., & Svrakic, D. M. (1997). Integrative Psychobiological Approach to Psychiatric Assessment and Treatment. *Psychiatry, 60*(2), 120–141.

Cloninger, C. R., & Svrakic, D. M. (2009). Personality Disorders. In B. J. Sadock, V. A. Sadock, P. Ruin (Eds.), *Kaplan, Sadock's Comprehensive Textbook of Psychiatry* (2nd ed.). New York, NY: Lippincott Williams & Wilkins.

Cloninger, S. C. (2008). *Theories of Personality: Understanding Persons* (5th ed.). Englewood Cliffs, New Jersey: Prentice Hall.

Costa P. T. Jr., McCrae, R. R., & Dye, D. A. (1991). Facet Scales for Agreeableness and Conscientiousness: A Revision of the NEO Personality Inventory. *Personality and Individual Differences, 12*, 887–898.

Covey, S. R. (2014). *7 návyků skutečně efektivních lidí. Zásady osobního rozvoje, ktoré změní váš život*. Praha: Management Press.

116   Daniel Lajcin

DeNeve, K. M., & Cooper, H. (1998). The happy personality: a meta-analysis of 137 personality traits and subjective well-being. *Psychological bulletin, 124*(2), 197.

Durdová, I. (2002). *Sportovní Management*. Ostrava: EF VŠB TU Ostrava.

Eysenck, H. J. (1960). *The Structure of Human Personality*. London: Methuen & Co.

Eysenck, H. J., & Eysenck, S. B. G. (1970). *Personality Sturcture and Measurement*. London: Routledge & Kegan Paul.

Eysenck, H. J., & Eysenck, S. B. G. (1993). *Eysenckovy osobnostní dotazníky pro dospělé: příručka*. Bratislava: Psychodiagnostika.

Fleeson, W., & Gallagher, P. (2009). The Implications of Big Five Standing for the Distribution of Trait Manifestation in Behavior: Fifteen Experience-Sampling Studies and a Meta-analysis. *Journal of Personality and Social Psychology, 97*, 6.

Gajdoš, J. (2007). Vrcholový manažér – požiadavky, nároky a zmeny v prístupe. In *Semafor*. Košice: Podnikovohospodárska fakulta EU so sídlom v Košiciach.

Hametová, L. (2004). Bochumský osobnostní intentář /BIP/. *Psychologie v ekonomické praxi 39*, 3–4, 161–170.

Hřebíčková, M. (2000). *Od pětifaktorového modelu k pětifaktorové teorii osobnosti. In Sociální procesy a osobnost* (pp. 65–72). Brno: Masarykova univerzita.

Hřebíčková, M., & Urbánek, T. (2001). *NEO pětifaktorový osobnostní inventář*. Praha: Testcentrum.

Hřebíčková, M., Urbánek, T., & Čermák, I. (2002). Psychometrické charakteristiky NEO osobnostního inventáře pro sebeposouzení a posouzení druhého. *Zprávy PsÚ AV ČR, 1*(8).

Judge, T. A., Martocchio, J. J., & Thoresen, C. J. (1997). Five-factor Model of Personality and Employee Absence. *Journal of Applied Psychology, 82*, 745–755.

Kolaříková, O. (2005). *Téma osobnostních rysů v psychologii dvacátého století*. Praha: Academia.

Kubeš, M., Spillerová, D., & Kurnický, R. (2004). *Manažerské kompetence. Způsobilosti výjimečných manažerů*. Praha: Grada Publishing.

Lojda, J. (2011). *Manažerské dovednosti*. Praha: Grada Publishing.

Lukeš, M., & Nový I. et al. (2005). *Psychologie podnikání – osobnost podnikatele a rozvoj podnikatelských dovedností*. Praha: Management Press.

Lukeš, M., & Stephan, U. (2004). Psychological Approaches to Entrepreneurship. In *Adaptační a rozvojové procesy firem po vstupu do EU* (pp. 279–287). Praha: Oeconomica.

McCrae, R. R., & Costa, P. (1986). Personality Coping and Coping Effectiveness in Adult Sample. *Journal of Personality 54*, 385–405.

Mesárošová, M. et al. (2008). *Komunikačné a manažérske spôsobilosti pre prax.* Košice: VÚSI.

Mikšík, O. (2007). *Psychologická charakteristika osobnosti.* Praha: Karolinum.

Mikuláštík, M. (2007). *Manažerská psychologie.* Praha: Grada Publishing.

Pervin, L. A., & John, O. P. (1999). *Handbook of Personality: Theory and Research.* New York: The Guilford Press.

Porvazník, J. et al. (2007). *Celostný manažment. Piliere kompetentnosti v manažmente.* Žilina: Poradca podnikateľa.

Porvazník, J. et al. (2013). Metodologické východiská ohodnocovania pracovných a manažérskych spôsobilostí (kompetentností). In *Celostná manažérska kompetentnosť – potreba, prístupy a metódy jej ohodnocovania* (pp. 7–21). Bratislava: Ekonóm.

Praško, J. et al. (2003). *Poruchy osobnosti.* Praha: Portál.

Procházka, J., & Smutný, P. (2010). *Čtyři pohledy na efektivního leadra. In Psychológia práce a organizácie* (pp. 388–397). Bratislava: Univerzita Komenského v Bratislave.

Říčan, P. (2010). *Psychologie osobnosti – Obor v pohybu.* Praha: Grada Publishing.

Ruisel, I. (2008). *Osobnosť a poznávanie.* Bratislava: Ikar.

Schmutte, P. S., & Ryff, C. D. (1997). Personality and well-being: reexamining methods and meanings. *Journal of personality and social psychology, 73*(3), 549.

Smékal, V. (2004). *Pozvání do psychologie osobnosti: člověk v zrcadle vědomí a jednání.* Brno: Barrister & Principal.

Šuleř, O. (2002). *Zvládáte své manažerské role? Jak rozhodovat, předávat informace, organizovat a motivovat své podřízené: testy.* Praha: Computer Press.

Van Den Berg, P. T., & Feij, J. A. (1993). Personality Traits and Job Characteristics as Predictors of Job Experiences. *European Journal of Personality, 7*, 337–357.

Vodák, J., & Kucharčíková, A. (2011). *Efektivní vzdělání zaměstnanců.* Praha: Grada Publishing.

Dawood Ahmad and Laila Mohebi

Adoption of E-Learning in Pakistani Schools: Learners' Viewpoints

1. Introduction

During the year 2021, e-learning was gaining momentum in various parts of the world, including Pakistan. E-learning refers to the use of electronic technology to deliver educational content and facilitate learning outside the traditional classroom setting. It is important to note that the situation may have evolved since my last update. To get the most current information on the adoption of e-learning in Pakistani public schools, it would be best to refer to recent reports, news articles, or government announcements. Every industry was impacted by the coronavirus's advent, which forced businesses to think about how technology fits into their daily operations. A number of nations have made major efforts to halt the virus's spread. According to World Health Organization (2020) assemblies were forbidden, social contact was reduced by upholding social-distance, and hygiene precautions were taken in accordance with World Health Organization safety requirements.

Institutions like Schools and businesses had to shut down out due to caution, and only essential services were provided (Jordan et al., 2021). By reducing infection rates and allowing the healthcare system more time to get ready for the peak of the pandemic, these approaches were able to flatten the curve. However, this action had a detrimental impact on other economic sectors. Access to digital and cutting-edge learning materials is made egalitarian and fair through e-learning (Ali, 2023). The historical injustices of apartheid result in a sizable digital difference. Due to its advantages, the shift to online teaching and learning is unavoidable (Tong et al., 2020), yet students from underprivileged areas (Ali, 2023) might not accept it as predicted. This essay's goal is to investigate the difficulties that students perceive.

In the age of rapid technological advancement, e-learning has emerged as a powerful tool, transforming educational landscapes across the globe. Many studies, such as those by Adnan and Anwar (2020), Bonk (2016), and Jordan et al. (2021), have highlighted the increasing importance and potential of online learning, especially in the context of global challenges like the COVID-19 pandemic. The advantages of e-learning and technology integration in classrooms are manifold, offering flexible learning environments, personalization, and improved access to resources (Chang & Cheung, 2001; Klein & Myers, 1999). However, while affluent educational institutions readily embrace these innovations, schools in underserved regions may face distinct challenges, particularly in countries like Pakistan.

While there is abundant research on e-learning's potential and benefits (Taherdoost, 2018; Marangunić & Granić, 2015), there is a shortage of focused literature on the difficulties public schools face in marginalized areas. Previous studies have discussed technology acceptance (Mirzajani et al., 2016) and the transformative potential of technology in bridging educational disparities (Ali, 2023). However, few have delved deeply into the specific challenges underserved schools in countries like Pakistan face from the student's perspective. Adopting e-learning tools and technology in Pakistani public schools, especially in underserved regions, presents unique challenges. These challenges are not only infrastructural but also encompass socio-cultural and economic dimensions (Raza et al., 2023). This research seeks to understand these multifaceted difficulties, specifically from the students' viewpoints, who are the primary beneficiaries of the educational process.

This study aims to enrich the existing body of literature by providing an in-depth look into the difficulties faced by underserved public schools in Pakistan when attempting to integrate new technologies. By emphasizing students' perspectives, this research offers invaluable insights into the ground realities of these schools, aiding educators, policymakers, and stakeholders in crafting more effective strategies for technology integration. Additionally, by adopting a case study approach, the research presents a unique lens through which the reactions and feedback of students to e-learning tools can be gauged, further illuminating the intricacies of this pressing issue. Therefore, this article explores the difficulties Pakistani public schools in underserved areas have in using new technologies, particularly e-learning.

2. Literature Review

Although technology has been around for thirty years, there are still issues with technology adoption in schools Academic scholars have sought to identify the elements that influence how technology is accepted and adopted. Information and communication technology (ICT) adoption, acceptability, and integration issues have been explored at many levels and venues within the context of Pakistani education (Mirzajani et al., 2016). According to several studies (Tabuni & Kusuma, 2019), adoption of effective technology, recognition, and incorporation are necessary for employee commitment and effective change administration. According to the literature, the adoption and acceptability of any invention by users – which depends on a number of important factors and perceptions – determines whether it succeeds or fails? The Unified Theory of Acceptance and Use of Technology (UTAUT) and the Technology Adoption Model (TAM) are the two most widely used theories and models that have been developed over time to better understand how users accept new technology (Taherdoost, 2018).

Understanding the emerging generation Z (Gen Z) of digitally engaged students is very important. E-learning is being used by a growing number of educational institutions (Zorman et al., 2011). Pakistani government has launched a number of technology initiatives and programs in recent years with the goal of educating teachers and students for a technologically enabled learning environment. These initiatives are aimed at giving students the abilities needed for the digital workplace. To support decision-making processes as well as classroom instruction and learning, many initiatives have aimed to make technological infrastructure, material, and relevant skills available (Raza et al., 2023).

However, because of a variety of variables, from socioeconomic issues to user-related difficulties, educators and students have not completely absorbed these innovations. Before implementing new technologies, it is important to provide thorough co-design technology methods and related adoption procedures while providing enough training. When adopting new technology in public schools, this is not efficiently done (Morelli et al., 2021). Empirical data also shows that when any type of technology is implemented in classrooms, change is not always well received. Technology implementation and acceptability in education are frequently hampered by obstacles and opposition (Mirzajani et al., 2016). Teaching and learning are directly impacted by technology. Studies on the adoption of technology by teachers have found that not all instructors are properly prepared to use it (Christensen & Knezek, 2017).

Additionally, there have been instances of thefts and break-ins that targeted gadgets, making access for students more difficult. Thus, it is necessary to investigate and assess the issues raised by technology in schools. By resolving the issues, obstacles may be utilized as a tool to increase adoption. According to Jantjies and Joy (2016), instructors are unable to fully use the utilization of technology to accomplish learning objectives because they have not received adequate technological training. This further influence how they see the application of technology in the classroom. It is difficult to incorporate technology in the majority of Pakistani schools, since most instructors lack the necessary skills. However, it is thought that with the right training, this difficulty might be addressed (Adnan & Anwar, 2020).

According to the study's findings (Joo et al., 2016), perceived usefulness will increase mobile learning's uptake and use over time. It is crucial to investigate and comprehend consumer expectations and perceptions regarding many elements of technology in order to increase technology adoption. According to Vershitskaya et al. (2020), researchers are very interested in e-learning. It has the ability to provide higher living standards by spreading education to a larger population. According to Navarrete et al. (2016), e-learning is currently a common practice in higher education.

Many researchers believe that e-learning is a digital revolution and a significant improvement in education (Martnez-Cerdá et al., 2020). The pleasure of learners has received a lot of attention, yet some academics have criticized it as being monolithic (Johnson et al., 2000). Chang and Cheung (2001), on the other hand, asserted that satisfaction is a multi-dimensional construct made up of perceptions, beliefs, attitudes, and interaction with online course material. Bonk (2016) suggested that modern education is increasingly individualized, digital, cozy, blended, visual, and game-based. The adoption of the e-learning in Pakistani public schools was gradually increasing due to several factors:

2.1. Technological Advancements and e-Learning

Digital devices such as smartphones, tablets, and laptops have not only become more accessible but also more affordable. Erdogdu and Erdogdu (2015) emphasized the significance of access to Information and Communication Technology (ICT) and its pivotal role in students' academic success. Furthermore, Manny-Ikan et al. (2011) evaluated the integration of technology, like interactive whiteboards, showcasing the possibilities of e-learning through technological tools.

2.2. Internet Penetration in Pakistan

The internet has grown widely with technology, reaching even the farthest corners of countries. Chang and Cheung (2001) highlighted internet intention and use determinants, implying its benefits, particularly in educational settings. Masimbe (2019) addressed mobile internet access and its affordability, indicating its potential to transform education in regions such as Pakistan.

2.3. Government Initiatives

Governmental support plays a fundamental role in promoting e-learning. While the article by Raza et al. (2023) discussed higher education perspectives between

Pakistan and China, it provides insights into how governmental interventions can shape educational landscapes, including e-learning adoption in public schools.

2.4. COVID-19 Pandemic's Role

The sudden onset of the COVID-19 pandemic drastically transformed the educational ecosystem. Adnan & Anwar (2020) and Jordan et al. (2021) have spotlighted how the pandemic led to an increased reliance on online learning, reflecting the global trend that Pakistan became a part of.

2.5. Flexibility and Accessibility

E-learning's allure often lies in its flexibility and accessibility. Marangunić and Granić (2015) thoroughly reviewed the Technology Acceptance Model, emphasizing how e-learning platforms can cater to diverse needs, making education more approachable and personalized.

2.6. Interactive Learning Platforms

Interactive e-learning platforms have been gaining popularity due to their engaging nature. Tong et al. (2020) have discussed the potential of data in ushering in a new era of e-learning, focusing on the importance of interactive tools like simulations and analytics in enhancing student engagement.

2.7. Challenges to E-Learning in Pakistan

Despite the evident progress, adopting e-learning in Pakistani public schools is fraught with challenges. Jantjies and Joy (2016) shed light on the issues of cultural and linguistic constraints, emphasizing the need for content localization. Furthermore, Mirzajani et al. (2016) touched upon teachers' acceptance of ICT, highlighting the broader issue of inadequate teacher training. Vershitskaya et al. (2020) highlighted the challenges of e-learning management, which can be extrapolated to understand infrastructure constraints in countries like Pakistan. Socio-cultural factors, as hinted by Navarrete et al. (2016), play a role in the acceptance and use of open educational resources, suggesting that traditional attitudes toward education might be a hindrance.

Therefore, while adopting e-learning in Pakistani public schools has seen considerable progress, fueled by technological advancements, internet penetration, and global events like the COVID-19 pandemic, challenges such as the digital divide, inadequate teacher training, and socio-cultural barriers still

124   Ahmad and Mohebi

need to be addressed. The literature provides a comprehensive overview of the opportunities and obstacles in this journey.

3. Research Methodology

The interpretivism paradigm was used to comprehend the alleged difficulties encountered by schools with the incorporation of technology. In order to understand how social actors use these processes to give their reality meaning and relate these meanings, beliefs, and intents to their social behavior, interpretivism, according to Klein and Myers (1999), aims to understand how these processes are used. A progressive mixed-method approach to data collection and analysis was employed to fully evaluate the challenges. As a part of a gamification experiment, some participants were subjected to semi-structured interviews. The data analysis employed a thematic approach. A questionnaire was created using the themes from the interviews and given to each participant. This study was conducted in the district of Faisalabad, Pakistan.

Pakistani education system has been divided into two main strands of education providing systems i,e Public sector schools and private sector schools. The study was done in private school sector. As private sector is considered more progressive than the public sector schools.

3.1. Participants of the Study

Random and non-random probability selection techniques were used to choose the sample from 12th grade pupils. The interview subjects were selected on purpose, and the entire sample in the experimental research study replied to the questionnaire. The respondents' gender wise dissemination is seen in Table 1.

Table 1 presents the distribution of participants based on gender. Of 139 learners, a slight majority are male, representing 53.96 % (75 learners). In contrast, females constitute a smaller proportion of the sample, accounting for 46.04 % (64 learners). The data illustrates a near-balanced gender representation among the participants, with a slight tilt towards males. This indicates that both genders are almost equally represented, making the sample relatively diverse in gender. Such a distribution might provide insights that are not overly skewed towards one gender, ensuring that the perspectives or responses collected could represent the broader population fairly. However, the marginal dominance of male participants could be acknowledged in further analysis to understand if this affects the study's outcomes.

Table 1. Participants distribution

Gender	Learners in Numbers	%
Male	75	53.96
Female	64	46.04
Total	139	100

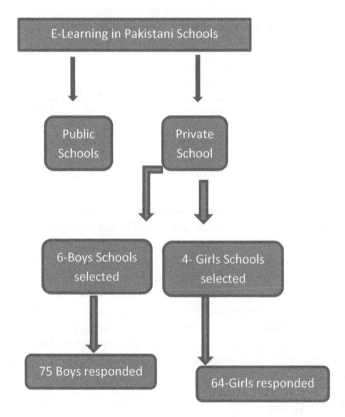

Figure 1. Depicts the selection and participating schools and students for the study.

4. Results

Participants were asked if they would be interested in participating in online training. They all expressed curiosity in the replies. But they also gave explanations on why they believe e-learning is not being utilized. A number of important criteria were identified after a study of the comments provided by students regarding the problems they saw as hurdles to e-learning. A significant threat was the availability of gadgets with internet access. The majority of homes do not have such gadgets, according to learners, who agree that availability is not an issue among instructors. The obstacles as viewed are shown in below Table 2:

Table 2. E-learning challenges

Factor	Male	Female	%
Not having access to devices	75	64	100 %
The price of data is excessive	84	55	100 %
E-learning is inefficient	65	74	100 %
Teachers are not enthusiastic	79	60	100 %

Table 2 delineates the e-learning challenges faced by both male and female participants. Both genders unanimously reported not having access to devices as a challenge, with 100 % of participants from each gender agreeing. A more significant percentage of males (84) felt that the data price was excessive compared to females (55). Conversely, more females (74) than males (65) perceived e-learning as inefficient. Similarly, more males (79) found a lack of teacher enthusiasm problematic, whereas 60 females echoed this sentiment. The data suggests that while there are shared concerns between the genders regarding e-learning challenges, there are also disparities in the intensity of these concerns, indicating that gender may influence perceptions and experiences related to e-learning barriers.

4.1. Device Access

Access to gadgets is a significant difficulty, according to all respondents. The school is located in a low-income neighborhood, hence poverty is the likely cause. "Sir, there is no one working at home, we survive on grants (social services support), and there is sometimes no food," one learner stated. We are unable to purchase a computer. Making teaching and learning simple and inspiring students are the goals of a teacher. Given this, it is pointless to instruct using a platform that is unavailable to the students. The fundamental internet-accessible gadgets and digital learning tools are taken into account in this study. Table 3 displays the various device access points and their proportions.

Table 3. Access of learners to the devices

Access	Learners in Numbers	%
Full access to devices	17	12.2 %
Shared devices (Domestic)	27	19.4 %
Shared devices (Public)	36	26 %
Nil/ None	59	42.4 %
Total	139	100

Interviews indicate that students are eager and ready to participate in online learning. However, they brought up important points that must be resolved first. They believe that if these problems are solved, they need to be exposed to such technology. Access to digital learning tools is the biggest problem facing students. 59 % of the 139 participants had no access to any digital devices, and only 17 % of them owned a smartphone, tablet, laptop, or desktop computer.

Because siblings frequently use a parent's smartphone, each sibling's access to time is limited. The current COVID -19 epidemic and the lockout in Pakistan make it challenging for students to access shared public devices. It will fail if the access problem is not addressed. Erdogdu and Erdogdu's (2015) examined the effect of access to ICT on student achievement, lends credence to this and additionally, having access to an ICT device improves student performance.

4.2. High Data Cost

Without adequate internet connectivity, e-learning in these places is ineffective. in the unorganized sector. Despite efforts to make internet access a fundamental necessity, it is seen as a extravagance owing to high statistics prices (Masimbe, 2019). This confirms the study's results that internet

4.3. Non-Effectiveness of: E-Learning

Majority of students don't believe that e-learning is successful. Whether it will be as beneficial as contact classes is a concern for them. Given that it is consistent with previous study findings, the learners' claim on the method's efficacy can be supported in this respect (Comi et al., 2017). They contend, as justification, that their homes do not provide favorable learning settings. 87 of the 139 students who participated in the survey acknowledged to living in an overcrowded household, and 52 reside in informal settlements. All of them made references to having an uncomfortable, distracting atmosphere at home that made it challenging to concentrate on their academics. They continue by saying that if they obtain resources, they might sell them to raise money for food and other necessities.

4.4. Lack of Interest

The majority of students contend that educators are not meeting their learning requirements, even though this was beyond the purview of this survey. Out of 139 respondents, 79 male and 60 female of respondents agreed that teachers weren't interested in employing instructional technology. These students raised the notion that their teachers' disinterest in using technology may be due to a lack of technological proficiency on their part. Therefore, it is advised that educators equip themselves with the ICT abilities needed for e-learning as well as for teaching and learning. Continuous professional growth can help with this.

5. Conclusion

To reach a conclusion, data from semi-structured interviews and questionnaires were employed. Although there are differing opinions on e-learning, it is important to recognize that most formerly underprivileged populations struggle with access to resources. Access to learning resources through e-learning need to be fair and egalitarian. However, due to the poor's lack of access to technology and the internet, educators' lack of enthusiasm, and the perceived ineffectiveness of online learning, this is not the case.

5.1. Recommendations

The results of this study suggest that before deploying e-learning, resources should be made available to underprivileged areas, and educators should receive the necessary training. It could be worthwhile to look into developing specialized devices with free access to online learning platforms in order to handle the problem of simultaneous device and data access. Such gadgets could just be useful for accessing learning, so there won't be much of a market for them beyond that. Promoting the adoption of e-learning in Pakistani schools can significantly enhance the education system and provide students with more comprehensive learning opportunities.

References

Adnan, M., & Anwar, K. (2020). Online Learning Amid the COVID-19 Pandemic: Students' Perspectives. *Online Submission*, 2(1), 45–51.

Ali, A. (2023). Exploring the Transformative Potential of Technology in Overcoming Educational Disparities. *International Journal of Multidisciplinary Sciences and Arts*, 2(1). And social measures in the context of COVID-19.

Bonk, C. (2016). Keynote: What Is the State of E-learning? Reflections on 30 Ways Learning Is Changing. *Journal of Open, Flexible, and Distance Learning*, 20(2), 6–20.

Chang, K. M., & Cheung, W. (2001). Determinants of the Intention to Use Internet/www at work: A Confirmatory Study. *Information and Management*, 39(1), 1–14.

Christensen, Rhonda, and Gerald Knezek. "Relationship of middle school student STEM interest to career intent." *Journal of education in science environment and health* 3, no. 1 (2017): 1–13.

Comi, S. L., Argentin, G., Gui, M., Origo, F., & Pagani, L. (2017). Is it the way they use it? Teachers, ICT and student achievement. *Economics of Education Review*, 56, 24–39.

Erdogdu, F., & Erdogdu, E. (2015). The Impact of Access to ICT, Student Background and School/Home Environment on Academic Success of Students in Turkey: An International Comparative Analysis. *Computers & Education*, 82, 26–49.

Jantjies, M., & Joy, M. (2016). Lessons Learnt from Teachers' Perspectives on Mobile Learning in South Africa with Cultural and Linguistic Constraints. *South African Journal of Education*, 36(3), 1–10. https://doi.org/10.15700/saje.v36n3a1274

Johnson, S. D., Aragon, S. R., Shaik, N., & Palma-Rivas, N. (2000). Comparative Analysis of Learner Satisfaction and Learning Outcomes in Online and Face-to-Face Learning Environments. *Journal of Interactive Learning Research*, 11(1), 29–49.

Jordan, K., David, R., Phillips, T., & Pellini, A. (2021). Education during the COVID-19: Crisis Opportunities and Constraints of Using EdTech in Low-Income Countries. *Distance Education Magazine*, 21(65), 1–15. https://doi.org/10.6018/red.453621

Joo, B. K., Lim, D. H., & Kim, S. (2016). Enhancing work engagement: The roles of psychological capital, authentic leadership, and work empowerment. *Leadership & Organization Development Journal*, 37(8), 1117–1134.

Klein, H. K., & Myers, M. D. (1999). A Set of Principles for Conducting and Evaluating Interpretive Field Studies in Information Systems. *MIS Quarterly*, 23(1), 67–93. https://doi.org/10.2307/249410

Manny-Ikan, E., Dagan, O., Tikochinski, T., & Zorman, R. (2011). [Chais] ysing the Interactive White Board in Teaching and Learning–an Evaluation of the Smart Classroom Pilot Project. *Interdisciplinary Journal of E-Learning and Learning Objects*, 7(1), 249–273. https://doi.org/10.28945/1523

Marangunić, N., & Granić, A. (2015). Technology Acceptance Model: A Literature Review from 1986 to 2013. *Universal Access in the Information Society*, 14(1), 81–95. https://doi.org/10.1007/s10209-014-0348-1

Martínez-Cerdá, J. F., Torrent-Sellens, J., & González-González, I. (2020). Socio-Technical E-Learning Innovation and Ways of Learning in the ICT-Space-Time Continuum to Improve the Employability Skills of Adults. *Computers in Human Behavior*, 107, 105753.

Masimbe, C. (2019). *Mobile Internet Access and Affordability among Youth in South Africa: Rethinking Universal Service and Access in the Age of "digital mobility"*. South Africa: University of Limpopo.

Mirzajani, H., Mahmud, R., Ayub, A. F. M., & Wong, S. L. (2016). Teachers' Acceptance of ICT and Its Integration in the Classroom. *Quality Assurance in Education*, 24(1), 26–40. https://doi.org/10.1108/qae-06-2014-0025

Morelli, M., Graziano, F., Chirumbolo, A. *et al*. Parental Mediation of COVID-19 News and Children's Emotion Regulation during Lockdown. *J Child Fam Stud* 31, 1522–1534 (2022). https://doi.org/10.1007/s10826-022-02266-5

Navarrete, R., Luján-Mora, S., and Peñafiel, M. (2016). Use of Open Educational Resources in E-learning for Higher Education. *Third International Conference on eDemocracy & eGovernment* (ICEDEG 2016), pp. 177–183, Quito (Ecuador), March 30–April 1, 2016.

Raza, H., Ali, A., Rafiq, N., Xing, L., Asif, T., & Jing, C. (2023). Comparison of Higher Education in Pakistan and China: A Sustainable Development in Student's Perspective. *Sustainability*, 15(5), 4327.

Tabuni, Y., & Kusuma, P. G. (2019). Evaluation of e-Government Use among Civil Servants Using Unified Theory of Acceptance and Use of Technology Model-A Case of Central Mamberamo Regency. *International Journal of Scientific & Technology Research*, 8(09), 1624–1631.

Taherdoost, H. (2018). A Review of Technology Acceptance and Adoption Models and Theories. *Procedia Manufacturing*, 22, 960–967. https://doi.org/10.1016/j.promfg.2018.03.137.

Tong, R., Wang, S., McBride, E., Kelly, H., & Cui, W. (2020). Data, Mark of a New Era. In *Radical Solutions and Learning Analytics* (pp. 17–35). Singapore: Springer.

Vershitskaya, E. R., Mikhaylova, A. V., Gilmanshina, S. I., Dorozhkin, E. M., & Epaneshnikov, V. V. (2020). Present-day Management of Universities in Russia: Prospects and Challenges of e-Learning. *Education and Information Technologies*, *25*(1), 611–621.

World Health Organization. (2020). *Considerations for Mass Gatherings in the Context of COVID-19: Annex: Considerations in Adjusting Public Health.*

Laila Mohebi and Mariam AlHammadi

Pre-Service and In-Service Teachers' Perceptions of and Satisfaction with Online Training Modules: A Case Study from Kenya

1. Introduction

1.1. Research Background

While online teacher training was prevalent before COVID-19, the pandemic made it exigent that education and learning institutes adopt the online training mode to ensure continuity of teacher training (Bashir et al., 2021). However, in the context of Africa, this thrust was encouraged by the pandemic, where online modes of operation were introduced in almost all sectors of the economy, including the education sector (Ferdig & Kennedy, 2014). As classrooms became increasingly online, so did the need for teachers to continue their training, for both pre-service and in-service requirements (Gumede & Badrisparsad, 2022). The need for high-quality teachers had already been felt in the country, owing to changes in educational policies that emphasized universal education for all. Kenya has a four-tiered teacher training program, starting from the early childhood level, primary level, diploma level and graduate level (Nyankanga et al., 2013). For each level, the country has well-structured programs for both pre-service and in-service teachers (Muthanje et al., 2019). These training programs were largely available in Kenya through the offline mode, although the COVID-19 pandemic encouraged the use of online teacher training in the country (Mahmood, 2021). However, even post COVID-19, the online mode of teacher training continued to be central to teacher training programs (Burquel & Busch, 2020). While online teacher training provides numerous advantages like savings in terms of time and cost and provides the benefit of convenience, there are concerns about its effectiveness in equipping teachers with standards of skills and knowledge as desired (Bashir et al., 2021). Also, since online teacher training on a larger scale is a recent phenomenon, there are very few studies that have audited such online programs or gauged the satisfaction level of teacher trainees. The current study, therefore, tries to answer the following research questions:

1. What are the perceptions of pre-service and in-service teachers about the online training module?

2. Do pre-service and in-service teachers find online training modules effective in improving their skills?

3. What are the factors that create satisfaction among pre-service and in-service teachers regarding the online training module?

2. Literature Review

2.1. Teacher Training Challenges in Kenya

Kenya faces significant challenges in teacher training due to inadequate investment and a lack of a strategic framework for targeted programs (Andiema, 2017). The limited ICT infrastructure further hinders online teacher training (Katitia, 2015). Underfunded educational institutions often lack sufficient teacher-educators and mentors, resulting in untrained individuals providing instruction to new teachers (Genvieve, 2017). Some institutions rely on short-duration programs for teacher recruitment, which compromises the quality of educators.

However, recent policy changes have brought positive developments, including funded continuous professional development programs for teachers, supported by The Centre for Mathematics, Science, and Technology Education in Africa (Mutenda, 2015). Scholarships and support initiatives encourage teachers to pursue higher education and ongoing development. Additionally, technology is being leveraged to create collaborative programs, addressing accessibility and mobility challenges (Odhiambo, 2021). These efforts aim to enhance teacher training and improve educational outcomes in Kenya.

The country is embracing the online mode of teacher training, mainly as teachers can access online training without having to take leave or lose a proportion of their salaries due to taking leave (Gathumbi et al., 2013). Online training programs are often conducted asynchronously, which further enables trainee teachers to access them at convenient times and locations.

Nevertheless, while there are substantial benefits to online teacher training programs, there is a need to evaluate their effectiveness in terms of providing high-quality knowledge and skill acquisition. Some studies have evaluated online teacher training programs in terms of their costs and benefits, and the review focuses on this in the next section.

2.2. Advantages and Disadvantages of Online Teacher Training

Online teacher training offers convenience, time-efficiency, and cost-saving benefits. It accommodates synchronous and asynchronous modes, allowing trainees to access training while managing their responsibilities (Dhawan, 2020). Asynchronous training, though lacking real-time interaction, fosters self-paced learning, shifting the focus towards teacher-trainee-centered education (Almahasees et al., 2021). The flexibility of online training extends to mobile device accessibility, enhancing convenience and autonomy for learners (Almahasees et al., 2021). Moreover, it reduces transportation and accommodation costs associated with in-person training.

However, concerns exist in the literature. Teachers may struggle to assess learning impact without access to trainees' body language or non-verbal cues, particularly in asynchronous settings (Mahyoob, 2020). Online learning inhibits personal bonding and rapport between teachers and trainees, which is valuable for coaching and learning (Mahyoob, 2020). Limited peer-to-peer interaction hampers knowledge sharing (Dhawan, 2020), and trainees can't be mentored in real-time while practicing theoretical skills (Mukhtar et al., 2020).

Furthermore, online teacher training faces technological infrastructure challenges. Students without internet access or devices may struggle to participate (Gumede & Badrisparsad, 2022). A lack of technical skills compounds these issues, hindering effective online learning participation.

2.3. Critical Success Factors for Online Teacher Training Success

While the rapid adoption of online teacher training in several Western countries filled an essential need for continuity, on the other, it also highlighted several concerns and problems related to training effectiveness. It becomes essential to explore factors that lead to effective and efficient online teacher training so these critical success factors can be imbibed into online training modules.

Numerous studies have been undertaken to evaluate perceptions of teachers regarding the effectiveness of training and their satisfaction with online training, with mixed results. For example, in a study by Sutiah et al. (2020), it was found teachers preferred having face-to-face training over the online mode. A major concern for teachers was fear regarding the ability to attain learning objectives using the online mode of training. Sutiah et al. (2020) used a survey of 750 teachers and concluded that online training could only be used as supplementary to regular face-to-face teaching and not as a complete substitute for the off-line mode. Additionally, researchers identified the need for training institutes to have technological capabilities to impart such online training.

Effective online learning relies on delivering relevant and need-based training (Phan & Dang, 2017). It should provide content that resonates with learners and covers both theoretical knowledge and practical skills (Yemini et al., 2019).

Traditional training involves real-time mentorship, which online training often lacks, making skill acquisition a challenge. Furthermore, the perception of training effectiveness is tied to trainers' belief that it contributes to personal growth and enhances career prospects (Ratheeswari, 2018). For online teacher training to succeed, it must address these factors, ensuring the content aligns with learners' needs, encompasses both theory and practice, and offers pathways to personal and career development.

Additionally, as noted in several studies, source credibility, authenticity and trustworthiness are considered essential for any learning to be effective (Collins & Mitchell, 2019). Further, online training effectiveness is also considered to be dependent upon the quality of the video in terms of audio-visual quality and length and structure of videos (Jung, 2020; Ratheeswari, 2018).

3. Research Methodology

3.1. Research Approach

A constructionist approach is adopted as it is most suited to the current research purpose of obtaining the perspective of the subjects. A constructionist paradigm allows for a plurality of reality and points of view, and as such, enables data collection and interpretation from participants in a rich and contextual manner (Gupta & Gupta, 2022).

3.2. Sampling

Sample size: 108 Kenyan pre-service and in-service teachers. The sample included 52 females, 42 males and 15 who preferred not to mention their gender. It can be presumed that the sample was slightly biased toward the female perspective. Sample selection included purposive sampling, and candidates selected were predominantly either first-degree or second-degree connections of the researcher. Purposive sample is found useful when the study aims to include participants that are likely to have the relevant and adequate information sought by the study (Refai et al., 2015).

3.3. Data Collection

Data was collected through a structured questionnaire that allowed respondents to give open-ended and detailed answers. The link to this online qualitative survey was sent to potential subjects, along with a consent form for them to read and accept. The survey was hosted on SurveyMonkey.

3.4. Data Analysis

A manual thematic content analysis was undertaken, where responses were read and coded to form categories, and categories were further consolidated in the form of themes. These themes are then discussed and used to answer the research questions.

3.5. Ethical Considerations

The research employed all ethical considerations to conform to ethical protocols required for studies with human subjects (Refai et al., 2015). The research questionnaire was preceded by an informed consent form which provided details of the study and its purpose and also informed potential participants about how their responses would be used. The participants were requested to agree to this voluntary participation before they could proceed to the questions. Also, since the research was conducted online, participants could give their answers from a location of their convenience and the time of their choice. There was, therefore, no possibility of any physical discomfort or harm to participants during the research. Further, all responses were maintained confidentially, and none of the participants were identified during the analysis or anywhere in the report. Their personal contact details were not collected, and only demographic data collected pertained to their age, gender, educational level and country. These details were kept private and not shared with any third party.

4. Findings and Discussion

The analysis of collected data revealed three themes, namely around the effectiveness of the online training.

4.1. Effectiveness of the Online Training

An analysis of the findings revealed that both male and female subjects provided somewhat similar responses regarding the effectiveness of training, except for one difference in how they found the training to be useful. In general, it was evident that respondents found the training to be useful in enabling them to learn how to conduct their classes, monitor students, relate to students and build a relationship with students that could help them make a more positive impact. Some of the quotes from the subjects are mentioned below:

> "I learned how to be a reflective practitioner." (Respondent 6)
> "The good way to monitor my class and make sure everything is in order." (Respondent 33)

Additionally, the participants also found they could understand how to elicit and bring out their children's learning and how to motivate them, as is evident from the following responses:

> I learned how to conduct Motivation of the learners. (Respondent 18)

They also mentioned they learned the importance of relating to students:

> The training taught me how to relate with children both social and emotional. (Respondent 20)

An important finding from this study is that the participants also reported that the online training module made them realize the importance of integrated teaching and the concept of multiple intelligence, and overall, provided them with creative ideas for making learning fun and engaging. It can be surmised from these findings that almost all the teachers found the online training useful, irrespective of their gender. However, there was no detail on how male participants seemed to differ from female participants. More male participants than females noted the online training made them realize the importance of technology to teaching and learning and that they looked forward to using technology in their future teaching endeavors. For example, according to Respondent 97, "Digital learning is a way to go," and in the words of Respondent 58, "I realized the advantages of incorporating videos during teaching." While this finding may not directly relate to perceptions of participants regarding how online training can make them effective practitioners, it does indicate participants' willingness to use the online method as an effective approach to teaching.

The above findings also highlight the fact participants found the training to be effective in most of the areas that are crucial to teachers' skills, classroom management and teachers' ability to engage (Kebritchi et al., 2017; Böttcher-Oschmann et al., 2021), encourage and monitor classrooms (Gorozidis et al., 2020) and provide effective tools for learning (Garzon et al., 2020).

The next theme that emerged was beyond just the effectiveness of online training and underscores the unique and new learning participants perceived they acquired with the online training.

4.2. New Learning from the Online Training

The majority of participants mentioned they learned about development theory and cognitive behavior theory, and understood the fact that learning happens at different paces and levels. The participants also found the novel concept of differentiated learning and integrated classrooms, as seen from the following excerpts:

"The way of understanding...the way children process the information." (Respondent 76)
"My most unique learning is around the understanding of the differentiated learning."
(Respondent 26)
"I learned the theory of cognitive development...that was new." (Respondent 72)
"I learned about children knowledge and the way they process information."
(Respondent 38)
"Identify and integrate strategies to motivate children." (Respondent 38)

The above responses highlight that participants found the online training to be grounded in theoretical sturdiness, which leads them to have a deeper understanding of the subject at hand. In addition to the theory, participants also reported they found new ways of conducting themselves in their classrooms and acquired specific skills for classroom management. For example, according to Respondent 62, "I learned how to keep myself always intact during my lessons," and Respondent 61, "It was new to see how I could relate well with my class in order to let them become effective."

4.3. Factors that Created Satisfaction with the Online Training

Another theme that emerged was around what makes the online training useful to participants, or the critical success factors for the online training module. Under this theme, it was observed the majority of respondents found the videos to be "trustworthy" as seen from the following responses:

This training is nice and to be trusted. (Respondent 16)

Another factor noted by participants was that the training was need-based or that it filled a need. This is seen from the following comments made by the participants:

"This is really what we need for our schools." (Respondent 2)
"This training is what we need." (Respondent 60)
"I am 100% sure that we needed this." (Respondent 27)

Similarly, a relevant factor also mentioned as leading to satisfaction with training was that it provided participants with skills to improve their performance. Another critical factor for satisfaction was the perception that training could lead to career advancement and promotion, as mentioned by Respondent 72, "Very nice to use as an advancing course." The content's clarity was also cited by some of participants as a factor that ensured their satisfaction with the training.

However, additional factors were mentioned that had the potential to create dissatisfaction, and these related to the quality as well as the duration of the videos. For example, Respondent 81 suggested, "Reduce attaching many videos together," while Respondent 92 mentioned, "making the video more interesting." Similarly, there were perceptions regarding the length of the video, with some participants suggesting a shorter video would be sufficient, while others wanted videos to be longer.

Overall, the critical success factors related to perceptions of satisfaction with online training can be summarized as those related to relevance and applicability of the content, and those related to quality and duration of the videos. Critical success factors are further classified below.

Table 1. Critical factors for Teachers' satisfaction with online training

	Critical Success Factors
Content Related CSF	– Trustworthy – Need-based – Skill enhancing – Leading to career advancement – Content clarity
Video Related CSF	– Duration of the video – Presentation (Interesting and engaging audio-visuals)

5. Conclusion

The research answered the first research question *"What are the perceptions of pre-service and in-service teachers about the online training module?"* by providing evidence that pre-service and in-service teachers of both genders found online training to be effective. In fact, as noted in the literature, teachers find training effective if it directly provides them with the theoretical background as well as specific and targeted skills to improve their performance (Böttcher-Oschmann et al., 2021). In the current study, participants reported they perceived the online training to have many elements – the explanation of the underlying theory of development, differentiated learning, the importance of an integrated learning environment and flexible classrooms; as well as providing them with the specific skills. This answer the second research question *"Do the pre-service and in-service teachers find online training modules effective in improving their skills?"* The findings indicate participants gained practical and applicable skills like managing themselves during lessons so as to create an environment of engagement, integrated learning and personalized learning to a certain extent. Participants also learned to manage data and use online tools like videos and creative approaches to make learning fun for their students.

Skills like the ability to create an inclusive classroom with individual attention and monitoring (Yemini, 2019), the ability to engage students through fun and creative approaches and tools (Böttcher-Oschmann et al., 2021) and the ability to stay in control and self-regulate one's emotions and conduct (Mahmood, 2021) have already been found in literature to be essential skills for better student outcomes.

The above findings have highlighted participants were largely satisfied with the online training in terms of its effectiveness in providing them with both theoretical understanding and practical skills. The critical success factors noted in the current study in response to the research question "*What are the factors that create satisfaction among pre-service and in-service teachers regarding the online training module?*" included trustworthiness or source credibility, need-based content, content that led to actual skill-development and improved chances of career growth and clarity of content. However, some of the factors identified as lacking in the online training module, but which were also cited as critical for participants' satisfaction with the training, were related to the video appearance as less engaging and attractive and its duration. However, it could not be elicited from responses whether shorter duration videos or longer duration videos were expected, as participants provided mixed responses.

5.1. Research Limitations Recommendations

A limitation of the research is that data was collected online, through a self-report method. While open-ended answers were requested, participants were not inclined to provide as detailed, in-depth or thought-out answers as could be expected in a face-to-face interview method. This limitation can be overcome in future research by using Zoom-based interviews or conducting face-to-face interviews.

5.2. Recommendations

A recommendation from the research is to explore the gender-based differences in perceptions of online training effectiveness and factors that cause satisfaction. In the current study, male participants emphasized the potential of technology in education and training, while female teachers had not focused on this aspect. This leads to a scope of exploring differences based on gender, which may lead to varying expectations or perceptions of trainee teachers regarding their online training.

5.3. Acknowledgment

This study was financially supported by Zayed University's Research Incentive Fund (RIF) under grant number 20121.

References

Almahasees, Z., Mohsen K., & Amin, O. A. (2021). *Faculty's and Students' Perceptions of Online Learning During COVID-19.* Retrieved online on 24 February 2023 from https://doi.org/10.3389/feduc.2021.638470.

Andiema, N. C. (2017). ECDE Teachers Training and Its Effect on Learning in Selected Pre-Schools Centres in West Pokot County, Kenya. *European Journal of Education Studies, 3*(11), 113–117.

Bashir, S., Murtaza, G., Ullah, S., Ahmed, M., & Adam, S. (2021). LEARNING EXPERIENCES OF STUDENTS ABOUT ONLINE TEACHING AND LEARNING DURING COVID-19 PANDEMIC IN BALOCHISTAN. *PalArch's Journal of Archaeology of Egypt/Egyptology, 18*(10), 1692–1704.

Böttcher-Oschmann, F., GroßOphoff, J., & Thiel, F. (2021). Preparing Teacher Training Students for Evidence-Based Practice Promoting Students' Research Competencies in Research-Learning Projects. In *Frontiers in Education* (Vol. 6, p. 642107). Frontiers Media SA.

Burquel, N., & Busch, A. (2020). Lessons for International Higher Education Post COVID-19. [online] *University World News.* Available at: https://www.universityworldnews.com/post.php?story=2020042408501836. Accessed 28 November 2022.

Collins, L., & Mitchell, J. T. (2019). Teacher Training in GIS: What Is Needed for Long-term Success? *International Research in Geographical and Environmental Education, 28*(2), 118–135.

Dhawan, S. 2020. Online Learning: A Panacea in the Time of COVID-19. *Journal of Educational Technology, 49*(1), 5–22.

Ferdig, R. E., & Kennedy, K. (Eds.). (2014). *Handbook of Research on K-12 Online and Blended Learning.* ETC Press.

Garzon, A. E., Martínez, T. S., Ortega Martin, J. L., Marin Marin, J. A., & Gomez Garcia, G. (2020). Teacher Training in Lifelong Learning – The Importance of Digital Competence in the Encouragement of Teaching Innovation. *Sustainability, 12*(7), 2852.

Gathumbi, A. W., Mungai, N. J., & Hintze, D. L. (2013). Towards Comprehensive Professional Development of Teachers: The Case of Kenya. *International Journal of Process Education, 5*(1), 3–14.

Genvieve, N. (2017). Challenges of Administering Teacher Education Programme in Kenyan Universities. *Journal of Education and Practice, 8*(14), 30–33.

Gorozidis, G. S., Tzioumakis, Y. S., Krommidas, C., & Papaioannou, A. G. (2020). Facebook *group* PETCoN (Physical Education Teacher Collaborative Network). An Innovative Approach to PE Teacher In-service Training: A Self-Determination Theory Perspective. *Teaching and Teacher Education, 96,* 103184.

Gumede, L., & Badrisparsad, N. (2022). Online Teaching and Learning through the Students' Eyes. Uncertainty through the COVID-19 Lockdown: A Qualitative Case Study in Gauteng Province, South Africa. *Radiography, 28,* 193–198.

Gupta, A., & Gupta, N. (2022). *Research Methodology.* SBPD Publications.

Jung, C. D. (2021). Perceptions of Collaborative Video Projects in the Language Classroom: A Qualitative Case Study. International Journal of Instruction, 14(4), 301–320.

Katitia, D. M. O. (2015). Teacher Education Preparation Program for the 21st Century. Which Way Forward for Kenya? *Journal of Education and Practice,* 6(24), 57–63.

Kebritchi, M., Lipschuetz, A., & Santiague, L. (2017). Issues and Challenges for Teaching Successful Online Courses in Higher Education: A Literature Review. *Journal of Educational Technology Systems,* 46(1), 4–29.

Mahmood, S. (2021). Instructional Strategies for Online Teaching in COVID-19 Pandemic. *Human Behavior and Emerging Technologies,* 3(1), 199–203.

Mahyoob, M. (2020). Challenges of E-Learning during the COVID-19 Pandemic Experienced by EFL Learners. *Arab World English Journal, 11*(4), 351–362. https://dx.doi.org/10.24093/awej/vol11no4.23.

Mukhtar, K., Javed, K., Arooj, M., & Sethi, A. 2020. Advantages, Limitations and Recommendations for Online Learning during COVID-19 Pandemic Era. *Pakistan Journal of Medical Sciences, 36*(COVID19-S4), S27–S31. https://doi.org/10.12669/pjms.36.COVID19-S4.2785.

Mutende, R. A. (2015). *Re-Orientation of Science and Mathematics Teachers' Instructional Strategies for Information Communication Technology Integration.* Department of Mathmatics, Kibabi University Institutional Repository. Retrieved from: http://crepository.kibu.ac.ke/handle/123456789/1183

Muthanje, K. A., Khatete, I., & Riechi, A. (2019). *Influence of Teacher Professional Qualifications on Acquisition of Learner Competencies in Early Childhood Development and Education in Public Primary Schools in Embu County,* Kenya.

Nyankanga, M. E., Joshua, B. N., Wekesa, N., Ongaga, E., & Orina, F. (2013). The Changing Trends in the Development of Teacher Education in Kenya: The Role of the Teacher's Service Commission. *Journal of Research on Humanities and Social Sciences,* 3(19), 82–86.

Odhiambo, D. (2021). Teacher Education in Kenya; Successes, Challenges, Policy Recommendation and Way Forward in the 21st Century. *Institute for Educational Development*. Researchgate, 1–12

Phan, T. T. N., & Dang, L. T. T. (2017). Teacher Readiness for Online Teaching: A Critical Review. *International Journal on Open and Distance e-Learning, 3*(1).

Ratheeswari, K. (2018). Information Communication Technology in Education. *Journal of Applied and Advanced Research, 3*(1), 45–47.

Refai, D., Klapper, R. G., & Thompson, J. (2015). A Holistic Social Constructionist Perspective to Enterprise Education. *International Journal of Entrepreneurial Behavior & Research, 21*(3), 316–337.

Sutiah, S., Slamet, S., Shafqat, A., & Supriyono, S. (2020). Implementation of Distance Learning during the Covid-19 Pandemic in Faculty of Education and Teacher Training. *Cypriot Journal of Educational Science, 15*(1), 1204–1214.

Yemini, M., Tibbitts, F., & Goren, H. (2019). Trends and Caveats: Review of Literature on Global Citizenship Education in Teacher Training. *Teaching and Teacher Education, 77*(1), 77–89.

Laila Mohebi and Nessrin Shaya

Discussion Paper on the Power of Universities as Learning Organizations in Achieving ESD Competencies

1. Introduction

Since the UN's release of Agenda 2030 in 2016, global sustainability awareness has surged, with universities recognizing their role in the development of a more sustainably oriented society (Boyon, 2019). *Education takes on the role of an agent of change brought about by altering people's attitudes and mindsets. Raising awareness and understanding is essential for achieving sustainable education. Universities should adapt to sustainable models and perspectives to build contemporary knowledge and assess sustainability matters.* Within this perspective, higher education institutions (HEIs) are increasingly addressing societal needs beyond research and teaching, including sustainable development (Nolting et al., 2020). *For universities to incorporate sustainable curriculum into their programmes, they must first act as learning organizations. In* this paper, we argue that universities must function as learning organizations to foster sustainability.

With the adoption of the learning organization framework, educational communities have gradually shifted their focus to sustainability. Sustainability is a growing concept that encompasses economic viability, environmental sustainability, and social responsibility. Universities are making significant progress in incorporating sustainability into their curricula, with examples including assessing Corporate Social Responsibilities (CSR) education in Europe, applying Bloom's Taxonomy of Educational Objectives, educating educators, and examining alumni's corporate sustainability practices. Courses are also being developed on organizational change management and engineering for sustainable development (Lozano et al., 2017). Redirecting university education towards sustainability is crucial as it shapes community leaders and decision-makers within its walls. But what are the strategies that effectively accelerate change? Limiting education to classical methods and mindsets will only enable us to fall short of our global goals for development. Managing change involves capitalizing on desirable changes, understanding mental representations, establishing relationships through public networks, and fostering learning individuals and organizations (Wheeler, 2007).

This is one of the few studies that tries to link universities as learning organizations to Education for Sustainable Development (ESD). ESD pledges to create a world that is suitable for both the current generation and the ones to come. We seek to offer useful insights into the intricate implementation of ESD and how education, through learning organizations, can assist institutions in fostering sustainability and balancing their rights with their desires. We aim at answering the following main research question:

1. What is the role of the university as a sustainable learning organization in conveying Education for Sustainable Development (ESD) competencies through developing faculty to nurture students as sustainability "change-agents"?
2. How are the key competencies in education for sustainable development being operationalized in pedagogies and assessment?

This paper offers an in-depth analysis of the existing literature on education for sustainable development (ESD), learning organisations (LOs), professional development, and higher education. It examines the existing literature on ESD, learning organizations and higher education, then offers a novel approach to strengthen the capabilities of higher education systems into embedding ESD in a way that facilitates meaningful transformation in the educational system, rather than simply the incorporation of sustainability-focused content.

The scope of the paper is constrained to the essential role of institutions as learning organizations in ensuring commitment to a supportive learning culture and continuous learning opportunities, fostering collaboration and collaborative learning, setting up systems to capture and disseminate learning, and integrating the university organization with its surroundings. This paper aims at fulfilling a gap in the literature. ESD is seen as a powerful force for societal transformation through the education it provides to future leaders and professionals across all industries. At present, universities struggle to embed ESD into mainstream teaching practice and the education they offer to academic staff, or to incorporate ESD into their institutional pedagogical strategic priorities (Mula, 2017). Numerous ESD initiatives continue to focus on addressing challenges related to SD research and providing specializes training or modules in sustainability topics.

2. Literature Review

2.1. Issues of Practices of ESD in HEIs

Sustainability has gained global recognition in recent years, aiming for improved living standards, equality between generations, and public health. It is defined as a nation's joint consent to achieve growth without compromising other societies' rights (Wiek et al., 2015). Education is a crucial aspect of sustainable development, as it promotes life-changing learning and defies current models. Universities play a crucial role in promoting sustainability, acting as learning organizations that foster sustainability (Wiek et al. 2015). *Bokharri (2017) notes that sustainable development cannot be attained in isolation from the close relationship between higher education and its institutions, specifically universities, and society. Mass educational transformation is needed to equip the next generation of sustainability specialists with problem-solving strategies, systems thinking, methodical expectations, value-loaded reflections, evidence-based methods, and strong government-organization cooperation* (Wiek et al., 2015).

In 2010, the UAE launched blueprint for a knowledge-oriented economy with over 100 higher education institutions affiliated to various universities with distinctive programs scattered around the world . The UAE has made significant efforts to promote sustainable development (SD) through various sectors, including the Ministry of Water and Environment, Ministry of Energy, and Ministry of Education (Al-Naqbi, 2018). Higher education in UAE has experienced a substantial rise in the quantity, variety, and quality of programs and providers. The UAE is now an international hub for higher education, a significant player in global education and pioneer in promoting sustainability education (Jose, 2017).

In educational contexts, competencies describe desired outcomes (Lozano et al., 2017). Competencies are dispositions to self-organization, consisting of psycho-social components, acquired gradually, and reflected in successful actions. Competency in sustainability may be illustrated as "complexes of knowledge, skills, and attitudes that enable successful task performance and problem solving with respect to real-world sustainability problems, challenges, and opportunities" (Wiek et al., 2011). A converging set of crucial skills in sustainability was advocated by multiple scholars such as (Wiek et al., 2011). These crucial competencies are (Wiek et al., 2011) Systems thinking competence, Futures thinking competence, Values thinking competence, Strategic thinking competence, and Interpersonal competence.

Wick and colleagues (2011) conducted a comprehensive literature review of higher education competencies in ESD and developed a set of five core competencies in the field of sustainability: Systemic Thinking Competency, Anticipatory Thinking Competency, Preparatory Competency, Prescriptive Competency, Strategic Competency, Interpersonal Competency, Meta Competency. Graduates can effectively communicate teamwork, stakeholder involvement, and joint efforts in professional sustainability cooperation, integrating expertise and leading groups in professional settings.

Higher education courses should channel these key sustainability competencies to prepare graduates for societal complexities and a sustainable future. Nevertheless, these major competencies are often vague, leading to slow embedding of sustainability into curricula. (Thomas & Day, 2014).

2.2. The Power of Learning Organizations

Learning organization refers to the concept of an organization that facilitates, supports, or arranges learning in a workplace or organizational context. The organization can learn as an individual or as a collective (Örtenblad, 2018). Senge introduced the concept of a learning organization in 1990, promoting continuous growth, nurturing new thinking patterns, and learning together. Senge's concept of "the learning organization" includes five disciplines: personal mastery, mental models, team learning, shared visions, and system thinking. Acquiring personal mastery requires reflective practice . Mental models require systematic knowledge of management approaches. A shared vision promotes systems mentality and team learning, while systems thinking focuses on interrelationships and patterns of change. Senge's system thinking, his final discipline, forms the conceptual cornerstone, integrating other disciplines into a comprehensible body of theories (Yeo, 2005).

Organizations, work teams, and academic work societies are expected to resemble learning organizations, utilizing job experiences to apply to different hierarchies . Education in learning organizations can encourage critical reflection and challenge current perspectives and unsustainable methods.

3. Advancing ESD through Higher Education, Lifelong Learning, and Professional Development

3.1. Institutional Learning Organizations

Numerous organizations and countries are adopting sophisticated strategies that prioritize organizational learning that shift their attention from human capacity building to organisational learning and change (Bamber et al., 2014; Gibbs, 2013). ESD embraces this broader overview, where that aims at providing the sort of professional development that prompts faculty not only to integrate new elements into existing curricula and structures, but also to amend the system. Faculty are encouraged to rethink and reframe their own teaching approaches and priorities, as well as to facilitate academic change processes at the programme, departmental, and/or institutional level (Hoffner & Tilbury, 2013; Sterling, 2011; Ryan & Tilbury, 2013).

Embedding sustainability requires a paradigm shift in education, reorienting systems, policies, and practices to engage learners with sustainability issues and make informed decisions. This requires significant organizational change and a multidisciplinary approach involving humanities, social sciences, and natural sciences (Sterling & Thomas, 2006). Ethical values, such as justice, fairness, and shared destiny, are essential for promoting change and transformation, fostering a sense responsibility for actions (McKeown, 2002; Barth, 2015). Growing public awareness of sustainability issues does not instinctively lead to altering behaviour (Sterling, 2001; Vare & Scott, 2007). ESD involves fostering a moral code for sustainable living (McCann & McCloskey, 2009).

In this manner, the authors argues that a sustainable institution (i) incorporates this commitment into their mission and academic objectives, (ii) embraces the concept of environmentally conscious practises in teaching and research, (iii) prompts students to think critically about environmental issues, (iv) demonstrates sustainable practises that lessen their ecological footprint, (v) promotes support services for students, and (vi) creates regional and international partnerships to advance sustainability.

Despite the growth in financing for research and development as a response to competition amongst HEIs, Zilahy et al. (2009) notes that the challenges related with the allure of students, the calibre of professors, and budgetary concerns have delayed the inclusion of SD in HEIs. The main hindrances to the advancement of SD in HEIs, which have an impact on their innovation strategies, include (e.g., Barth et al., 2015; Lee et al., 2013; Lozano et al., 2013; Shriberg & Harris, 2012; Stephens et al., 2008; Velazquez et al., 2005) (a) a lack of managerial support, human resources, and infrastructure to promote their development; (b) misunderstanding and misrepresentation of the notion associations; (c) a lack of financial resources; and (d) aversion to change.

In light of the above, the authors conclude that aspects of Education for Sustainable Development (ESD) align with the Learning Organization model's lifelong learning and continuous learning approaches provided by the learning organisation model. The embedding of sustainability is described as a paradigm shift, and curriculum change in universities is a complex process that requires consideration of institutional culture as an integral step in the process.

The learning organization is the entity that translates new concepts related to sustainability into enhanced outcomes that are in line with current industry trends. By incorporating (SD) and (ESD) competencies, learning organisations empower faculty and administrative staff to consistently develop their capacity to produce the results they genuinely desire. Such institutions enable the staff to see the big picture and liberate new, expansive aspirations. Integrating ESD into higher education enable students to engage with the major changes of our time from a scientific perspective ,assess their consequences from a sustainable perspective rethink our relationships to nature and take responsibility for being able to actively participate in society's transformation toward sustainability (Nolting et al., 2020).

A Learning culture is an organizational environment that fosters the development of learning. These characteristics are closely related to those associated with innovation, and a Learning culture implies a focus on the future and external factors. Learning Organizations, in particular, possess a strong Learning Culture, which fosters an understanding of the environment and encourages senior teams to take time to reflect on the future for the extensive use of external resources and advisors. A university's Learning Culture is a key factor in the successful implementation of (ESD). A supportive culture encourages the development of values, processes, and tools that allow the institution to effectively teach students about sustainability, equipping them to tackle the complex issues that confront the world (Barth et al., 2015). A university's learning culture can be instrumental in the successful incorporation of (ESD) through:

1. *Alignment of Values and Mission.* Incorporating sustainability into a university's learning culture is essential in order to ensure that the institution's values and mission are in line with the objectives of (ESD). When a university emphasizes sustainability, it conveys to its faculty, personnel, and student body that sustainability is an integral part of the university's identity and mission.
2. *Curricular Integration.* Having a strong learning culture is key to integrating sustainability principles into the curriculum across various disciplines. This includes adding sustainability-related material to already-existing courses and developing brand-new courses that are exclusively concerned with sustainability.
3. *Interdisciplinary Collaboration.* ESD frequently requires inter-disciplinary collaboration to address complex issues. The learning environment at a university can foster an all-encompassing approach to sustainability education by encouraging cross-disciplinary cooperation between faculty, researchers, and students.
4. *Pedagogical Approaches.* The pedagogical practises used to engage students in current sustainability issues should be encouraged by the learning environment. Project-based learning, field trips, and service-learning opportunities are a few examples of this.
5. *Institutional Support.* ESD initiatives are more likely to receive funding and faculty time at universities with a strong learning culture centred

on sustainability. It might also include scholarships, grants, and research institutions with a focus on sustainability.

6. *Assessment and Evaluation.* Evaluation of sustainability skills and outcomes is valued in a productive learning environment. Universities should continually enhance their ESD programmes by establishing clear learning objectives, assessing student learning, and applying the results.

7. *Student Engagement.* Student involvement in sustainability initiatives is encouraged by an inclusive learning environment. This could entail participation in sustainability-focused activities, student representation on sustainability committees, and student-led sustainability clubs.

8. *Community Engagement.* Effective ESD frequently reaches out into the larger community in addition to the university campus. Universities with a strong commitment to learning can support collaborations and community engagement initiatives to tackle sustainability issues.

9. *Long-Term Commitment.* ESD should become a long-term commitment rather than a passing fad thanks to a learning culture that places a high value on sustainability. The strategic planning and governance frameworks of the university should include sustainability objectives and initiatives.

3.2. Life-Long Learning and Professional Development for ESDs

ESD promotes an education vision that encourages young and old alike to take on the personal responsibility for building a sustainable future (Combes, 2005; Huckle, 2015; Elfert, 2019). As development issues are interdependent and complex, educators can play an essential role in building critical consciousness of students and in teaching justice and sustainability. The cross-curricular and interdisciplinary nature of ESD necessitates educators to recognise the potential in their subject areas and to interconnect disciplinary and pedagogy strategies to create a holistic experience of ESD for the learner. Sustainability and citizenship issues are seen as an essential component of science education and increasingly feature in science curricula. (Gresch et al., 2013).

This introduces a layer of complexity to the technical issues that need to be addressed, which can then be broken down into parts (see, for example, [UE4SD], 2016b):

- Comprehending the potential applications of new pedagogies in various professional fields and disciplines;
- Connecting ESD pedagogies to the specialist content taught.
- Redefining what optimal learning results might entail through an ESD lens;
- Re-evaluating student performance and learning outcomes.

- Recognising how sustainability ideology and technique articulates in multiple industries and professions;
- Challenging relationships of power in learning.
- Stimulating learners at all levels of the constantly evolving learning process.
- Gaining insight into strategies for attaining educational transformation in educational institutions.

Therefore, the challenge and need for effective implementation of ESD in the curriculum lies in the building process.

Most professional development initiatives in higher education to date have focused solely on enhancing teaching techniques; they have not questioned the fundamental purposes of academic training or impacted the strategic priorities of the academic system. This suggests pedagogical change at two interconnected levels: new classroom procedures and curriculum redesign, as well as a change in the higher education system's overall educational priorities. Efficient ESD in higher education necessitates alternative learning dynamics and also aims to have a greater impact on educational practises, changing what academic staff and education providers consider to be "excellence" and "quality" in the learning experiences they provide.

Multidisciplinary Education, Interdisciplinary Education, and Transdisciplinary Education all play a role in the process of integration, dissemination, and institutionalisation of SD in higher education institutions (Lozano, 2006). According to a 2013 study by Disterheft and colleagues, the transition for sustainable HEIs may ultimately depend on the Science of Sustainability (SS) and education for sustainable development (ESD). Capacity building can thus consider the following elements: The development of engagement and learning opportunities for both staff and students should be pursued in order to increase recognition of (ESD) initiatives, to improve the co-curricular and extracurricular experiences of students, and to develop and strengthen the sustainability teaching capacity of academic staff. Additionally, existing ESD initiatives should be established and connections set up between them to encourage interdisciplinary teaching methods. Building staff capacity would adhere to the Competencies for Educators framework.

4. Conclusion

This paper provides a critical review of the literature on higher education, professional development, learning organisations, and ESD. It investigates and suggests an innovative strategy that aims to enhance higher education educators' capacity to incorporate ESD into academic practise at the individual, disciplinary, and institutional levels. It guarantees educational change in ESD, not just the inclusion of sustainability-related content in learning opportunities. The contributions to this special issue show the need for greater understanding of the multi-level task of integrating SD into the mission and main practices of the institution, along with the need to rethink the professional development activities, not just for individual impact in the classroom but to advance institutional change and decisively influence the teaching and learning discourse of higher education.

References

Al-Naqbi, A. K., & Alshannag, Q. (2018). The Status of Education for Sustainable Development and Sustainability Knowledge, Attitudes, and Behaviors of UAE University Students. *International Journal of Sustainability in Higher Education*, 19(3), 566–588.

Bamber, G. J., Stanton, P., Bartram, T., & Ballardie, R. (2014). Human Resource Management, Lean Processes and Outcomes for Employees: Towards a Research Agenda. *The International Journal of Human Resource Management*, 25(21), 2881–2891.

Barth, W., Hulek, K., Peters, C., & Van de Ven, A. (2015). *Compact Complex Surfaces* (Vol. 4). Springer.

Bokhari, A. A. (2017), "Universities" Social Responsibility (USR) and Sustainable Development: a Conceptual Framework. *International Journal of Economics and Management Studies*, 4(12), 8–16. doi: 10.14445/23939125/ijems-v4i12p102.

Boyon, N. (2019). Awareness of United Nations Sustainable Development Goals Is Highest in Emerging Countries. *Ipsos*. Available at: www.ipsos.com/en/awareness-united-nations-sustainable-developmentgoals-highest-emerging-countries.

Cohen, M., Wiek, A., Kay, B., & Harlow, J. (2015). Aligning Public Participation to Stakeholders' Sustainability Literacy A Case Study on Sustainable Urban Development in Phoenix, Arizona. *Sustainability*, 7(7), 8709–8728.

Combes, B. P. (2005). The United Nations Decade of Education for Sustainable Development (2005–2014): Learning to Live Together Sustainably. *Applied Environmental Education and Communication*, 4(3), 215–219.

Elfert, M. (2019). Lifelong Learning in Sustainable Development Goal 4: What Does It Mean for UNESCO's Rights-Based Approach to Adult Learning and Education?. *International Review of Education*, 65(4), 537–556.

Gibbs, G. (2013). Reflections on the Changing Nature of Educational Development. *International Journal for Academic Development, 18*(1), 4–14.

Gresch, H., Hasselhorn, M., & Bögeholz, S. (2013). Training in Decision-Making Strategies: An Approach to Enhance Students' Competence to Deal with Socio-Scientific Issues. *International Journal of Science Education, 35*(15), 2587–2607.

Hoffner, S., & Tilbury, D. (2013). *Towards a post-United Nations Decade of Education for Sustainable Development (DESD) Framework.*

Huckle, J., & Wals, A. E. (2015). The UN Decade of Education for Sustainable Development: Business as Usual in the End. *Environmental Education Research, 21*(3), 491–505.

Jose, S., & Chacko, J. (2017). Building a Sustainable Higher Education Sector in the UAE. *International Journal of Educational Management, 31*(6), 752–765.

Kamel Boulos, M. N., & Wheeler, S. (2007). The Emerging Web 2.0 Social Software: An Enabling Suite of Sociable Technologies in Health and Health Care Education 1. *Health Information & Libraries Journal, 24*(1), 2–23.

Lee, Y., Park, J., Ryu, C., Gang, K. S., Yang, W., Park, Y. K., ... & Hyun, S. (2013). Comparison of Biochar Properties from Biomass Residues Produced by Slow Pyrolysis at 500 C. *Bioresource Technology, 148*, 196–201.

Lozano, R. (2006). Incorporation and institutionalization of SD into universities: breaking through barriers to change. *Journal of cleaner production, 14*(9–11), 787–796.

Lozano, R., Lukman, R., Lozano, F. J., Huisingh, D., & Lambrechts, W. (2013). Declarations for Sustainability in Higher Education: Becoming Better Leaders, through Addressing the University System. *Journal of Cleaner Production, 48*, 10–19.

Lozano, R., Merrill, M. Y., Sammalisto, K., Ceulemans, K., & Lozano, F. J. (2017). Connecting Competences and Pedagogical Approaches for Sustainable Development in Higher Education: A Literature Review and Framework Proposal. *Sustainability, 9*(10), 1889.

McCann, G., & McCloskey, S. (2009). *Od lokálneho ku globálnemu. Kľúčové rozdiely rozvojových štúdií.[From Local to Global. Key Differences in Development Studies].* Bratislava: Nadácia Pontis, 2011. ISBN 978-80-968229-3-4.

McKeown, R., Hopkins, C. A., Rizi, R., & Chrystalbridge, M. (2002). *Education for Sustainable Development Toolkit* (p. 2002). Knoxville: Energy, Environment and Resources Center, University of Tennessee.

Mulà, I., Tilbury, D., Ryan, A., Mader, M., Dlouhá, J., Mader, C., Benayas, J., Dlouhý, J., & Alba, D. (2017). Catalysing Change in Higher Education for Sustainable Development: A Review of Professional Development Initiatives for University Educators. *International Journal of Sustainability in Higher Education*, 18(5), 798–820.

Nölting, B., Molitor, H., Reimann, J., Skroblin, J. H., & Dembski, N. (2020). Transfer for Sustainable Development at Higher Education Institutions – Untapped Potential for Education for Sustainable Development and for Societal Transformation. *Sustainability*, 12(7), 2925.

Örtenblad, A. (2018). What Does "learning organization" Mean?. *The Learning Organization*, 25(3), 150–158.

Ryan, A., & Tilbury, D. (2013). Flexible Pedagogies: New Pedagogical Ideas. *Higher Education Academy*.

Shriberg, M., & Harris, K. (2012). Building Sustainability Change Management and Leadership Skills in Students: Lessons Learned from "Sustainability and the Campus" at the University of Michigan. *Journal of Environmental Studies and Sciences*, 2, 154–164.

Stephens, G. L., Vane, D. G., Tanelli, S., Im, E., Durden, S., Rokey, M., ... & Marchand, R. (2008). CloudSat Mission: Performance and Early Science after the First Year of Operation. *Journal of Geophysical Research: Atmospheres*, 113(D8).

Sterling, S. (2011). Transformative Learning and Sustainability: Sketching the Conceptual Ground. *Learning and Teaching in Higher Education*, 5(11), 17–33.

Sterling, S. R., & Orr, D. (2001). *Sustainable Education: Re-visioning Learning and Change* (Vol. 6). Totnes: Green Books for the Schumacher Society.

Sterling, S., & Thomas, I. (2006). Education for Sustainability: The Role of Capabilities in Guiding University Curricula. *International Journal of Innovation and Sustainable Development*, 1(4), 349–370.

Thomas, I., & Day, T. (2014). Sustainability capabilities, graduate capabilities, and Australian universities. *International Journal of Sustainability in Higher Education*, 15(2), 208–227.

Vare, P., & Scott, W. (2007). Learning for a change: Exploring the relationship between education and sustainable development. *Journal of Education for Sustainable Development*, 1(2), 191–198.

Velazquez, L., Munguia, N., & Sanchez, M. (2005). Deterring sustainability in higher education institutions: An appraisal of the factors which influence sustainability in higher education institutions. *International Journal of Sustainability in Higher Education*, 6(4), 383–391.

Wiek, A., Withycombe, L., & Redman, C. L. (2011). Key Competencies in Sustainability: A Reference Framework for Academic Program Development. *Sustainability Science, 6,* 203–218.

Yeo, R. K. (2005). Revisiting the Roots of Learning Organization: A Synthesis of the Learning Organization Literature. *The Learning Organization, 12*(4), 368–382.

Zilahy, G., & Huisingh, D. (2009). The Roles of Academia in Regional Sustainability Initiatives. *Journal of Cleaner Production, 17*(12), 1057–1066.

Ileana Hamburg and David Sommer

The Role of Cybersecurity Educational Frameworks on the Improvement of Cybersecurity Awareness

1. Introduction

Digital technologies should support economic development of countries, qualification of employees and should also improve national and international Due to the COVID-19 pandemic this importance grows because people used intensively digital means for work, life and social relations. So, interest was great and big investments have been done in digital research also in connection with cybersecurity. But, using evolving digital approaches, cybersecurity attacks increase, became more sophisticated and affect users in different ways (Herjavec, 2019). Many cyber-attacks are a consequence of human errors and of missing of security measures. Within small and medium sized companies (SMEs) situation is very bad due to weak resources, missing skills and awareness of employees about necessary training. This situation requires urgently not only more cybersecurity professionals but also trained employers and employees to act corresponding. Research studies show that one urgent measure is to increase cybersecurity awareness of them. Progress has been made in consulting cyber experts, developing some security policies, and improving qualification of their security professionals. Networks, operating systems and digital programs have been developed. But not enough has been invested to increase cybersecurity awareness of all digital technology's users. So, criminals know it and developed advanced hacking techniques based on corresponding user behaviours.

National and international educational frameworks are necessary to assure countries resilience and support awareness development in their countries in order to continue their business, to assure information systems security and organizational resilience. It means to have the ability to deliver planned outcomes despite experiencing challenging cyberattacks, natural disasters or economic slumps.

This paper presents shortly some cybersecurity frameworks and cybersecurity training strategies particularly for employers and employees from SMEs for improving their cybersecurity awareness. Approaches to develop cybersecurity education and training programs for individuals taking into consideration also their future careers.

The Goal-Question-Metric (GQO) +Strategies (Breitinger et al., 2021) helps to describe cybersecurity competencies required to fulfil the National Cybersecurity Strategic Plans and adapt the improvement process of cybersecurity education and training curricula to national strategic goals.

Frameworks, e.g., developed by NIST (Newhouse et al., 2017) or ENISA (ENISA, 2022) will be shortly discussed. They present requirements also for education frameworks but do not give methods for their development to support user's awareness. Intervention Mapping (IM) (Adamson, 2019; Debate et al., 2017; Chowdhury et al., 2022) and Interdisciplinary approaches (Hussain et al, 2009; O'Brien et al., 2022; Hamburg, 2023) can be used in this context. An example is given in this paper how the Cybersecurity Framework developed within the InCyT project (www.incytproject.eu) and the cybersecurity training modules for SMEs managers and employees can be improved and used to support also awareness development (Hamburg & Sommer, 2022).

2. Cybersecurity Frameworks and Training Strategies

Agencies for the development of national cybersecurity frameworks are paid by big companies and institutions in their which would like their own frameworks or to have one some adapted to their specific situation. But SMEs do not have the manpower, know-how and do not understand the necessity to create their own cybersecurity frameworks.

Some of known developments will be listed below.

- Centre for Critical Security Controls (CIS) is oriented to common forms of data breaches and attacks (https://www.cisecurity.org/controls).
- Control Objectives for Information and Related Technologies (COBIT) is issued by ISACA, a non-profit organization known as "Information Systems Audit and Control Association" (https://www.isaca.org/resources/cobit).
- International Standards Organization (ISO) frameworks ISO/IEC 27001 and Agencies the world, can be adapted also to small businesses (https://www.isms.online/iso-27002/).
- The National Initiative for Cybersecurity Education Cybersecurity Workforce Framework (NICE Framework describes and classifies skills and competencies requirements for cybersecurity workers. The framework allows employers, employees, developers, job seekers and trainers to determine specific work roles as well as the skills, competences and knowledge to the work roles (https://niccs.cisa.gov/workforce-development/nice-framework).

- SPARTA Cybersecurity Skills Framework (SPARTA CSF) uses the structure of the NICE Framework with EU specific adaptations. The Framework has been tested and validated for applicability, adaptability by industry and academia and proposals for improvements have been done (https://www.sparta.eu/training/).

The European Union Agency for Cybersecurity (ENISA) (ENISA, 2022) assures cybersecurity in Europe since 2004 and supports the development of crossworder communities throughout the EU. Since 2019, a cybersecurity certification scheme has been developed (www.enisa.europa.eu).

The NIST National Initiative for Cybersecurity Education NICE shows the shortage of "people with the interdisciplinary knowledge, skills and abilities to perform the tasks required for cybersecurity work". But a workforce with interdisciplinary skills to solve the problem of communication between educators, researchers and people using information technologies which is necessary in this context is difficult to develop. Cooperation and communication between such groups is necessary due to complexity of cybersecurity problems. Particularly within SMEs with fewer resources and many tasks communication is missing. So, SMEs need help at determining the necessary skills and gaps of their employees, at using digital methods to improve the existing situation by developing training opportunities to reskill their employees and increase their awareness for cybersecurity. In the following we present two examples of cooperation in this context.

The REDCYBERSG Erasmus + project does not develop a Cybersecurity framework but aims to improve cybersecurity management skills of SMEs by filling gaps in SMEs in partner countries and to provide a comprehensive guide for integrating best practices into their procedures in order to mitigate cyber risks. This is achieved by focusing on direct target groups as VET teachers and trainers, SME managers and employees and other stakeholder organizations related to the SME sector. They can use developed intellectual outputs respectively by educating students (future employees), training employees or, in case of stakeholder organizations, by sustaining and disseminating information regarding the education and training solutions in cybersecurity.

Within the Erasmus+ INCyT project with partners from Universities, SMEs, vocational education and training (VET), consulting firms, a Cybersecurity Framework has been developed for vocational training and SME business to describe the competencies and skills that managers and employees, are required to have in order to prevent cyberattacks. Advantages of interdisciplinary training and mentoring programs are used, particularly in the area of cybersecurity and so the team project developed and tested digitally supported an interdisciplinary mentoring and training program and a collaborative e-learning platform for SMEs. This training program will be customized for VET and for development of a European transferability model.

This Framework has been developed and validated interactively in cooperation with managers and employees of some SMEs from the seven European partners, selected by partners and with cybersecurity SME consultants.

The proposal of European Commission i.e., The Digital Competence Framework 2.0 (Dig Comp 2.0 https://ec.europa.eu/jrc/en/digcomp/digital-competence-framework) has been used within InCyT particularly in order to prepare employees for digital transformation in their countries.

One problem is that despite many cybersecurity frameworks and projects which have been developed, the vulnerability of user computers is growing also because the significance of the missed training in cybersecurity awareness and because management did not understand the importance. So, it is necessary to include awareness approaches into cybersecurity frameworks/projects, to give concrete examples and develop corresponding cybersecurity training. Indeed, very often SMEs employees are prime targets of cyberattacks by using. i.e., various online applications and social platforms. Many of them have no knowledge about cybersecurity or do not recognize cyber-attacks and act to protect their devices from malware, viruses, and scams. In the following we give an example how to improve this situation.

3. Intervention Mapping

Holistic cybersecurity education frameworks and training for the development of cybersecurity competencies of professionals, managers and employees as well as their awareness should include identification of stakeholder's roles, implementation paths for competence development, and training methods to achieve corresponding competencies.

Intervention Mapping (IM) (Bartholomew Eldridge et al., 2016) uses this and helps to build theory- and evidence-based approaches taking into consideration ecological aspects, the participation of stakeholders, and the application of theories and evidence.

Intervention Mapping is an iterative process not a linear one: the IM steps are revised during the intervention development, it is also cumulative, each phase being built on the previous ones. The IM planners use theoretical models and empirical evidence in behavioural and environmental determinants related to a target problem, selecting the most appropriate theoretical methods and practical applications to address the identified determinants.

IM has been first developed and used for health and later adapted to other domains due to its applicability and efficiency for development and evaluation of corresponding training approaches (Kok et al., 2011).

Following steps for planning a training program development and its assessment can be used.

(Bartholomew Eldridge et al., 2016):

1. The assessment of stakeholder inclusion in the work process through social measures. In this context, the future learners are requested to answer questions including expectations, needs, and topics of interest.
2. The identification of desired performance and necessary changed objectives based on scientific analyses of problems and their causes. Cybersecurity behaviours which should be changed and missing awareness in cybersecurity measures should be identified as important factors threats to both individual and organizational security (Canham et al., 2022).
3. The use of intervention methods, based on theoretical analysis and practical applications to change behaviour and improve awareness of training participants. Technical scenarios should be developed for the participants as well as corresponding training materials (lectures, audiovisual, group exercises and individual assignments).
4. The development of training program components. It means the intervention strategies and planning their realisation. NIST framework, and ENISA recommendations will be used. Available or new toolsets should support an efficient transfer of knowledge and awareness training.
5. The development of a plan for program adoption, implementation, and sustainability support.
6. The planning of process evaluation and impact measures.

4. Interdisciplinary Approaches

Due to the numerous cyber-attacks, the Cybersecurity Policy Review (https://www.redscan.com/services/cyber-policy-review) underlines the necessity for measures to develop cybersecurity awareness of workforce and an interdisciplinary expertise and skills. They should recognize and prevent potential threats faced by organizations and individuals. The challenges due to technology misuse and abuse require a better understanding of cybersecurity connections with other disciplines.

But Holt (2016) points out that it is difficile to situate a cybercrime threat or vulnerability in a multidisciplinary context. In this context, a holistic approach to cybersecurity considering many disciplines for training experts, employees, managers together are required. Such an approach should consider contributions of different subfields. So, cybersecurity professionals must develop an expertise within their individual subfield and understand how their work can be integrated together with other ones. Also, nonprofessional employees and manager should understand it.

The study (Borg, 2005) explained the "interdisciplinarity" of cybersecurity that contributes to the direction, content and techniques involved in the development of cybersecurity education and training. It is also underlined the contribution of other disciplines to the field of cybersecurity by analysing relevant theories to understand cyber security in the context of legal, economics and criminology perspectives.

Understanding the technical nature of the cyber environment, the networked systems, operating systems and the security threats around them is necessary. The behaviour of human actors and their decision-making process play a vital role in a cyber-attack to be successful and should be more considered (Ramirez, 2017). This will help institutions or organizations to develop/adapt educational programs and to consider more the human decisions. Criminology theories try to clear the motivations of crimes, different behaviours, and practices used (Jaishankar, 2007).

One condition to understand the cyberattacks, is to analyse interconnections and economy factors that cyber attackers use in destroying process. The economic structural analysis is used by cyber attackers and is important also for cyber defenders (Borg, 2005). An efficient cyber defence program and training should include more not only consider some individual cyber-attack scenarios.

A comprehensive approach to cybersecurity based on the internet structure and emerging cyber threats requires also a continuous development, interpretation and use of legal areas and instruments. Cyber incidents politically motivated increased and this require that cybersecurity be is of more interest for national governments and international organizations and to develop an approach combining considerations of threat, deterrence and response from different political areas and responsibilities.

Based on considering cyber related interdisciplinary theories, the need for a comprehensive approach to cybersecurity is essential (Jacobson et al., 2012).

As an example of interdisciplinary connections presented within InCyT training, social engineering is an important topic and phishing attacks a verry often threat in cybersecurity. The networked world, the intensive use of the internet and digital technologis are a basis for social engineering attacks. The Federal Bureau of Investigation's internet crime underlined the increased use of social engineering attacks and business email fraud schemes having as a consequence loss of a lot of money during the last years (Abbate, 2020). To fight against methods of hackers, it is necessary to use an interdisciplinary approach to understand their methods, complexities and how it affects businesses. Literature reviews highlight perspectives from different disciplines: information technology, psychology, business and ethics. Figure 1 illustrates this view (Washo, 2021) and gives some explications.

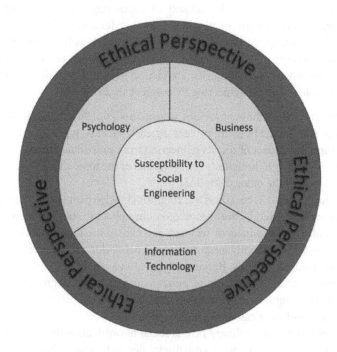

Figure 1. Social engineering from an interdisciplinary view (Washo, 2021)

- Social engineering should be considered in the context of the actual digital systems and their use in the business. Multi-factor authentication is an effective way for organizations to confirm that the person accessing the systems has permission. A login process with username and password is an effective way for the user to be authenticated. An additional factor could be the use of a virtual private network (VPN) login to better validatation of the user.

• Social engineering is connected with deception, so a psychological approach of the concept is important for understanding behaviours of both the attacker and victim. The use of psychological methods is important to social engineering to support the protections such as firewalls and systems used to identify intruders (Bullee et al., 2018).

• Social engineering attacks impact many businesses and have implications for the structure and management. The topic can be considered from the business perspective to determine the factors that impact social engineering attacks.

• Ethics is important in the context of social engineering and should be researched because the manipulating another human violates many ethical principles. The qualities of an ideal employees such as trust, the willingness to please others such as managers, customers, co-workers, and visitors, and the readiness to obey authority, are characteristics that make an individual susceptible to social engineering (Mouton et al., 2015).

Each of these disciplines, provides information on how to understand and interpret the topic, how to protect against various types of attacks, and understand the impact of social engineering from individual and organizational standpoint. But each discipline's interpretation of the topic should be considered in the context of the other disciplines.

Another example is social networking, which helps people and organizations to connect with friends, are means of communication, help to launch a new business idea, sell products or services, and extend the reach of an own brand. Sure, there are also disadvantages of social networking like decreases face-to-face communication skills. Because organizations use intensively social media platforms, attackers use trust and public nature of these platforms to attacks. Social networking security is important for business and private success so that training of employees can have a big contribution.

The related interdisciplinary field is social network analysis (SNA) including knowledge from other social science disciplines such as sociology, anthropology, psychology, communication. SNA belongs to a larger interdisciplinary field of studying all types of networks called network science including physics, computer science, data science, biology, engineering, mathematics, and other fields. The relationship between these fields is showed in Figure 2 (https://bookd own.org/omarlizardo/_main/1-2-what-is-a-social-network.html).

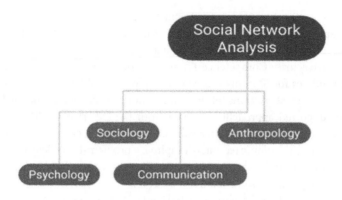

Figure 2. Relationships between fields in SNA (https://bookdown.org/omarlizardo/ _main/1-2-what-is-a-social-network.html)

5. Cybersecurity Awareness and InCyT project

Until now, cybersecurity awareness has been a topic mostly in higher education to better understand students' attitude, knowledge, behaviour, and other relevant impacting factors.

One conclusion is that the major problem with security awareness is not missing security knowledge but that this knowledge is few applied in real-world situations. So higher education institutions should use it to develop policies and procedures that motivate students to find own responses to avoid cyber-attacks.

Such measures are missing but necessary also in companies and cybersecurity awareness should be included within training of employees and employees. Studies are necessary, to find cybersecurity awareness methods and training topics to be applied in companies in providing information on cybersecurity awareness. The methods should be suitable for users (Abawajy, 2014), particularly within SMEs which are few resources and time. In education and training, cybersecurity awareness can be conducted i.e., using text-, game-, and video-based delivery methods with the aim of determining user preferences. A combination of different delivery methods would be most effective. More work is necessary to determine how to improve awareness of employers and employees through including it into corresponding training approaches.

Building a company-wide cybersecurity culture and active participation is necessary: decision-making and application of cybersecurity best practices should become daily tasks for end-users at all levels.

The Cybersecurity Competence Framework developed InCyT as well as the training modules for SMS managers and employees will be improved be using IM. Individual roles, responsibilities, and required skills will be better linked; evidence supported approaches, derived from the experience within the first phase of training within InCyT, to ensure competencies in the awareness context will be used. Digital-supported interdisciplinary problem-based learning (IPBL) will be further used for the training program supporting the development of critical thinking (Hamburg, 2022).

Based on the next results of investigated level of security awareness within some SMEs, it is planned that the InCyT training program will be extended with a module using IM evidence-based practices and interactive presentations of consequences of careless cyber habits of common internet/technology users to increase the awareness of SME managers and employees. It is intended to use GQM+Strategies approach in improvement of training program to determine the learning methods and outcomes which fit better into cybersecurity companies' strategies.

6. Conclusions

Many countries understood that cybersecurity is an important and actual topic and developed guidelines for training within private and public sectors. Cybersecurity training programs also to increase awareness about the impact of cyber breaches or attacks have been developed. But particularly within SMEs, continuous maintain and training to improve the awareness among employees is missing. Awareness of cybersecurity best practices for employees and employers through suitable training topics should be a continuous duty. It is important to keep the users of digital developments motivated to be aware of cybersecurity measures to prevent cyber-attacks, raise their interest and participation in the training. It demands cooperations between SMEs, cybersecurity consultants, educators, VET representatives, developers to find the right methods.

References

Abawajy, J. (2014). User Preference of Cyber Security Awareness Delivery Methods. *Behaviour & Information Technology*, 33(2014), 237–248.

Abbate, P. (2020). *Internet Crime Report 2020*. https://www.ic3.gov/Media/PDF/AnnualReport/2020_IC3Report.pdf

Adamson, K. (2019). *Strategy Mapping: An Essential Tool for New Academic Faculty – Faculty Focus | Higher Ed Teaching & Learning*. https://www.facul tyfocus.com/articles/faculty-development/strategy-mapping-an-essential-tool-for-new-academic-faculty. Accessed on 07/21/2021.

Bartholomew Eldridge, L. K., Markham, C. M., Ruiter, R. A. C., Fernàndez, M. E., Kok, G., & Parcel, G. S. (2016). *Planning Health Promotion Programs; An Intervention Mapping Approach*. San Francisco, CA: Jossey-Bass.

Borg, S. (2005). Economically Complex Cyberattacks. *IEEE Secur. Privacy,* 3(6), 64–67.

Breitinger, F., Tully-Doyle, R., Przyborski, K., Beck, L., & Harichandran, R. S. (2021). First Year Students' Experience in a Cyber World Course–an Evaluation. *Education and Information Technologies, 26,* 1069–1087.

Bullée, J-W., Montoya, L., Pieters, W., Junger, M., & Hartel, P. (2018). On the anatomy of social engineering attacks: A literature-based dissection of successful attacks. *Journal of Investigative Psychology and Offender Profiling,* 15(1), 20–45. https://doi.org/10.1002/jip.1482

Canham, M., Posey, C., & Constantino, M. (2022). Phish Derby: Shoring the Human Shield through Gamified Phishing Attacks. *Frontiers in Education, 6,* 807277. https://doi.org/10.3389/feduc.2021.807277

Chowdhury, N., Katsikas, S., & Gkioulos, V. (2022). Modeling Effective Cybersecurity Training Frameworks: A Delphi Method-based Study. *Computer Security* 113, 102551. https://doi.org/10.1016/j.cose.2021.102551.

DeBate, R., Corvin, J. A., Wolfe-Quintero, K., & Petersen, D. J. (2017). Application of the Intervention Mapping Framework to Develop an Integrated Twenty-First Century Core Curriculum – Part One: Mobilizing the Community to Revise the MPH Core Competencies. *Front Public Health 5,* 287. https://doi.org/10.3389/fpubh.2017.00287.

ENISA. (2022). *European Cybersecurity Skills Framework*. https://www.enisa.europa.eu/topics/cybersecurity-education/european-cybersecurity-skills-framework/ecsf-pro files-v-0-5-draft-release.pdf.

Hamburg, I. (2022). Using Interdisciplinary Problem-Based Learning and Critical Thinking in Cyber Training (Abstract). In European Association of Erasmus Coordinators (Eds.), *Abstract Booklet 2022 of the Eracon & Career EU on 27th June – 1st July 2022 (7)*. Thessaloniki.

Hamburg, I., & Sommer, D. (2022). Cyber-Sicherheitstraining für kleine und mittelständische Unternehmen – Das Erasmus+-Projekt InCyT. *Forschung Aktuell, 2022* (12). Gelsenkirchen: Institut Arbeit und Technik, Westfälische Hochschule Gelsenkirchen Bocholt Recklinghausen. https://doi.org/10.53190/fa/202212

Herjavec. (2019). *2019 Official Annual Cybercrime Report.*

Holt, T. J. (2016). *Cybercrime Through an Interdisciplinary Lens.* Taylor & Francis, Milton Park.

Holt, T. J., Burruss, G. W., Bossler, A. M. (2010). Social Learning and Cyber-Deviance: Examining the Importance of a Full Social Learning Model in the Virtual World. *Journal of Crime and Justice, 33*(2), 31–61.Hussain, O., Mohd, B., Ahmad, E., Selamat, A., & Sulaiman, A. (2009). Problem-based Learning across Diverse Engineering Disciplines at Universiti Tun Hussein Onn Malaysia. *International Journal of Learner Diversity, 1*, 113–126, 12.

Jacobson, D., Rursch, J., & Idziorek, J. (2012). Security across the Curriculum and Beyond. *Proceedings of the 2012 IEEE Frontiers in Education Conference (FIE),* pp. 1–6. IEEE Computer Society.

Jaishankar, K. (2007). Establishing a Theory of Cybercrimes. *International Journal of Cyber Criminology, 1*(2), 7–9.

Kok, G., Lo, S. H., Peters, G.-J. Y., & Ruiter, R. A. (2011). Changing Energy Related Behavior: An Intervention Mapping Approach. *Energy Policy 39,* 5280–5286. https://doi.org/10.1016/j.enpol.2011.05.03.

Mouton, F, Malan, MM, Kimppa, KK & Venter, HS. (2015). Necessity for ethics in social engineering research. *Computers & Security,* Vol 55, 114–127.

Newhouse, W., Keith, S., Scribner, B., & Witte, G. (2017). National Initiative for Cybersecurity Education (nice) Cybersecurity Workforce Framework. *NIST Special Publication, 800,* 181. https://doi.org/10.6028/NIST.SP.800-181.

O'Brien, E., & Hamburg, I. (2022). About Training Educators to Become Drivers for Change. In A. Kaplan (Ed.), *Digital Transformation and Disruption of Higher Education* (pp. 316–332). Cambridge: Cambridge University Press & Assessment.

Pratt, T. C., Holtfreter, K., & Reisig, M. D. (2010). Routine Online Activity and Internet Fraud Targeting Extending the Generality of Routine Activity Theory. *Journal of Research in Crime and Delinquency 47*(3), 267–296.

Ramirez, R. B. (2017). *Making Cyber Security Interdisciplinary: Recommendations for a Novel Curriculum and Terminology Harmonization.* Massachusetts Institute of Technology.

Schreider, T. (2019). *Building an Effective Cybersecurity Program* (2nd ed.). Brookfield, CT, USA: Rothstein Publishing.

Washo, A. (2021). *An Interdisciplinary View of Social Engineering: A Call to Action for Research.* https://www.researchgate.net/publication/353448049_An_interdisciplinary_view_of_social_engineering_A_call_to_action_for_r esearch.

Machyudin Agung Harahap, Susri Adeni, Titien Yusnita and
Arifin Saleh Harahap

Improving Family Communication of Child Marriage in Family Resilience

1. Introduction

The number of child marriages in Indonesia is worrying. Data from the Religious Courts shows that in 2021 there were 65 thousand cases recorded and in 2022 there were 55 thousand applications (Biro Hukum dan Humas, 2023). This is also what happened in West Java Province, especially in Bogor Regency. Child marriages in Bogor Regency have increased since 2019. Data shows that there were 136 reports of marriage dispensation cases during 2019, increasing rapidly in 2020 to 387 filings, in 2021 there were 362 reports and in 2022 there were 295 (Imam, 2023).

The high number of cases of child marriage will of course have an impact on many things. The security of child marriage families is very vulnerable. Research conducted by Akhiruddin (Akhiruddin, 2017) in Bone Regency regarding the impact of young marriage shows that several negative impacts include risky pregnancies due to too young an age, the emergence of prolonged psychological trauma in the child's soul and which is difficult to heal, threats to family harmony. due to the immature mindset of couples, and the increasing population density of couples of childbearing age (Akhiruddin, 2017).

Another research conducted by Suryaningsih in Bantul Regency said that couples who married at a young age had unstable emotional levels, early marriages were more vulnerable to arguments and domestic violence, because they adjusted to their partner. very difficult to do (Suryaningsih et al., 2023). Raj also revealed that child marriage has a health impact on women, including increasing the risk of postnatal death and stillbirth, premature babies and low birth weight, as well as morbidity and mortality of babies and children (Raj, 2010).

Kartikawati conducted research on the impact of child marriage in Indonesia, and found that there are several factors that influence child marriage, including educational factors, lack of understanding of reproductive health in adolescents, which causes risky sexual behavior among children, economic factors (poverty), cultural factors (traditions/customs), and arranged marriage (Kartikawati, 2014). These factors will also have an impact on the child's home life. For example, in the economic aspect, child marriage makes the child trapped in a "poverty cycle" as a result of dropping out of school. In social and psychological aspects, child marriage increases the potential for infidelity and divorce due to unstable emotions, and women are even very vulnerable to experiencing subordinate treatment in the form of domestic violence. Furthermore, from a health perspective, child marriage has the potential to endanger the lives of mothers and babies, one of which is due to the reproductive organs not being ready due to their young age (Kartikawati, 2014; Musfiroh, 2016).

The results of the research above show that child marriage has an impact on many things. Likewise what happened in Pamijahan Regency, especially in Cibitung Wetan Village. Child marriage is rampant due to various factors, including culture, economics and societal stigma which says that if you are 18 and unmarried, you are considered an old maid. In fact, there are many impacts of child marriage, as has been studied by previous researchers.

Family resilience, which is the basis of marriage, can be vulnerable due to marriage at a young age. The concept of family resilience involves processes that foster relational resilience as a functional unit. Challenges faced in families can range from a series of normative transitions in the life cycle, such as retirement, divorce, or remarriage, to sudden job loss or the untimely death of an important family member, or a prolonged series of migration or inner-city violence (Walsh, 1996). Another opinion says that, first, resilience appears when facing difficulties. It involves the way individuals respond to adversity. Without struggle, resilience will not exist. Second, resilience brings the property of buoyancy. This approach assumes that individuals who demonstrate resilience are able to "bounce back" from adversity, reaching or exceeding pre-crisis conditions (Hawley, 2000).

For this reason, a family needs a way to face the challenges that occur. In family resilience, communication is important. This is because resilience involves many processes that vary and repeat over time, from the family's approach to the threat of crisis to the disruption that occurs immediately afterwards and long-term adaptation. Experts also say that relational resilience in families involves organizational patterns, communication and problem solving processes, community resources, and confirmation of belief systems (Walsh, 1996).

Based on the background above and the phenomena that occur in Cibitung Wetan Village, it is urgent to carry out this research to explore family communication and family resilience for child marriage couples. The significant impact of child marriage makes researchers also interested in knowing how religious or community leaders view and overcome the problem of child marriage.

2. Literature Review

2.1. Family Communication

Family communication is very important. If communication is not good in the family then family harmony will definitely not be good. Communication patterns in each family are different. Family communication can be defined as readiness to discuss openly everything in the family, both pleasant and unpleasant, as well as being ready to resolve problems in the family with discussions carried out in patience, honesty and openness (Friendly, 2002 in Permana & Ramadhana, 2020)

This pattern of communication within the family contains two dimensions, namely conversation and conformity which focuses on interactions between parents and children rather than interactions between children or between parents, because it is during these intergenerational exchanges that parents socialize their children regarding the concept of communication family (Koerner & Fitzpatrick, 2002 in Permana & Ramadhana, 2020; Savitri & Ramadhana, 2020).

Furthermore, there are four types of family communication patterns according to Fitzpatrick and Koerner (Campbell-Salome et al., 2019; Fitzpatrick & Ritchie, 1994; Permana & Ramadhana, 2020; Putri & Supratman, 2021; Savitri & Ramadhana, 2020; Watts & Hovick, 2023), namely: Consensual, Pluralistic, Protective and Laissez-Faire families. These four types of family communication patterns are of course different:

1. Consensual family communication patterns; where the family has a high conformity orientation. Consensual type families tend to talk a lot to family members, but for family authority it is usually parents who make decisions. These families experience an emphasis on valuing open communication, while also wanting clear parental authority.
2. Pluralistic; where the family has a high conversation orientation and a low conformity orientation is given. In this type of family, there is a lot of open discussion, but family members will choose for themselves what decisions to make on the basis of these discussions. Parents in this family feel no need to control their children in making decisions for their children. Instead, parents' opinions are evaluated based on the merits of those arguments, and everyone participates in family decision making.
3. Protective Pattern; families tend to be low in conversation orientation and high in conformity orientation. There is a lot of emphasis on obedience to parental authority but little on communication with family members. Parents in this type of family believe that they should make decisions for the family and family members.

4. Laissez-Faire Pattern; Families with low conversation orientation and low conformity orientation. Members of this type of family don't want to be much involved in what other family members are doing and don't want to spend time talking about it. Parents believe that all family members should make their own decisions and have little interest in their children's decisions.

The communication patterns mentioned above are an illustration of how families interact and communicate. This pattern of communication within the family contains two dimensions, namely conversation and conformity which focuses on interactions between parents and children rather than interactions between children or between parents, because it is during these intergenerational exchanges that parents socialize their children regarding the concept of communication. family (Koerner & Fitzpatrick, 2002 in Permana & Ramadhana, 2020).

The effectiveness of the communication that is formed will also reflect the intimacy that exists within the family. Schrodt, Witt, and Messersmith (2008 in Setyawan & Psi, n.d.) underline the results of their research, that in general family communication patterns have a meaningful relationship with various cognitive activities and relational behavior, as well as individual well-being.

2.2. Family Resilience

Family resilience is necessary for the continuity of life in the family. Family resilience is the resilience of a husband and wife in maintaining and maintaining their family intact and not resulting in divorce (Indriyani, 2021). Meanwhile, according to Black and Lobo, family resilience is the success of family members in overcoming difficulties which allows them to develop with warmth, support and cohesion (Black & Lobo, 2008). Furthermore, family resilience is described as a family's success in overcoming life transitions, stress or difficulties (McCubbin & McCubbin, 1988, 1996 in Black & Lobo, 2008). The concept of family resilience was originally developed in studying children's positive adaptation in adverse circumstances (Rutter, 1999).

McCubbin and Mc-Cubbin (1988 in Hawley, 2000; Hawley & DeHaan, 1996) define family resilience as "family characteristics, dimensions and traits that help families to be resilient to disruption in the face of change and adaptive in the face of crisis situations". The family resilience perspective recognizes parental strengths, family dynamics, reciprocal relationships, and the social environment (Black & Lobo, 2008). This strengths-based approach views family stress and challenges not as destructive, but as opportunities to promote healing and growth (McCubbin & McCubbin, 1988; Walsh, 1996).

Consistent with the individual resilience perspective, family resilience is an ongoing process and often emerges within families and is not a stable trait. Family resilience is similar to the regenerative power of families, especially when good outcomes follow situations of significant risk that a family faces (Patterson, 2002).

Family resilience is also a condition of sufficient and sustainable access to income and resources to meet various basic needs such as food, health services, educational opportunities, housing, time to participate in society, and social integration (Frankenberger, 1998 in Muhammad et al., 2023). Indonesian Government Regulation Number 21 of 1994, family resilience is a dynamic condition of families that have tenacity, physical, material, mental abilities and toughness to live independently (Muhammad et al., 2023). Family resilience includes the family's ability to manage resources and problems to achieve prosperity.

From the opinions of these experts, family resilience is very important. When a family is able to maintain their family conditions, it will have an impact on the children. A focus on family resilience seeks to identify and promote key processes that enable families to cope more effectively and become more resilient to crises or persistent stress, whether originating from within or outside the family. In building family resilience, strengthening the family as a functional unit and enabling the family to foster resilience in all its members (Walsh, 1996).

2.3. Child Marriage

The definition of child marriage is a child who marries before the age of 19 years. In Indonesia, marriage is regulated in law number 16 of 2019 which regulates the minimum age for women to marry, namely 19 years and men 19 years. Definition of child on the basis of law no. 23 of 2002 are under the age of 18, including children who are still in the womb. Child marriage, or often referred to as early marriage, is defined as a marriage that occurs before the child reaches the age of 18, before the child is physically, physiologically and psychologically mature to be responsible for marriage and the children resulting from the marriage (Hakiki, Gaib et al., 2020).

However, in practice, child marriage occurs in Indonesia both in urban and rural areas. Regarding child marriage, Law 35/2014 explicitly states the obligations of parents to prevent child marriage. The Indonesian Government's commitment to preventing child marriage was then realized with the issuance of Law 16/2019 which amended the Article regarding the minimum age limit for child marriage in Law 1/1974 concerning Marriage. With the issuance of Law

16/2019, the minimum age for marriage for women increased from 16 years to 19 years (Hakiki, Gaib et al., 2020).

There are many reasons and arguments when parents marry off their children at a young age. Families who marry children at a relatively young age, namely 16–18 years, for several reasons for getting married include dropping out of school, wanting to be alone, no longer wanting to go to school, feeling ready to settle down, and some even being forced by their parents (Hikmah, 2019). Apart from that, according to Kartikawati, several factors that influence child marriage are educational factors, lack of understanding of reproductive health in adolescents which causes risky sexual behavior among children, economic factors (poverty), cultural factors (traditions/customs), and arranged marriages (Hikmah, 2019; Kartikawati, 2014).

There are many problems that usually arise in cases of child marriage. One of them then has an impact on fulfilling the family's economic needs, for the most part only the husband works in an effort to fulfill the family's needs. There is a lack of fulfilling economic needs, by taking refuge in parents in the form of living with their parents. This choice can be interpreted as an economic lifeline for families who engage in child marriage (Sarradian & Hasibuan, 2015; Sinabutar et al., 2023).

Furthermore, some of the implications of this are, firstly, young families who already have children even entrust their children to be looked after by their parents, secondly it has an impact on efforts to fulfill children's nutrition, and thirdly it has an impact on children's parenting patterns. These young families generally receive support from parents to carry out child marriages, of course with consideration and readiness from the parents (Sinabutar et al., 2023).

The families of child marriage couples are very vulnerable because both partners are not yet physically or mentally ready to live a married life. Married couples with children do not have enough formal knowledge (drop out of school) and informal knowledge because they are young and do not yet have the skills to earn a living, making it difficult to achieve family functioning (Yusnita, 2021).

3. Research Methods

Qualitative research was carried out in this study to explore how children marry and the resilience of their families. So family communication factors are also important to examine, how young couples communicate in overcoming their problems that occur. Family resilience is also crucial in child marriage.

Bogor Regency, which is one of the districts in West Java, had a percentage of child marriages reaching 13.3% in 2019. BPS (2014 in Yusnita, 2021) stated that the number of child marriage couples less than 19 years old reached 21,304 people, while the number of child marriage couples was increased by 29,327 people in 2019. The increase occurred in the age range between 16–19 years where there was a weakening of parental supervision of their children. This data did not significantly change to a decrease in cases of child marriage. From this data, it became the research location is Cibitung Wetan Village, Pamijahan District. This location was chosen because of the high number of child marriages. There are three sub-districts with the highest number of child marriage cases in Bogor Regency, especially in the West Bogor region, namely Cigudeg, Pamijahan and Leuwiliang (Yusnita, 2021).

The informants in this study were 3 child married couples after going through a purposive informant selection process using the criteria of being female and married before the age of 19 years. Researchers also interviewed community leaders and village officials regarding child marriage cases in Cibitung Wetan Village. Primary data obtained from interviews with informants was then analyzed qualitatively. Meanwhile, secondary data was obtained by collecting various scientific reading sources related to the research topic.

4. Results and Discussion

The research location is Cibitung Wetan Village with a typology of rice fields and the majority of occupation are farmers, farm laborers, entrepreneurs and casual daily laborers. The education level of the majority is elementary school for both women and men (Pamijahan District, n.d.). The location for this research was chosen due to the high rate of child marriage in Pamijahan District and especially in Cibitung Wetan Village. The characteristics of the informants are:

Table 1. Informant data

No	Inisial	Age now	Age when married	Education	Occopation	Role
1.	ER	39	14	Ementary school	Housewife	Informant child marriage
2.	DE	34	16	Junior High School	Housewife	Informant child marriage
3.	DA	41	14	Ementary school	Housewife	Informant child marriage
4.	DH	35	24	MA Isamic School	Village Staff	Informant for village officials
5.	EN	55	22	Ementary school	Village Head	Informant for community leaders

Table 1 shows data from informants interviewed by researchers regarding their children's marriages. All child marriage informants, namely ER, DE and DA, were married under the age of 19 years. They married based on their own initiative with their partner.

4.1. Why Marry at a Young Age?

The results of interviews with informants can be seen in Table 1 that the informants married under the age of 19 years. ER and DA married at the age of 14 while DE married at the age of 16. When asked further why she married at such a young age, ER explained that she married on her own initiative because she was no longer in school, and also because of having a boyfriend and finally decided to get married. ER's parents at that time also agreed to their marriage. Meanwhile, DE decided to marry young because she was worried about being the topic of discussion among people/neighbors because she had a boyfriend and her status was unclear, as DE stated as follows: "I'm worried about what the neighbors will say about me. If you're dating, your status isn't clear. So it's better to just get married so that the status is clear. I got married on my own initiative too." DA also said the same thing that he felt it was better to be married than alone and to have a clear status when married. DA also married on his own initiative.

If they were asked further, they married at the young age is due to several other factors, namely because they are no longer in school. Dropping out of school is one of the reasons for getting married because of their parents' inability to pay for their further education. Dropping out of school was also due to economic factors, where the informant's parents were previously only agricultural laborers or casual laborers with an uncertain income. Marriage is also considered to be a solution for their children because their daughters will be supported by their husbands. However, in reality this is not the case. After getting married, they don't have stable finances and their own house to live in, so they live with their parents.

Apart from economic factors, culture also influences the decision to marry. As the informants said, if you are over 19 and unmarried, you are considered an old maid and there is something wrong with the woman. This thinking is wrong, but because the culture has existed for a long time, the mindset of the people there has not changed. This is in line with research conducted by Inayati that from a traditional and cultural perspective, underage marriages often occur due to cultural encouragement in a community which positions women as second class where society avoids the stigma of being called a spinster and tries to speed up marriage for various reasons (Inayati, 2015).

Some of the factors mentioned above are in line with previous research conducted by Hikmah in 2019. The results of Hikmah's research state that the factors causing child marriage in Muara Wis village, Kutai Kartanegara Regency include: 1. Economic factors; 2. Educational factors; 3. Customs and customs factors (Hakiki, Gaib et al., 2020; Hikmah, 2019; Suryaningsih et al., 2023).

Another opinion states that, in general, marriage at an early age cannot be separated from certain factors such as old traditions that have been passed down from generation to generation which consider marriage at an early age to be normal. In fact, in certain areas, it is ironic that if a girl does not find a match immediately, the parents will feel embarrassed because the girl is not yet married. There are various kinds of exploitative culture towards children, one of which is economic or material. There are parents who marry their children to people who are considered respected without caring whether their child's future husband is married or not and whether their daughter is physically, mentally and socially ready or not, this is based on a sense of prestige or self-esteem (Muhammad et al., 2023). Meanwhile, Kartika said that the factors causing child marriage were education, poverty and tradition or culture and religion (Kartikawati, 2014).

According to Hollean (in Lestari, 2015), the factors that influence the occurrence of young marriages are: 1. Family economic problems 2. Parents of girls ask the male family if they want to marry off their girls 3. That with child marriage – the child, then in the girl's family there will be one less family member who is responsible (food, education, etc.).

The large number of cases of child marriage shows that parents also do not have a good understanding of the impact of child marriage. The culture that also influences child marriage has not been able to change and change the mindset of parents. Followed by the behavior of children who are willing and obedient to marry at a young age. This complexity has become a protracted problem and requires a strategy to change the mindset of the community, especially in Cibitung Wetan Village.

4.2. Child Marriage and Family Resilience

The researcher then also asked about the family resilience of informants who married young. This was because the age of the informants when they married were still very young and the informants' knowledge was deemed inadequate regarding marriage and family resilience.

ER as informants said that they got their understanding of marriage from their parents because their parents approved of their marriage. There is no special learning to be gained before marriage. ER also said that if there is a problem in the family, they will discuss it together as much as possible, even if the communication is done in an angry or high tone. ER and her husband try to defend their household from various problems. They do this because they remember that they already have children and do not want their children to become victims of their household problems.

The same thing happened with informant DE who revealed that their household had been fine even though there were problems that they were facing. DE admitted that they both agreed to run a household together and always communicate regarding any problems. Even though DE thought about divorcing her husband, DE said she would hold on for the sake of their children. A glance at DE's statement shows that the resilience of their family was shaky and fragile, but because they had children, difficulties were overcome for the sake of the continuity of the household.

This is different from DA who said that she should not let other people know about the household problems she is facing. So DA also finds out for herself various information on how to build a household with her partner. The DA did not say what media was used to obtain information about the household. DA also said that there were various problems they faced, but that did not make them separate. Third people are not allowed to enter and interfere in DA's family so DA tries not to talk about his household problems.

Many families cannot fulfill their needs, both physically, psychologically and socially (Lestari, 2015). So that the family's resilience can be shaken and they cannot build a harmonious and prosperous family. A marriage that is based on maturity when choosing to get married and being ready physically and mentally will have problems that cannot be solved. What about those who choose to marry as teenagers. In fact, currently there are many families in Indonesia whose level of family resilience cannot be met properly so they cannot form a harmonious and prosperous family. What is interesting about these three informants, even though they married at a very young age, they were able to maintain their family and marriage until they were more than 20 years into their marriage. This means that even though they married young, they learned an understanding of family resilience as they lived their married life. Child marriage is inherently vulnerable to family resilience. This is due to various influencing factors.

Family resilience can be seen from the conditions or circumstances within the family itself. Communication between family members, meeting family needs, affection between family members, and family health (Lestari, 2015). Apart from that, what is called a strong and successful family is another meaning of family resilience which is as follows (Puspitawati, 2013 in Lestari, 2015): 1. Health aspects 2. Economic aspects 3. Healthy family life, 4. Aspects education

5. Aspects of social life, 6. Responding to differences in society through personal interaction skills with various cultures. If the three informants can overcome problems related to family resilience, then their family is a strong family and is able to communicate well within the family.

4.3. Family Communication in Child Marriage

Family communication is a communication activity that takes place within a family, namely the way a family member communicates with other family members, as a place to instill and develop the values needed to guide life (Rahmah, 2018 in Asiyah & Ni'am, 2022).

Family communication during child marriage is an interesting matter because basically a relatively young age will influence communication and thinking. As stated by ER informants, the communication they had with their partners was rude, with a high tone and anger due to selfish factors and age. After being married for several years, communication went quite well because they had entered a relatively established age.

Likewise, what was experienced by DE and DA, poor communication at the beginning of marriage was due to the age factor which made both partners feel self-righteous and selfish. Existing problems are resolved with good communication. This is because family communication is an organization that uses words, body attitudes, voice intonation, actions to create images of hope, express feelings and share mutual understanding. If the communication that occurs is not good, then the results will not be good and will not match expectations. This is also a major factor in family resilience. Good communication on both sides greatly influences the continuity and functioning of the family.

Judging from the family communication patterns mentioned by experts, the decision to marry children was based on good communication between parents and children. Parents invite their children to talk about marriage plans, the children do not refuse and agree.

4.4. Community Figures and Village Officials in Child Marriage

Furthermore, researchers also interviewed community leaders and Cibitung Wetan village officials regarding child marriage cases. According to DH, village officials have informed them that the age limit for marriage is over 19 years. Likewise with EN. However, relatively speaking, society still practices child marriage. This is caused by many factors as mentioned above. Economic factors are the main thing when child marriage takes place. Parents assume that by getting married, their children will be free from their parents' responsibility. In reality, the opposite applies. Because children are very young and do not have decent work, they live with their parents.

The poverty of the Cibitung Wetan village community combined with low levels of education means that cases of child marriage continue to increase. Society does not fully realize the importance of education for their children's future. So according to DH, even though there is a special program that invites people not to engage in child marriage, it still cannot be completely successful. Socialization is carried out very frequently by the village, including up to 4 meetings with Cibitung Wetan residents, but child marriages still exist and are ongoing.

DH also added that there is a Youth Counseling Information Center (*PIKR*) for teenagers to receive education regarding marriage and reproductive health. This activity is carried out for teenagers under 19 years of age. The aim is to open teenagers' minds about the importance of education in the future. So teenagers are encouraged not to marry at a young age. EN also suggests that before marriage, couples who marry children receive guidance and education about the household. However, unfortunately EN does not forbid children from marrying young because according to him it is not good to date erratically and it is better to just marry according to religious law.

Cultural issues also influence child marriage. Women who are over 19 years old and unmarried are considered spinsters and "unsellable". So this is a social pressure that applies in the Cibitung Wetan Community that marriage is over 19 years old because no one likes the woman, aka "not selling".

DH also said that child marriage has an impact on the lives of the children themselves. The impacts that occur include disruption to the reproductive health of girls, domestic violence due to selfishness and unstable communication, problems with babies being born such as stunting, there are many other impacts. This is in line with previous research that child marriage will have an impact on their lives.

Basically, according to DH, village officials are maximally encouraging the community not to carry out child marriages. This is also what EN as a community figure said. However, that's still not what happened. So continuous outreach must be carried out and invite the community to dialogue and look at various cases of child marriage which have negative impacts so that the community is convinced that there are negative impacts caused by child marriage.

5. Conclusion

The ongoing child marriages in Cibitung Wetan Village affect children's life patterns. Family communication is an important foundation in resolving family problems so that family resilience can be guaranteed. Child marriage is vulnerable to family resilience. For this reason, education is needed for children before marriage and socialization of marriage after the age of 19 years. This means that the child is ready to enter married life with all its problems.

Various factors also influence child marriage, including economics, poverty, education, culture, social encouragement and pressure. Children choose to marry because their parents also approve of their wishes. Children are not directed enough to continue their education and are decided to marry young.

Further research is needed to see the culture in Cibitung Wetan Village and the community's understanding that women who are not married before the age of 19 are women who are "unsold" and will become spinsters. It is necessary and interesting to explore further.

The recommendation from the results of this research is to continue conducting outreach or social campaigns regarding the impact of child marriage. Education and peer groups or education centers for teenagers that have been carried out in Cibitung Wetan Village still need to be activated and carried out continuously.

References

Akhiruddin. (2017). *Implikasi Sosial Pernikahan Usia Muda di Kabupaten Bone.* https://journal.unismuh.ac.id/index.php/equilibrium/article/view/967

Asiyah, S., & Ni'am, M. (2022). Ojo Kawin Bocah Peran Komunikasi Keluarga dalam Pencegahan Pernikahan Anak di Kecamatan Keling Kabupaten Jepara. *Kifah: Jurnal Pengabdian Masyarakat, 1*(2), 107–118. https://doi.org/10.35878/kifah.v1i2.536

Biro Hukum dan Humas, K. (2023, January 27). *Kemen PPPA : Perkawinan Anak di Indonesia Sudah Mengkhawatirkan* [Siaran Pers Nomor: B- 031/SETMEN/HM.02.04/01/2023].

Black, K., & Lobo, M. (2008). A Conceptual Review of Family Resilience Factors. *Journal of Family Nursing, 14*(1), 33–55. https://doi.org/10.1177/1074840707312237

Campbell-Salome, G., Rauscher, E. A., & Freytag, J. (2019). Patterns of Communicating About Family Health History: Exploring Differences in Family Types, Age, and Sex. *Health Education & Behavior, 46*(5), 809–817. https://doi.org/10.1177/1090198119853002

Fitzpatrick, M. A., & Ritchie, L. D. (1994). Communication Schemata Within the Family: Multiple Perspectives on Family Interaction. *Human Communication Research, 20*(3), 275–301. https://doi.org/10.1111/j.1468-2958.1994.tb00324.x

Hakiki, Gaib, Ulfah, A., Khoer, M. I., Supriyanto, S., Basorudin, M., Larasati, W., Prastiwi, D., Kostaman, T. K., Irdiana, N., Amanda, P. K., & Kusumaningrum, S. (2020). *Pencegahan Perkawinan Anak: Percepatan yang Tidak Bisa Ditunda.*

Badan Pusat Statistik (BPS), Badan Perencanaan Pembangunan Nasional (Bappenas), UNICEF, dan Pusat Kajian dan Advokasi Perlindungan dan Kualitas Hidup Anak Universitas Indonesia (PUSKAPA).

Hawley, D. R. (2000). Clinical Implications of Family Resilience. *The American Journal of Family Therapy*, 28(2), 101–116. https://doi.org/10.1080/01926180 0261699

Hawley, D. R., & DeHaan, L. (1996). Toward a Definition of Family Resilience: Integrating Life-Span and Family Perspectives. *Family Process*, 35(3), 283–298. https://doi.org/10.1111/j.1545-5300.1996.00283.x

Hikmah, N. (2019). *Faktor-faktro yang Menyebabkan terjadinya Pernikahan Dini di Desa Muara WIS Kecamatan Muara Wis Kabuoaten Kutai Kertanegara*, 7(1).

Imam. (2023, January 29). Tingginya Pernikahan Dini Memicu Stunting di Kabupaten Bogor. *Radar Bogor*. https://www.radarbogor.id/2023/01/29/tingginya-pernikahan-dini-memicu-stunting-di-kabupaten-bogor/

Inayati, I. N. (2015). *Perkawinan Anak Di Bawah Umur Dalam Perspektif Hukum, Ham Dan Kesehatan*, 1.

Indriyani, F. (2021). *Pola Ketahanan Keluarga Pernikahan Dini Perspektif Maqasid Al-Syari'ah (Studi asus di Desa Gondang ecamatan Watumalang abupaten Wonosobo)*. Universitas Islam Negeri (UIN) Prof. K.H. Sifuddin Zuhri Purwokerto.

Kartikawati, R. (2014). *Dampak Perkawinan Anak di Indonesia*. 3(1).

Lestari, R. P. (2015). Hubungan Antara Pernikahan Usia Remaja dengan Ketahanan Keluarga. *JKKP (Jurnal Kesejahteraan Keluarga dan Pendidikan)*, 2(2), 84–91. https://doi.org/10.21009/JKKP.022.04

McCubbin, H. I., & McCubbin, M. A. (1988). Typologies of Resilient Families: Emerging Roles of Social Class and Ethnicity. *Family Relations*, 37(3), 247. https://doi.org/10.2307/584557

Muhammad, H. S., Nurcahyanti, F. W., & Salahuddin, M. (2023). *Problem Solving Dalam Praktek Pernikahan Dini Terhadap Pembangunan Ketahanan Keluarga*, 15(1).

Musfiroh, M. R. (2016). *Pernikahan Dini dan Upaya Perlindungan Anak di Indonesia*, 8(2).

Patterson, J. M. (2002). Understanding Family Resilience. *Journal of Clinical Psychology*, 58(3), 233–246. https://doi.org/10.1002/jclp. 10019

Permana, D. J., & Ramadhana, M. R. (2020). *Pola Komunikasi Keluarga antara Orantua dan Anak Anggota Komunitas Motor N-BBC Cirebon*, 7(2).

Putri, K. R., & Supratman, L. (2021). *Pola Komunikasi Keluarga Ibu Tunggal pada Anak Remaja saat Pandemia COVID-19*, 8(5).

Raj, A. (2010). When the Mother Is a Child: The Impact of Child Marriage on the Health and Human Rights of Girls. *Archives of Disease in Childhood*, *95*(11), 931–935. https://doi.org/10.1136/adc.2009.178707

Rutter, M. (1999). Resilience Concepts and Findings: Implications for Family Therapy. *Journal of Family Therapy*, *21*(2), 119–144. https://doi.org/10.1111/ 1467-6427.00108.

Sarradian, & Hasibuan, E. J. (2015). Pola Komunikasi pada Pasangan Pernikahan Dini di Desa Kelambir Kecamatan Pantai Labu Kabupaten Deli Serdang. *Jurnal Simbolika*, *i*, 1.

Savitri, Y. E., & Ramadhana, M. R. (2020). Pola Komunikasi dalam Penerapan Fungsi Keluarga pada Anak Pelaku Tindak Aborsi di Jakarta Pusat. *Jurnal Ilmu Komunikasi*, *3*.

Setyawan, I., & Psi, S. (n.d.). *Merancah Family Well-Being Melalui Komunikasi Keluarga*.

Sinabutar, M. J., Sari, R., & Ramadhani, T. (2023). *Perkawinan anak dan Dinamika Ketahanan Keluarga (Studi Pada Aktor Pernikahan Usia Anak di Desa Peradong, Bangka Barat)*.

Suryaningsih, E. K., Astuti, T. W. P., & Hidayah, N. (2023). *Pengalaman pernikahan usia dini terhadap ketahanan dalam keluarga: Studi kasus, 1.*

Walsh, F. (1996). The Concept of Family Resilience: Crisis and Challenge. *Family Process*, *35*(3), 261–281. https://doi.org/10.1111/j.1545-5300.1996.00261.x

Watts, J., & Hovick, S. R. (2023). The Influence of Family Communication Patterns and Identity Frames on Perceived Collective Psychological Ownership and Intentions to Share Health Information. *Health Communication*, *38*(6), 1246–1254. https://doi.org/10.1080/10410236.2021.1999573

Yusnita, T. (2021). *Pola Komuniasi Keluarga Perkawinan Anak dan Keberfungsian Keluarga di Kabupaten Bogor*. IPB University.

Ilona Jokhadze

Organizational Change Management Effectiveness: Framework and Measurement

1. Introduction

Based on that changes are vital for companies, it is important to describe practical and theoretical examples of its management. The Paper's main aim is to outline the modern aspects of change management and analysis of the practice of transformations from the example of Georgian companies. This paper should be outlined change management's negative and positive aspects, existing contradictions, and their possible ways of solutions.

With the abovementioned criteria, it is important to focus on the main topics to be discussed:

- The essence of organizational changes;
- Methods implementing organizational changes;
- Analysis of change management on the example of Georgian companies;
- Analysis of contradictions arising in companies;
- Development of organizational change management guidelines and recommendations.

1.1. Subject and Object of Research

The subject of research is organizational processes and implementation of changes. Managers and employees' attitudes towards changes and contradictions arising from the implementation of changes in the process. One of the objects of the research would be the Georgian company LTB LLC.

1.2. Organizational Changes

Before we focus on organizational changes, it is necessary to emphasize the role of the corporate culture, which is part of the identity of any company and without which successful work is doomed. Corporate culture is a kind of indicator of what standards of behavior are agreed upon on the one hand by the company as an employer, and on the other hand by all those employees who are involved in the processes for the company and personal well-being (Golembiewski, 1993).

Change management in some cases includes organizational change, which in turn is related to both internal and external factors. Although internal factors may seem easier to deal with, since administrative topics enter here, in which the company is more or less competent, in some cases, external factors may have a direct impact on the company's internal factor. Human resources can be affected by both political and economic factors, so both internal and external factors are linked with each other (King, N., & Anderson, N. 1995).

Implementation of changes is difficult because first of all, it needs thinking about changes, and using new experiences. In some cases, change is possible to arouse such emotions as uncertainty and fear.

Conflict among employees is one of the implementations of changes. It is a continuous process, so the manager must ensure these conflicts. Changes without proper planning are a waste of time. Every step and every stage of change must be calculated and possible risks should be minimized.

When we introduce a new system we have to compare its compliance with the old system and only after that analyze what kind of changes are needed and what should be done immediately or step-by-step (Weick, 1999).

The reasons for organizational changes can be different be, they can be caused by ideological, economic, organizational, personal, informational, etc. Changes in organizations can be divided into internal and external factors. Internal factors are subject to administration and control is much easier, but predicting external factors is not so easy.

The external environment of the company can be divided into the micro and macro environment. The microenvironment itself includes suppliers, consumers, competitors, intermediaries, and the target audience. The macro-environment influences indirectly impact the organization.

The PESTEL model consists of the following factors:

- Economic factors;
- Political factors;
- Social/cultural factors;
- Technological factors;
- Environment factors;
- Legal factors (Robert, 2009).

Economic factors: have a great influence on the organization's current processes and its functioning. The reason can be many economic factors like globalization of markets, level of purchasing, population welfare, current income, unemployment rate, inflation rate, etc.

Technological, political, and legal factors: helps the organization to remain competitive in the market and be compliant with environmental factors. Technological factors include: technologies level of use, level of development, etc. political factors belongs political stability in the country, freedom of property, freedom of speech, etc. legal factors include the degree of property protection, legislation, etc.

Social/cultural and ecological factors: affects indirectly of the process of making changes, but it is a big mistake to ignore these factors, because they may cause negative results in a long term.

Internal factors that lead to organizational change it is largely related to external factors. Organizational changes can be caused by the following internal factors: economic activity, quality growth assurance, organization legal form, to which legal entity it belongs, improvement of service, an increase of staff motivation in the organization, existing corporate culture, values, traditions, all these criteria creates company's internal factors, it consists of the following elements;

- Goals;
- Mission;
- Structure;
- Tasks;
- Employees;
- Processes (George & Jones, 2007).

Internal factors causing changes can be combined in the following three approaches:

- From the top level-the approach is used when the leader is the initiator of changes; he gives instructions about what needs to be done. Often, in this case, those employees who directly participate in the changes and are directly related to these changes can not affect the progress of the process.
- From the employees' level-the approach is used when the need for change arose from the employees. In the case of such an approach employees who are directly affected by this change, also participate in the implementation and formation of this change. In this case, there may be many different opinions, which can take a long time (Jones, 2004).
- Expert-during the expert approach, the process of the given case as a whole is in the hand of experts who have certain knowledge in particular fields. Experts do not make decisions; they give recommendations and information

about the situation in the organization. After that, the managers make the decision themselves (Rhodes, 2004).

A certain number of managers prefer to use a relatively mild method, illustrated by Deming's cycle called PDCA, which involves:

- Planning;
- Doing;
- Checking;
- Acting.

The planning phase is fundamentally important, as it determines what activities/ changes to be implemented for subsequent phases to work effectively towards the main goal.

For the successful implementation of the Deming cycle, it is necessary to mobilize employees, both on a professional and psychological level, so that they do not fall out of any stage and are ready for the expected results. When employees go through changes in the organization, they are also strongly connected, which makes it easier for them to work as well as the right involvement and participation in the processes improve the productivity of their work day-by-day (Edwards Deming, 1993).

2. Mandatory Pre-Written Questions as a Prerequisite for Changes

Two important aspects of change management are readiness for change and capacity, at which point it is necessary to ask the following questions:

- Why and for what the change is needed;
- Why the company needs a specific change;
- How ready is the company to implement the mentioned change;
- What ways should be used to carry out the changes;
- How ready are employees to adapt to change?

Each stage of change must be agreed upon with the management team, based on which managers and change initiators must determine at what stage and at what frequency their involvement in the processes should be carried out. It is also important to agree on the changes at the initial stage with the direction, and department, to whom the specific change directly or indirectly affects (Wang, G. G., & Sun, J. Y., 2012).

Kubler-Ross's "Grief Model" establishes five basic and significant aspects of employees' attitudes toward change:

1. **Denial**-when employees have fear and excitement about the news, look with skepticism and cannot imagine its positive aspects;
2. **Anger**-at this time, employees try to demonstrate their emotional state in different ways, deliberately come out with antagonistic views, and ask irrelevant questions;
3. **Bargaining**-at this time the perception of the employees is focused on the issues related to the case, they see their role, and more clarity comes in, which presents the processes in a more optimistic light;
4. **Depression**-on the one hand, the employees sharing the news at the mentioned time, after facing the reality, they seem not to change anything and continue to work with the same approaches, this situation is similar to immobility;
5. **Acceptance**-when employees become single-minded and, if they previously had pessimistic views, are now focused on achieving results (Christina Gregory, 2022).

3. Conclusion

For employees, all new challenges are a means of their professional and personal growth, and if the company is late in giving them new, difficult tasks, after a certain period it causes demotivation on them and increases the desire to go in search of bigger challenges in other environments. On the other hand, the company can no longer take advantage of the opportunity and spend more time with new employees than requires. That is why constant monitoring of employees is an unwritten law of managers.

To get from point "a" to point "b" managers should follow up on the planned methodology, which includes (whatfix.com/change-management):

1. Determine the reason for the change;
2. Set specific goals for the change;
3. Establish key performance indicators (KPIs) and milestones to monitor progress;
4. Refer to change management models;
5. Create a change management plan and implementation strategy;
6. Designate change leaders;
7. Implement change;
8. Gather feedback;
9. Analyze progress and results.

3.1. Applicant's Views

- In the process of changes, it is necessary to choose a courageous employee with leadership skills who will lead the processes and turn all negative or positive experiences in the company into opportunities and indicators of changes;
- Before change policy is implemented, it is necessary to create artificial barriers about certain issues so that employees feel the need to implement changes;
- Companies like crisis management, if they do not have a pre-developed standard, with what periodicity, in what format of meetings to review the changes, they will be constantly delayed in time;
- At any stage of change management, it should be compared with the company's main policy, so that the company does not lose sight of its core values, which ultimately create its identity;
- Employees, as the main players of the process, if they are denied from the change process, will never understand the essence of the goal to be achieved and will simply be victims of intimidating policies, which will demotivate them in the future;
- Since the obstacles from employees and the means to overcome resistance are in the hand of the managers, the managers should be free and strict in their decisions;
- Managers should always have extra time to consider the views of employees, to listen to them, to leave an impression in the perception of employees that they have been allowed to express their opinion equally and transparently;
- Employees, regardless of whether they express readiness or be careful about changes, it is still equally necessary to conduct certain training in the direction of the expected changes, so that they can experience the transformation.

References

Deming, W. E. (1993). *The New Economics*. MIT Press. Cambridge, MA.

George, J. M., & Jones, G. R. (2007). *Understanding and Managing Organizational Behavior* (5th ed.). New York: Pearson Education, Inc.

Golembiewski, T. R. (1993). *Approaches to Planned Change (Orienting Perspectives and Micro Level Interventions)*. New Brunswick: Transaction Publishers.

Gregory, C. (2022). An Examination of the Kubler-Ross Model, Ph.D. Thesis.

Jones, G. R. (2004). *Organization Theory, Design, and Change*. New York: Addison-Wesley Publishing Company.

King, N., & Anderson, N. (1995). *Innovation, and Change in Organizations*. London: Routledge.

Rhodes, C., & Scheer's, H. (2004). Developing People in Organizations: Working (on) Identity. *Studies in Continuing Education, 26*(2).

Robert, M. (2009). *The New Strategic Thinking: Pure & Simple*, McGraw-Hill.

Wang, G. G., & Sun, J. Y. (2012). Theorizing Comparative Human Resource Development: A Formal Language Approach. *Human Resource Development Review,* 11(3), 380–400.

Weick, K. E., & Quinn, R. E. (1999). Organizational Change and Development. *Annual Review of Psychology,* 50.

Tatiana Danescu, Radu-Bogdan Matei, Lavinia Constantinescu
and Roxana Maria Stejerean

Corporate Responsibility in Pharmaceutical Industry

1. Introduction

The current economic and pandemic context, the vulnerability of financial markets, the violation of peace agreements between states and the need for sustainable development are prerequisites and challenges for rethinking the business strategy, imperatively requiring effective social responsibility and corporate governance policies.

Corporate Social Responsibility (eng. Corporate Social Responsibility – CSR) must be seen as a new form of business management, offering, in addition to building an organizational culture and identity, an important component in the development of intangible assets such as the reputation and trust of customers and suppliers. Thus, CSR practices will attract, in the first stage, intangible benefits related to the maintenance of clientele, the interest of suppliers, the notoriety of the brand, and then they will be transformed into tangible internal benefits, transposed by attracting experienced and valuable human resources, by reducing operating costs and through the positive impact on turnover (Cosmulese, 2019).

Corporate governance (CG) is a topical concept in the economic literature, the fundamental objective being to provide a degree of assurance that the internal control system is effective and that the business is run in the interests of both shareholders and stakeholders. We believe that transparency is the essential element for the effectiveness of corporate governance systems, with information shared voluntarily contributing exponentially to a company's integrity and credibility in the marketplace.

The debates surrounding CSR address two opposing components: opponents of social responsibility practices believe that these activities reduce shareholder profits and refer to the general objective of any company to use the resources it owns in the most optimal way while proponents of CSR practices believe that the company's responsibility is also represented by meeting the needs of stakeholders, which are directly affected by management decisions. These days, CSR actions have become mandatory for the activity to be carried out ethically.

194 Tatiana Danescu et al.

2. Theoretical Background

According to studies by Giroud and Mueller (2011), companies with poor governance have poorer operational performance, lower revenues, and lower labor productivity than companies with effective governance, based on clear and respected structures and attributions (Giroud, 2011). Through the analysis carried out by Chen, Yu, and Hu (2018) it was found that, as a rule, companies with a high level of social performance are more able to capture added value, increasing thus financial performance (Chen, 2018). Through this attribute, social performance is seen as a key component in overall performance.

Through Wellalage, Locke, and Acharya (2018) studies of 30 top listed companies in Australia, France, UK and USA over a 10 years period, it was found that there is no direct link between the composition of the Board of Directors (CA) and the CSR score obtained by the analyzed companies (Wellalage, 2018). Through the research carried out on 71 companies listed on the Stock Exchange of Pakistan, a possible relationship between GC, CSR and the added value of the companies was confirmed (Butt, 2020). The results of the study showed a direct and significant relationship between company performance and CSR, and when GC was introduced as a moderator, the correlation between the variables decreased. CSR and GC practices are in synergy, joining political efforts to adapt companies to social and environmental needs (Rahim, 2013).

The determining factor in the generation of new accounting paradigms is represented by the emergence of multinational companies that have taken over the organizational model and culture from economically and socially developed states. They understood much faster that voluntarily adopted CSR policies help to build an image and strengthen the reputation in the market. CSR practices have become an integrated part of companies' strategy, thus their sustainability and development coexist in a unitary manner.

In the last decades, the objectives of companies have changed substantially because profit is no longer their main concern, being more and more attentive to what is happening around them in order to create an environment conducive and favorable to sustainable development. The phrase the 3 P's (People, Planet, Profit) appears, the order being established by current importance. Respect for human rights is the main mission of the United Nations (UN), these being included in all published agendas, since the Brundtland Report in 1987 and much more recently, the 2030 Agenda through the launch of the 17 Sustainable Development Goals (Dănescu, 2021). This action also launched a public question: "Will this planet survive?", which suggested the urgent need for action to limit climate change and the current irrational consumption of resources.

Investors are increasingly attentive to the non-financial information published by companies, their confidence being directly reflected in the share price. They understood that the company's profitability is insufficient for long-term economic predictions, and environmental and social information contributing to increasing transparency, strengthening risk management and improving communication with stakeholders (Gellidon, 2022).

CG appears in Romania in the business landscape after the 2000s, later than in other countries, the main reasons for the delay being related to economic, social, and political reforms. It brought significant improvements in a relatively short time, and the appearance and adherence of companies to the Corporate Governance Code of the Bucharest Stock Exchange (CGC BSE) was transposed by increasing informational transparency, something useful for all categories of stakeholders (Bătae,2020). CG is taking shape and gradually becoming an essential element, taking into account accountability in its essence, as well as the transparency it offers. Among the premises of the emergence are the numerous bankruptcies of famous companies (Enron, Lehman Brothers, Parmalat, WorldCom), the financial crises that marked the economic evolution of the states and the discrepancy between the compensation of the members of the Board of Directors and the performance of the companies as Feleagă (2011) presented, but also the scandal in the USA in the 70s – Watergate, where certain companies were involved in politics and distributed sums of money to political parties (Gulati, 2021).

The Covid 19 pandemic has generated a series of changes in the company's management approach, with specialists having to resort to integrated thinking in order to find viable solutions in order to continue the activity. Management should not be reduced to a simple set of rules, the act itself should follow certain guidelines, being dominated by individual traits. To be a good manager, the strategic objectives of the company must be achieved first, and training, experience and professional behavior are essential conditions.

3. Research Objective, Methodology and Data

Through this research we studied the existence of the relationship between CSR and the company's financial performance, with corporate governance as a moderator of influence. From the analysis of specialized literature, we start from the premise that there is a direct, positive and significant relationship between the analyzed variables. Regarding the elements used to determine the social and environmental performance of the analyzed companies, we used the ESG (Environment, Social and Governance) score, being considered a new global trend. Financial performance is difficult to establish using a single indicator, so we created a set consisting of profitability rates (Return on Assets – ROA, Return on Equity – ROE, Return on Sales – ROS), liquidity, labor productivity and solvency. The chosen sample was based on companies from the pharmaceutical industry listed on the Bucharest Stock Exchange on the regulated market. On this market at the time of the research, there were 82 companies, 4 of which were from the medical field. This field was chosen because we believe that it was not negatively affected by the Sars-Cov 2 virus pandemic, the period of analysis of financial statements, administrators' reports and sustainability reports being 2018–2020. It was also taken into account that the reporting of non-financial aspects was imposed on public interest companies that exceed the average number of 500 employees on the date of publication of the financial statements by Directive 2014/95/EU, so that, starting with 2017, the first sustainability reports appear .

The research questions set at the beginning of the scientific approach were the following:

• Is there a relationship between ESG score and company performance?
• Have the companies in the medical field aligned themselves with the provisions of Directive 2014/95/EU regarding the publication of non-financial information useful to interested parties?
• Does the structure of the management board and the shareholding influence the performance of the companies?

4. Results and Discussion

4.1. Empirical Research Applied to Companies in the Pharmaceutical Industry

More information about the companies selected and also the no. Pages of Administrator Report and the no. Pages of Sustainability Report can be found in the Supplementary file.

Regarding the age of the companies, it is noted that two of the companies are over 30 years old, thus marking the time of privatization of the formerly state-owned companies. Ropharma is the youngest company in the current research, the field in which it operates is the trade of pharmaceutical products through its own pharmacy chain. Two of the companies, respectively Antibiotice and Zentiva, are manufacturers of generic drugs, and MedLife integrates its own chain of pharmacies alongside the provision of medical services through its own hospital units.

We believe that a holistic approach is required for the successful implementation of sustainability reporting, the mechanisms being obliged to communicate and cooperate to create a average standard applicable to all companies.

According to the provisions of the CGC of BSE, any Board of Directors must consist of at least five members, two of whom are non-executive. It is also mentioned that the number of independent non-executive members must be greater than the number of executive members.

Table 1. The structural elements of the Board of Directors

BSE Symbol	No. Members	Executive Members	Non-executive Members	Female person	Average age	CEO = President of the Board	Ownership Structure
M	7	3	4	1	53	YES	Family Ownership – 41 %
ATB	5	1	4	1	48	NO	Romanian State – 53 %
RPH	7	3	4	1	59	YES	Arrow + Add Pharma– 48 %
SCD	5	2	3	2	56	NO	Zentiva Group – 96 %

Source: authors' own research.

All 4 analyzed companies are managed in a unitary system and comply with the main provisions of the CGC. The companies preferred to have 5 or 7 members in the CA, an odd number being used to avoid situations related to the non-meeting of the quorum in voting situations. Also, the number of non-executive members is higher than the number of executive members in all the analyzed companies. Every company has at least one female person in management, Zentiva being the only one that has two people in such positions, thus denoting an inclination towards equal opportunities for women to occupy a top management position. Regarding the average age of the board members, the most advanced team is found within Ropharma with an average of 59 years, followed by Zentiva with 56 years, MedLife with 53 years and Antibiotice with 48 years. Also, within the Antibiotice company, we find the youngest member of the Board of Directors, aged 37. Two of the companies, MedLife and Ropharma, considered it appropriate to offer the position of Chairman of the Board of Directors and CEO to one person, while Antibiotice and Zentiva preferred to allocate these positions to two people. The shareholding structure of the companies is very different, thus we meet a family business in the case of MedLife, which is owned in a proportion of 41 % by family ownership. The Antibiotice Company is majority owned by the Romanian state, and Ropharma and Zentiva are part of groups of companies managed from abroad. Thus, we considered it appropriate to study the structure of the shareholding, the diversity being able to make the results more efficient in terms of the global performance of the companies.

Clusters by age and education of Board members can be found in the Supplementary file.

From this analysis, the age of maturity is found between 46–55 years, being considered that, at that moment in life, the person has the experience and knowledge necessary for the effective management of companies. The most people were found in this category, namely 11. Also, 10 of the CA members are over 55 years old, and 3 of them between 36–45. There is no person under 35 years of age. Regarding the categories of studies followed by the members of the CA, all 24 people have higher education. Considering the medical field of which the analyzed companies are part, it was expected that most of them have studies in this field. However, most people, 8 in number, have higher education in the economic field, thus considered much more suitable and experienced for executive management. In second place is engineering with 5 people, followed by physics/chemistry with 4 each, coming from manufacturing companies. The medical and legal fields offer 3 representatives each among the members of the CA, and only one person holds studies in mathematics and informatics.

In order to answer the research hypotheses by testing the correlation between financial performance – sustainability – corporate governance, it was necessary to create a ranking of companies according to the ESG (Environment, Social, Governance) criteria, considered a true global trend regarding sustainable development, after an own model of the authors (TRL – ESG model). Through the scoring scale used, 1 point was given for the full presentation of information in a certain field, 0.5 points for partial presentation and 0 points where no information is found or the information is lacking in transparency. 21 indicators from three thematic areas were used, four companies being analyzed over the period of three years: 2018–2020, resulting in a total of 252 items. The three thematic areas and subsections used in the analysis are:

- Environment – environmental management, transparency on environmental sanctions, environmental investments, waste management;
- Social – volunteering, employee benefits, sports, education, ethics and anti-corruption, work accidents and training, Sars-Cov 2 pandemic;

• Governance and generalities: CG/CSR section, standards used, United Nations Global Compact alignment, sustainability CEO message, transparency of remuneration of CA members, compliance with the "Apply or explain" Declaration.

Table 2. The score of the TRL – ESG model obtained by the analyzed companies

Crt. No	BSE Symbol	Environment Score	Social Score	Governance Score	ESG Total Score	ESG Score %
1	M	0,5	6	4,5	11	52 %
2	ATB	3	8	8	19	90 %
3	RPH	0,5	0,5	2,5	3,5	17 %
4	SCD	2	3,5	3	8,5	40 %

Source: authors' own research.

After applying its own ESG scoring model, the Antibiotice company obtained the highest score in terms of sustainability reporting, with 19 of the 21 indicators being respected (90 %). We can state that this company is transparent from the point of view of published non-financial information, which is useful to stakeholders in making strategic decisions. Next in this ranking is MedLife with 11 respected indicators (52 %), Zentiva with 40 %, the last ranked being Ropharma which respects only 3 principles out of the 21, non-financial information being lacking in transparency and not currently a priority for the company

Table 3. Correlations between TRL – ESG model score, financial performance and Board of Directors structure variables

	ESG	FIN	No. Members	Average age	CEO= President	Ownership_ stru
ESG	1					
FIN	0,2634058	1				
No. Members	-0,580218	-0,808452	1			
Average age	-0,994385	-0,189076	0,492365964	1		
CEO= President	-0,580218	-0,808452	1	0,492365964	1	
Ownership_ stru	0,8761257	0,046676	-0,577350269	-0,852802865	-0,57735027	1

Source: Authors' projection using Data Analysis.

From the data integrated in Table no. 6, a relationship is observed between the ESG score and the financial performance of the companies, thus this hypothesis is confirmed. Pearson's R correlation coefficient had a value of 0.26, which indicates that there is a positive, direct relationship between the 2 variables, but of a low intensity.

Bearing in mind that in Romania, non-financial reporting has become mandatory since 2017 through the transposition of Directive 2014/95/EU, we considered it appropriate to analyze the evolution of this type of reporting for 3 years, considering that it is a sufficient period for companies to adapt to the new stipulations. On the basis of what was shown previously, we appreciate that the entities listed on the Bucharest Stock Exchange from the emerging market have aligned with these provisions and create non-financial reports useful to interested parties.

Regarding the influence of the structural elements of the management board in the global performance, from the analysis carried out on the 4 companies in the medical industry, there is no causal relationship between them. We believe that this study should be expanded to include all companies listed on the Bucharest Stock Exchange on the regulated market, the relationships between these variables may look different in that new configuration. Also, the company's shareholding structure was studied in relation to financial and non-financial performance, since Antibiotice is majority state-run, with the aim of ascertaining whether public institutions provide transparent information to stakeholders. The correlation between the shareholding structure and the ESG score obtained the value of 0.87, thus being considered a direct, positive and high-intensity relationship.

4.3. Highlighting the Importance of Research Results through Bibliometric Analysis

The bibliometric analysis was designed to improve the literature review process and to highlight the importance of the topic under investigation. For this purpose, the classical method of identifying scientific articles using famous databases was combined with the visualizations provided by VOS viewer to outline a clearer picture of the empirical results obtained from the research conducted and published so far.

Integrating the traditional literature review methods with the recently developed ones, the Figure below shows the graphical representation of the network resulting from the study of the relevant keywords in the title and abstracts. In order to study the most relevant keywords, 7500 articles from the Dimensions database were used.

Following the mapping of all the resulting words, we obtained a number of nine clusters, i.e. 169 keywords that are part of them, with a total of 1338 links between them. It can be seen that the dominant topics or keywords were: governance, accountability and social performance, these being the most discussed topics by the researchers during the period analysed. We believe that nodes or keywords that do not intertwine or network closely enough with other keywords have the potential to become new research topics in the future.

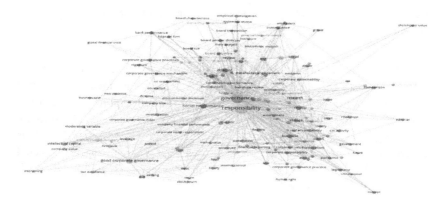

Figure 1. Keywords found in the bibliometric analysis. Source: authors' projection using VOSviewer software.

The study of the bibliometric network also reveals the period in which the most articles on Corporate Social Responsibility have been published, with corporate governance as a mediator. Thus, the period 2017–2018 was a vast period of research in terms of the frequency with which this was published.

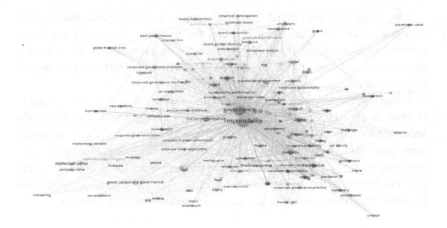

Figure 2. Frequency of publication of papers in the field studied. Source: authors' projection using VOSviewer software.

Collaborative scientific networks are a hallmark of contemporary academic research. Researchers are no longer independent actors, but members of teams bringing together complementary skills and multidisciplinary approaches around common goals. Social network analysis and co-authorship networks are increasingly used as powerful tools to assess collaborative trends. For this analysis we considered a minimum of 5 co-authored papers. Following the selected options, we have drawn up the bibliometric analysis map of co-authorship which is shown in the figure below.

Figure 3. Co-authorship based on bibliometric analysis. Source: authors' projection using VOSviewer software.

One of the most cited papers in this research area is Mark Orliszky's, with approximately 4630 citations. The article is entitled Corporate Social and Financial Performance: A Meta-Analysis and was published in 2003. Also with over 4000 citations, David Yermack's paper, Higher market valuation of companies with a small board of directors, is in second place and presents evidence consistent with the theories that small boards are more effective.

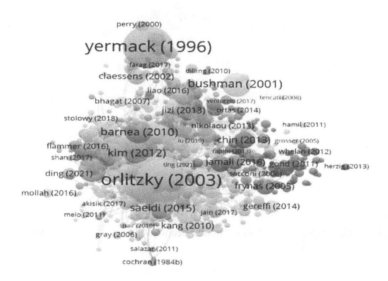

Figure 4. Citation analysis based on bibliometric research. Source: authors' projection using VOSviewer software

We also used VOSviewer to view the map of the co-authorship network by country and the international collaboration of publications in this field of research. The largest set of connected countries consists of 51 countries in 12 clusters. Clusters are formed by the frequency of co-occurrence of terms representing each country, the more often terms tend to co-occur, the more they are colored in clusters. The size of the circles represents the number of publications from that country, and the thickness of the lines represents the size of the collaboration. Countries with similar colors form a single cluster. For example, the blue cluster shows collaborative links from China, the Czech Republic, Denmark, and New Zealand representing authors affiliated with these countries.

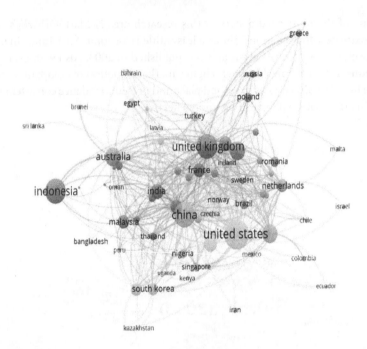

Figure 5. Geographical distribution of published works. Source: authors' projection using VOSviewer software.

5. Conclusion

CSR and CG are considered the pillars of a company's sustainability and that of the whole economy. Social responsibility is approached from the perspective of a modern management, adaptable to organizational changes, becoming in a relatively short time since its emergence in Romania, a key tool for achieving objectives and mitigating risks, as shown in the bibliometric analysis where the dominant keywords were: governance, responsibility and social performance. These were the most discussed topics by researchers during the period analysed. The management of the company must adapt to new conditions, decisions must be made in the shortest possible time, because the volatility of the market is significant. Accounting information must be the basis of any decision, so for effective governance, the fundamental contribution of accounting is needed. The accuracy, relevance and timing of the information can significantly influence the future of the company.

The need for transparent reporting addresses non-financial perspectives, incorporating environmental, social and governance aspects under the umbrella of sustainability reporting which is considered the foundation of company success and survival. Approaching ESG aspects in a balanced way is the catalyst for sustainable development, materialized by satisfying the needs of stakeholders and shareholders.

Specifically, for the pharmaceutical sector studied, the empirical results obtained indicate a direct and positive link between ESG score and companies' financial performance, which is the answer to the first research question.

The research on the disclosures in the integrated reports of the companies studied revealed compliance with the requirements of Directive 2014/2005 regarding the disclosure of non-financial information in meeting the needs of stakeholders, which is the answer to the steps taken for the second research question.

In addition, we note that the management board and shareholder structure is in a direct, positive, high intensity relationship with the EGS score, which constitutes to the third research question.

Therefore, today the relationship between business and society is taking on new dimensions, with a clear link between social responsibility and financial performance, a link that is supported by the quality of the management process, proven by targets and achievements towards financial performance, but also towards the needs of a sustainable society. Therefore, we clearly believe that the need for transparent reporting addresses the non-financial perspective, incorporating environmental, social and governance aspects under the umbrella of sustainability reporting which is considered the foundation of the company's success and survival. Addressing ESG issues in a balanced way is the catalyst for sustainable development, materialised by meeting the needs of stakeholders and shareholders.

For prospective research, comparative analysis of corporate responsibility in the pharmaceutical industry globally is proposed, with a focus on investigating corporate responsibility practices and performance in different geographical regions and countries. The aim is to identify significant differences in approaches, strategies and outcomes to highlight global best practices in corporate responsibility in the pharmaceutical industry.

A future research direction is also envisaged with a focus on assessing the social engagement of pharmaceutical companies and its impact on local communities. Through this research approach, the aim is to gain a deeper understanding of the impact of pharmaceutical companies' social engagement on local communities and to identify the most effective corporate social responsibility practices for enhancing the well-being of the communities involved.

References

Bătae, O., & Feleagă, L. (2020). Corporate Governance in Listed and State-Controled Companies in the Romanian Energy System. *Audit Financiar, 18*(2), 395–410.

Butt, A., Shahzad, A., & Ahmad, J. (2020). Impact of CSR on Firm Value. The Moderating Role of Corporate Governance. *Indonesian Journal of Sustainability, Accounting and Management, 4*(2), 145–163.

Chen, C., Yu, C., & Hu, J. (2018). Constructing Performance Measurement Indicators to Suggested Corporate Environmental Responsibility Framework. *Technological Forecasting and Social Change, 135,* 33–43.

Cosmulese, C. (2019). The Effects of CSR and Accumulation of Intangible Assets on Competitive Advantage of the Company. *Accounting and Accounting Education in the Digital Society, 8,* 223–229.

Dănescu, T., Matei, R., & Constantinescu, L. (2021). Evolutionary Benchmarks in Sustainability Reporting. Incursion from the Brundtland Report to the Sustainable Development Goals. *Acta Marisiensis, Seria Oeconomic, 2,* 37–60.

Feleagă, N., Feleagă, L., Dragomir, V., & Bigioi, A. (2011). Corporate Governance in Emerging Economies: The Case of Romania. *Theoretical and Applied Economics Magazine, 18*(9), 3–15.

Gellidon, J., & Soenarno, Y. (2022). Comparative Study of Sustainability Reporting in the Banking Industry in Several Countries. *Financial Audit, 166*(2), 261–272.

Giroud, X., & Mueller, H. (2011). Corporate Governance, Product Market Competition and Equity Prices. *The Journal of Finance, 66*(2), 563–600.

Gulati, J., & Brown, L. (2021). The Personal Is Political: Reconsidering the Impact of Scandals on Congressional Incumbents. *Congress & Presidency, 48*(1), 25–49.

Rahim, M. (2013). *The Impact of Corporate Social Responsbility on Corporate Governance: The Rise of Standardization of CSR Principles.* Berlin: Springer.

Wellalage, N., Locke, S., & Acharya, S. (2018). Does the Composition of Board of Directors Impact on CSR Scores? *Social Responsibility Journal, 14*(3), 651–669.

Muna Mohamed Alhammadi and Zeina Hojeij

Perceptions of College Students with Disabilities Regarding the Accessibility of the UAE's E-Learning System

1. Introduction

Experience during the COVID-19 pandemic has encouraged many higher education institutions to show significant interest in improving their e-learning systems to meet the needs of their students, including those with disabilities. For most students, the sudden transition to distance learning in 2020 due to the COVID-19 pandemic was not an easy shift, and this transition was even more difficult for students with disabilities. These students generally faced challenges in obtaining the necessary technology, technical support, and training, and in using a learning management system (e.g., Blackboard and Moodle) and accessing educational resources (Scott et al., 2020; Ro'fah et al., 2020; Akyıldız, 2020).

One of the basic elements of online learning that was not considered sufficiently during the pandemic was the accessibility of the online system. According to Kim and Fienup (2022), online learning requires access to the necessary technology, including Wi-Fi and computers, and access to the necessary support to use the technology, such as professional training and technical support. Additionally, Ro'fah et al. (2020) argue that online learning can only become accessible if it is thoughtfully delivered, considering the diversity of learners' needs, including those with disabilities. This requires consideration of course content, teaching and learning strategies, the choice of online platforms and apps, accessibility of study materials, accessibility of digital audio and video content, flexible time limits for online exams, and sufficient human resources and support.

Educational institutions in the United Arab Emirates (UAE) started to pay more attention to improving their online learning systems following the outbreak of the COVID-19 pandemic. During the pandemic, the UAE's schools and universities relied entirely on online learning systems to offer their educational programs (The UAE Government Portal, 2022). However, as in other countries, these educational institutions did not have enough time to prepare their students for online learning or even to ensure that the special needs of students with disabilities were addressed. Nevertheless, most college students in the UAE developed positive attitudes towards online learning as it provided an easier and more flexible environment for them to manage their studies, and saved time and money. Furthermore, a majority of students surveyed reported no difference in the quality of education between online and face-to-face education (Ali, 2021).

In contrast to these mainly positive findings, students with disabilities reported varying experiences with online learning in UAE higher educational institutions (Juma, 2020; Lottin et al., 2021; Meda & Waghid, 2022). Lottin et al. (2021) conducted a qualitative study of student experiences in the UAE's Higher Colleges of Technologies. They found that many instructors did not have enough experience or knowledge to accommodate the special needs of students with disabilities through e-learning, and that those special needs were not fully considered in online assessments. Juma (2020), on the other hand, found that students with disabilities had both positive and negative experiences with online learning. Regarding the advantages of e-learning, some students reported that online learning provided them with a flexible environment, which saved them time and helped them to better manage their health conditions. It also allowed students with social anxiety to participate more actively because the classes were not face to face. Regarding the disadvantages, some students with disabilities mentioned a lack of interaction with others, losing attention during online classes, and technical challenges (Juma, 2020).

Given these findings, the present study aims to assess the level of accessibility of the e-learning system in UAE higher educational institutions during the COVID-19 pandemic. The study identifies the most common accessibility challenges faced by students with disabilities during online learning and explores how the universities that took part in this study tried to overcome those challenges. The study also examines the perceptions of students with disabilities regarding the accessibility of online learning. Finally, it provides some recommendations to UAE higher educational institutions to improve the accessibility of e-learning for students with disabilities.

2. Methodology

2.1. Research Design and Data Collection Instruments

A mixed-methods approach (qualitative and quantitative) was adopted for this study. Data were gathered through two research instruments: an online survey and interviews.

Online Survey. An online survey was circulated to 600 students with disabilities who were registered for disability support services at three different universities in the UAE. A total of 107 students with disabilities completed the questionnaire, of whom 70.7 % identified as women and 29.3 % identified as men. The main disabilities represented in the sample were vision impairment (22.8 %), learning disabilities (21.9 %), physical disability (19.4 %), hearing impairment (17.5 %), and attention deficit hyperactive disorder (ADHD) (10.5 %), while a very small percentage had other disabilities. The survey responses were collected anonymously through SurveyMonkey. The survey questions mainly focused on investigating the accessibility level of e-learning based on the student's experience, specifically accessibility of online classes, the Blackboard learning management system, online exams, study materials, and the online library. The survey questions were presented in both Arabic and English.

Semi-Structured Interview. Individual online interviews were conducted with 21 research participants (9 disability support staff members and 12 students with disabilities). Most of the interviews were conducted in Arabic rather than English (17 in Arabic and 4 in English). All the interviews were audio recorded with the participants' permission, and the recordings were transcribed. The transcripts for the interviews conducted in Arabic were then translated into English by the principal investigator. All interviews were conducted virtually using Zoom, an online virtual meeting platform, after obtaining consent from the participants. Each interview lasted between 30 and 60 minutes. The interview questions mainly focused on investigating the accessibility challenges faced by students with disabilities during online learning and how the university supported staff to accommodate special education needs during distance learning.

Data Collection Procedure. Data for the study were gathered in the Spring and Fall Semesters of 2021, more than a year after shifting to distance learning and before the students resumed face-to-face classes on campus. This enabled the study to investigate the students' online learning experiences after they had got used to the new system, but while still studying online. Data were gathered from three different UAE universities with specialized disability departments. The names of the universities are not disclosed in this study. Therefore, to differentiate between the students' experiences in these universities, the universities are referred to as University A, University B, and University C.

Data analysis. The survey data were analyzed using the Statistical Package for Social Science (SPSS), Version 28 for demographic information using frequencies and percentages, whereas the interview data were analyzed qualitatively using thematic analysis. The interview recordings were transcribed verbatim before being summarized and prepared for quoting. Different themes were identified to address the research questions.

3. Results

3.1. Access and Ability to Use the Necessary Technology

Survey analysis indicated that 73.8 % of the participants stated that they were able to access the technology they needed, while 15.4 % specified that they did not have access to the AT they needed. However, only 64.3 % of the students in the former group stated that they could use AT independently (Table 1).

Table 1. Access to assistive technologies

Survey item	Strongly agree	Agree	Neither agree nor disagree	Disagree	Strongly disagree
During the remote learning period, I was able to access the assistive technology I needed for my classes and schoolwork.	45.2 %	28.6 %	10.7 %	7.1 %	8.3 %
I am able to use the assistive technology I need for my classes and school work by myself and without any help.	36.9 %	27.4 %	23.8 %	4.8 %	7.1 %

The interview responses showed that most students with disabilities in the UAE were able to obtain the needed technologies. However, some students, especially those with vision impairment, experienced a challenge in learning how to use them.

One important factor that affected students' knowledge when using technology was the previous training they had received from the department for students with disability at their respective universities. Both University A and University B had an AT specialist who helped students in improving their AT skills as part of an individualized educational plan that was set when they joined their university. Thus, most of these students knew how to use the necessary technology before the outbreak of the pandemic. In contrast, University C did not have an AT specialist, so many of its students – especially those with vision impairment – did not acquire the necessary skills for using AT before starting online education.

3.2. Home Access to Wi-Fi

Analysis of the survey responses indicated that 64.3 % of the students who completed the survey stated they had no trouble with their Internet connection, while 18.1 % stated they had problems with their Wi-Fi connection and could not access the Internet easily.

Some of the interviews with students and disability support staff indicated that not all students' homes were equipped with high-quality Wi-Fi because the transition to online learning was so sudden. Even the universities' systems were not set up to handle large numbers of users simultaneously. Consequently, the students were repeatedly disconnected during their online classes or even while doing their exams. Some students said that their families had upgraded their home Wi-Fi connection a few months after shifting to distance learning, whereas others reported that Wi-Fi coverage remained an obstacle throughout the distance learning period.

3.3. Accessibility of the Blackboard Learning Management System

Overall, 78.6 % of the students found the Blackboard learning management system accessible and easy to use, while only 4.8 % did not. Furthermore, 76.2 % of the students agreed that they could use Blackboard without any help.

The interviewees' responses did not indicate any accessibility issues with Blackboard itself, although some students with disabilities did not know how to use it independently. Some students pointed out that they had not received any training on how to use Blackboard from their universities before the pandemic. The students who said they knew how to use the technology were able to learn that by themselves during the pandemic, whereas those students who could not use the technology independently struggled with using it.

3.4. Accessibility of the Online Platform and Online Classes

To investigate the perceptions of students with disability about the accessibility of the online platform, the participants were asked about their experiences logging into their online classes, and how easy it was for them to participate in online activities during their classes.

The survey results indicated that most students (78.6 %) found it easy to log in to their online classes. In contrast, only 52.4 % agreed that it was easy for them to take part in activities during online classes, 21.4 % had a negative experience participating in class activities, while 26.2 % had a neutral opinion (see Table 3).

Table 2. Accessibility of online classes

Survey item	Strongly agree	Agree	Neither agree nor disagree	Disagree	Strongly disagree
I can regularly log into my online classes without any problems.	48.8 %	29.8 %	14.3 %	3.6 %	3.6 %
It is easy for me to participate in online class activities.	22.6 %	29.8 %	26.2 %	9.5 %	11.9 %

The interview responses indicated that various accessibility issues with the online platform affected the students' abilities to participate in online classes. For instance, the first online platforms used by the three universities – Adobe Connect and Microsoft Teams – were not fully accessible for users with disabilities. In particular, students with physical disability could not use the keyboard focus, while there was no option for Communication Access Realtime Translation (CART) captioning, so students could not translate spoken language to text. This feature was needed by students with mild or moderate hearing loss, or with specific learning difficulties.

Moreover, there were no accessibility features for hearing-impaired users. For example, University B had the largest number of students who were deaf. Although this university employed a few sign language interpreters, it was difficult for them to attend the online classes and translate the material into sign language. Another problem at University B was that its platform, Microsoft Teams, lacked a feature to display two screens at the same time (e.g., one for the lecturer and another for the sign language interpreter). Thus, the sign language interpreters had to join the lecturer's online class as an attendee, and translate spoken English into sign language via another screen using a different account. Consequently, students with hearing impairments had to use two different devices to attend their classes: one to attend and the other to see the sign language interpreter. University B continued with this system until it switched to Zoom as the online platform.

The interview responses, however, showed that many accessibility issues disappeared once Zoom was adopted as the online platform. Zoom provided various accessibility features, such as CART captioning, and it was easy to provide sign language interpretation within the same class without the need to join the class from another account. Most of the participants also described Zoom as user friendly.

Nevertheless, some students with disabilities continued to face challenges in the online classes due to insufficient accommodation and modification. These issues concerned difficulties in participating in online activities, challenges in understanding the content of some classes, and lack of interaction with instructors and other students during the online classes.

3.5. Access to the Study Materials and Online References

Considering access to study materials and their institution's online library, only 42.8 % of the participants indicated that they could easily access the references they needed from the university's library. On the other hand, most students (79 %) indicated that the study materials for their courses were provided in accessible formats (Table 4).

Table 3. Accessibility of online library and study materials

Survey item	Strongly agree	Agree	Neither agree nor disagree	Disagree	Strongly disagree
I can easily access the online references I need from the university's library website.	21.4 %	21.4 %	32.1 %	13.1 %	11.9 %
During my online learning time, I was provided with the study materials I needed in an accessible format.	38.3 %	40.7 %	12.3 %	4.9 %	3.7 %

The interview responses with the disability support staff at the three universities indicated that there is great interest in providing course materials for students with disabilities in accessible formats, although transforming Arabic materials into accessible formats like Microsoft Word remains a challenge. In particular, optical character recognition (OCR) software is not as accurate for Arabic text as English text, making it harder to convert Arabic printed material into digital formats. In addition, many students could not use the necessary technology independently (Table 1), which hindered their ability to use the online library and search for sources for their assignments. Finally, some students reported that they struggled to obtain the support they needed to do their assignments. As one student with learning disability stated:

> One of the challenges I faced during distance learning is getting support to do my assignments. I was able to contact the university volunteers directly, but now I have to book an appointment and wait a few days to get an appointment.

3.6. Accessibility of Online Exams

The students were asked about their satisfaction with the level of support provided during online exams, such as the provision of extra time, test writers, and accessible exam materials. Overall, 71.6 % of the participants reported a positive experience with online exams, while 21 % responded neutrally, and only 7.4 % respondents disagreed that online exam support had been sufficient.

In contrast, analysis of the interview responses indicated that online exams were generally not fully accessible for students with disabilities. For example, the interviewees reported accessibility issues when using LockDown Browser, the secure exam software for Blackboard. Issues included problems using the speech-to-text feature, keyboard focus, screen reader, and Braille devices. Another challenge reported by many students with vision impairment was facing the camera during online exams. Some students stated that they did not have sufficient skills in using computers and other AT devices independently. Finally, some students with specific learning difficulties felt uncomfortable doing their exam on a computer, preferring to write their exams on paper.

The interview responses also indicated that the three universities' departments for students with disabilities created various solutions to accommodate the special needs of their students. This may explain the high rate of student satisfaction with online exams in the survey responses. One disability specialist at University B stated:

> We offered the online exams to our students who have disabilities in different modes: online on LockDown Browser with extra time, online on Blackboard without using LockDown Browser, on a Word document while the exam was monitored on Zoom or Teams, and orally on Zoom or Teams, either with their instructors or with a test-writer.

4. Discussion

This study investigated the perceptions of university students with disabilities regarding the accessibility of the e-learning system established in the UAE during the COVID-19 pandemic. The findings highlighted the common accessibility challenges faced by these students and revealed how the participating universities tried to overcome them.

Students with disabilities reported positive experiences in terms of accessing the technology they needed, indicating that this had not been a barrier for them. Similarly, about two-thirds of students with disabilities (64.4 %) stated that they had experienced no issues with their Internet connection. Based on the interview responses, Blackboard, the learning management system used in the UAE, seemed to be easy and accessible to use. This is probably because its design takes account of the Web Content Accessibility Guidelines (WCAG 2.1 AA), which provides an international accessibility standard (Blackboard, n.d.). Regarding online lesson platforms, the students found Zoom more accessible than the other platforms used in the UAE during the pandemic. Zoom incorporates several accessibility features for individuals with disabilities, which the students found very useful, such as "captioning & transcription options. screen reader support, keyboard shortcuts for easy navigation, customize the font size of chat and captions" (Zoom, 2022).

The results also identified other factors that play a major role in the ability of students with disability to access the e-learning system. These include access to the necessary technology, access to Wi-Fi, and access to training. Similar findings also were reported by Kim and Fienup (2022) and Ro'fah et al. (2020). Accessing training in how to use the technology, the Blackboard system, and the online platform found to be the most difficult barrier reported by the students at the three universities in this study. Ro'fah et al. (2020) stated: "online learning requires students to be able to control and navigate technology and learning content independently, and this may not be possible for some students with certain disabilities" (p. 15).

However, findings of the study indicated that students with disabilities did not find online examinations entirely accessible due to the use of LockDown Browser within Blackboard. The accessibility issues reported by the participants included using speech-to-text capability, keyboard focus, screen reader, and Braille devices, and facing the camera during online tests for visually impaired users. Stevanović et al. (2021) point out, the most significant drawback of remote learning for students with disabilities is online assessment, mainly because of issues with test design, the possibility of cheating, intensified anxiety, and technical issues. These problems were further aggravated during the COVID-19 pandemic by the abrupt transition from in-person to online classes, especially because many instructors had never taught online classes before and did not receive the necessary training to conduct online assessments. Thus, results varied from unfairness to serious inequities in academic integrity (Eaton, 2020).

Although mobile apps can be very helpful when teaching students with disabilities, any technology intended to support their learning must be designed not only with the user, aim, and setting in mind, but also in terms of accessibility and affordability in the user's community (Kumm et al., 2021).

5. Conclusion and Recommendations

Focusing on the UAE, this study showed that students with disabilities faced various accessibility challenges with online learning during the COVID-19 pandemic, which should be addressed before delivering future online courses. Several recommendations can be made based on these results. First, universities should follow a universal design for online learning considering the diverse needs of students with disabilities. Second, before starting their online courses, students with disabilities should be trained to access and use AT, online platforms, the course learning management system, and the university email system independently. Faculties and instructors also need to be trained to accommodate the special needs of students with disabilities in online classes, provide accessible study materials, and differentiate the assessments to meet the additional needs of such students. Finally, when educational institutes decide to implement virtual learning, they should choose a platform that is accessible to students with all forms of disabilities. That is, this platform should first be tested for ease of use.

Funding: This work was supported by Zayed University, United Arab Emirates (Grant Award Code: R22032).

References

Ali, L. (2021). The Shift to Online Education Paradigm Due to COVID-19: A Study of Students' Behavior in UAE Universities Environment. *International Journal of Information and Education Technology, 11*(3), 131–136. https://doi.org/10.18178/ijiet.2021.11.3.1501

Akyıldız, T. (2020). College Students' Views on the Pandemic Distance Education: A Focus Group Discussion. *International Journal of Technology in Education and Science, 4*(4), 322–334. https://doi.org/10.46328/ijtes.v4i4.150

Blackboard. (n.d.). *Accessibility at Blackboard.* https://help.blackboard.com/Accessibility

Eaton, S. E. (2020). Academic Integrity during COVID-19: Reflections from the University of Calgary. *International Studies in Educational Administration, 48*(1), 80–85. https://prism.ucalgary.ca/handle/1880/112293

Juma, M. (2020). *The Advantages and Disadvantages of Distance Learning for Students with Special Educational Needs and Disabilities during Covid-19 at University in UAE* (Masters dissertation, British University in Dubai). https://bspace.buid.ac.ae/bitstream/handle/1234/1767/20180999.pdf?sequence=3&isAllowed=y

Kim, J. Y., & Fienup, D. M. (2022). Increasing access to Online Learning for sTudents with Disabilities during the COVID-19 Pandemic. *The Journal of Special Education*, *55*(4), 213–221. https://doi.org/10.1177/002246692 1998067

Kumm, A. J., Viljoen, M., & de Vries, P. J. (2021). The Digital Divide in Technologies for Autism: Feasibility Considerations for Low- and Middle-income Countries. *Journal of Autism Development Disorder*, *52*(5), 2300–2313. https://doi.org/10.1007/s10803-021-05084-8

Lottin, J., Alzahmi, E., Wiseman, A., Sukker, H., Eltoum, M., Alayyan, M., Quirke, P., Al Aghar, T., Alghourani, A., & Anand, A. (2021). Reduce Academic Fatigue and Enhance Retention for the Determined Ones (TDOs) in Online Learning. *Sustainable Leadership and Academic Excellence International Conference* (SLAE), 1–5. https://doi.org/10.1109/SLAE54202.2021.9788087

Meda, L, & Waghid, Z. (2022). Exploring Special Need Students' Perceptions of Remote Learning Using the Multimodal Model of Online Education. *Education and Information Technologies*, *27*(6), 8111–8128. https://doi:10.1007/s10639-022-10962-4

Ro'fah, R., Hanjarwati, A., & Suprihatiningrum, J. (2020). Is online learning accessible during COVID-19 Pandemic? Voices and Experiences of UIN Sunan Kalijaga Students with Disabilities. *Nadwa: Jurnal Pendidikan Islam*, *14*(1), 1–38. https://doi.org/10.21580/nw.2020.14.1.5672

Scott, S., Ahead, & Aquino, K. (2020). COVID-19 Transitions: Higher Education Professionals' Perspectives on access Barriers, Services, and Solutions for Students with Disabilities. *The Association on Higher Education and Disability*. https://higherlogicdownload.s3.amazonaws.com/AHEAD/38b602f4-ec53-451c-9be0-5c0bf5d27c0a/UploadedImages/COVID-19_/AHEAD_COVID_Survey_Report_Barriers_and_Resource_Needs.pdf

Stevanović, A., Božić, R., & Radović, S. (2021). Higher Education Students' Experiences and Opinion about Distance Learning during the Covid-19 Pandemic. *Journal of Computer Assisted Learning*, *37*(6), 1682–1693. https://doi.org/10.1111/jcal.12613

The United Arab Emirates Government Portal. (2022). *Distance Learning in Times of COVID-19*. https://u.ae/en/information-and-services/education/distance-learning-in-times-of-covid-.19#:~:text=From%20March%202020%2C%20UAE%20has,protect%20students%20from%20COVID%2D19

Zoom. (2022). *Zoom Is for Everyone*. https://explore.zoom.us/en/accessibility/

Marijana Bubanić and Dina Korent

Clusters of the European Union's Countries Total Tax Burden

1. Introduction

Tax policy, as part of overall fiscal policy, is a set of instruments devised and implemented by a country's government that pertain to various aspects of taxation in it. Tax policy establishes a set of rules that determine the amount of tax liabilities (tax burden in the narrower sense), on the one hand, and the manner in which they are fulfilled (tax administrative burden), on the other (Ravšelj et al., 2019). As a result, the aforementioned dimensions represent the total tax burden borne by the taxpayer.

In the context of entrepreneurs, it is important that the total tax burden be as low as possible, so that not only the tax liability, but also the administrative cost, is minimized. The European Union's (EU) open borders allow companies to relocate their operations to a country with a lower total tax burden. As a result, the question of which EU countries has the lowest total tax burden appears.

The main goal of the study is to identify which EU countries are similar in terms of total tax burden, more specifically, to determine the clusters of EU countries in terms of total tax burden. The study attempts also to achieve specific goals. The first refers to determining how to measure the tax burden in the narrower sense and the administrative tax burden, allowing international comparisons, while the second refers to determining the cluster of EU countries with the lowest total tax burden.

Following an introduction of the research problem and objectives in the first chapter, the second chapter provides a literature overview of the measures on tax burden (in narrower sense) and administrative tax burden. The third chapter explains the research methodology, and provide a presentation and discussion of the findings. The final chapter state the contribution of the research, its limits, and recommendations.

2. Literature Review

A review of the literature in the context of entrepreneurship revealed the presence of a distinction between the tax burden in the narrower sense and the tax administrative burden (Ravšelj et al., 2019). Consequently, the total tax burden consists of two dimensions: tax burden in the narrower sense, and administrative tax burden.

The first dimension, the tax burden in a narrower sense, refers to the amount of tax paid, or tax costs, and is determined by tax bases, tax rates, and other primary and secondary direct characteristics of relevant tax forms (Ravšelj et al., 2019). The fundamental issue is how to evaluate the tax burden in a narrower sense while making it internationally comparable. The nominal and effective tax burdens are primarily distinguished when measuring the tax burden. According to Dias and Reis (2018) citing Slemrod and Bakija (2008) the nominal tax rate is regulated by law and is applied to the taxable base to calculate tax liability. It's the most fundamental measure of the tax burden (Devereux et al., 2002). Because data on the statutory tax rate is widely available, it enables for a quick comparison of countries' tax burdens, which is why they present a rough means of attracting foreign investments. (Bubanić & Korent, 2020). Nominal rates are a relatively good but rough measure of the tax burden because they do not take into account the tax base, which is why effective tax rates differ from legal rates. (Bubanić & Korent, 2020; Kukić, 2006). When estimating the effective tax burden, two approaches are distinguished: ex ante and ex post. According to Nicodeme (2001), one of the key differences between these methodologies is the information used in their calculation. Given that the purpose of the study is to compare the tax burdens of EU countries, an approach that allows for international data comparison is required. Without going into detail, we focus on the ex-ante approach. As stated by Kukić (2006), this approach can be used for international comparisons of effective tax rates, and Leibrecht and Hochgatterer (2012) agree, arguing that effective tax rates based on this approach can be calculated for domestic and international investments. Ex ante effective tax rates (ex-ante approach, forward-looking approach), Kukić (2006) characterizes as tax regulations-based measures. According to Leibrecht and Hochgatterer (2012), they calculate the tax burden imposed on a hypothetical, possible investment project, using data on the tax rate and tax base obtained directly from present and future (anticipated) tax regulations. As explained by Adamczyk (2012), the ex-ante approach relies on theoretical assumptions. Given that corporate taxation influences decisions about a company's location, the measure of the effective tax burden must reflect the decision-making process on investment strategies, so this approach is used in the context of observing corporate taxation as a factor in choosing a company's location (Overesch, 2005). This approach distinguishes two measures of the effective tax burden: Effective Marginal Tax Rate (EMTR) and Effective Average Tax Rate (EATR). According to Adamczyk (2012), EMTR is the rate that burdens a marginal investment project, that is, a project with a marginal rate of return on the last invested unit of capital equal to the project's marginal capital costs. EMTR evaluates the net present value of investment income and costs, and by equating them, the marginal investment is obtained, from which the needed rate of return before taxation may be calculated. (Devereux & Griffith, 1998). EATR, in contrast to EMTR, measures the tax burden on a hypothetical infra-marginal investment project, that is, a project that generates a positive economic rent (Leibrecht & Hochgatterer, 2012). The primary idea behind calculating EATR is to subtract the NPV of the investment project after taxation from the NPV of the project before taxation and divide the difference by the NPV of the project before taxation (Adamczyk, 2012). Overesch (2005) asserts that EATR is an essential predictor of an investment location's attractiveness. The European Commission includes both EATR and EMTR in its annual European report on tax policies as potential decision-making components on investment location (European Commission, 2020; Spengel et al., 2021).

In addition to the aforementioned, Doing Business is an indispensable study that enables international comparability of the total tax burden. The World Bank Group's Doing Business studies are annual surveys that measure aspects of business regulation and their influence on individual business areas of small and medium-sized domestic companies. Doing Business 2020 is the 17th and last study in the series, its replacement B-READY is in preparation. In the Doing Business research, the tax framework that determines the cost of taxes in a company's daily operations is evaluated on the basis of the tax burden in the narrower sense, i.e. all taxes and mandatory contributions that a representative company must pay or suspend in a given year, as well as the administrative burden of paying taxes and contributions and compliance with subsequent procedures (VAT refund and tax control). (World Bank, 2020) The overall score in the area of tax payment is determined by the scores of four individual indicators for a representative company: total tax and contribution rate (in% of commercial profit), number of tax and contribution payments in a year (adjusted for electronic and joint submission and payment), time required to fulfill the tax obligations related to the three main taxes (in hours per year), and the index of subsequent submission of tax returns. The first refers to the tax burden in the narrower sense, and the remaining three to the tax administrative burden. (World Bank, 2020)

The administrative tax burden is the second dimension of the total tax burden, and it refers to the costs for fulfilling tax obligations that are determined by, often complex, tax rules or tertiary tax aspects. As a result of the above, the complexity of the tax system might influence the administrative tax burden. The fulfillment of tax obligations is defined as the willingness of taxpayers to act in accordance with tax legislation without the use of coercive measures (James & Alley, 2009). As a result, the costs of meeting tax obligations include all expenditures originating from administrative obligations that entrepreneurs must execute in compliance with tax legislation (Ravšelj et al., 2019). The mentioned costs are substantial, according to the Global Competitiveness Report, and include the expenses of time and other resources, such as financial resources, employees with suitable knowledge and skills, and infrastructure for tax regulation implementation (Schwab, 2015). These are the costs of collecting information on tax laws and procedures, the costs of tax obligations (registration, declaration, invoicing, payments, and refunds), tax accounting, tax audits, and litigation. This costs also include the fees charged by external service providers such as tax lawyers and consulting companies. Furthermore, costs include both employee costs (such as salary, social security, and fringe benefits) and non-personnel costs (such as computers). Actual tax costs, costs of developing and maintaining the financial accounting system, costs of management accounting and reporting systems, and costs of information systems are not included in the costs of performing the company's tax obligations. (European Commission et al., 2022) The specified costs are fixed business costs that are unrelated to the profitability of companies. (Block, 2021). The preceding implies that the administrative tax burden is not strictly necessary for the total achievement of the public interest, and that a portion of that cost might be reduced without affecting tax revenue collection (Buckley, 2016). That part of the tax administrative burden can be defined as tax bureaucracy (Ravšelj et al., 2019). In terms of the latter, numerous EU countries face the challenges of modern tax legislation, which is frequently excessive, confusing, and designed to apply to all types of companies in a similar way. (European Commission et al., 2022; Ravšelj et al., 2019) Studies of the administrative tax burden are still in its early stages. Nonetheless, the previously referenced Doing Business research (World Bank, 2020) includes certain indications of the administrative tax burden. In addition to the foregoing, the study Tax compliance costs for SMEs: An update and a complement Final Report (European Commission et al., 2022), conducted in 2021, provides the most comprehensive assessment of the tax administrative burden of small, medium, and large companies in EU member states and the United Kingdom for 2019.[1] However, the already mentioned complexity of the tax system affects the administrative tax burden. Hoppe et al. (2023) create the Tax Complexity Index (TCI), a comprehensive measure of the complexity of the corporate tax system

---

[1] For more information, see European Commission et al. (2022).

encountered by multinational corporations from various countries. It is based on surveys of highly experienced tax consultants from the world's top tax services networks. The TCI is made up of two subindices: a tax code subindex that covers tax regulations and a tax framework subindex that covers tax processes and features. The Tax Complexity Index is a DFG-funded research project called "Accounting for Transparency" (Accounting for Transparency, 2020).

3. Research Methodology

3.1. Sample Selection and Data Collection

The literature review reveals the existence of two key components of a company's total tax burden: the tax burden in the narrower sense and the administrative tax burden. Furthermore, it also reveals that there are studies that generate and analyze indicators for assessing these dimensions that are also internationally comparable. Because the purpose of the study is to cluster the members of the EU based on indicators of the dimensions of the total tax burden, the entities of the system that is trying to be clustered are the countries of the EU. As a result, a database of indicators of the dimensions of the total tax burden for EU countries was established. The sample comprises all countries for which data on all variables' indicators were available. The data were collected from previous studies, therefore they served as the input for this study, and they are accordingly of a secondary character. Data on individual variable indicators include data from the most recent versions of Doing Business 2020 research (World Bank, 2020), Effective Tax Levels Using the Devereus/Griffith Metohodology (Spengel et al., 2021), Tax Complexity Index (Accounting for Transparency, 2020) and Taxation trends in the EU (Directorate-General for Taxation and Customs Union et al., 2022). The study includes 26 EU member countries[2]. Estonia is left out of the sample since no Tax Complexity Index data is available for it.

3.2. Variables

Several variable indicators were chosen based on findings of previous studies as well as their internationally comparability to measure the dimensions of the total tax burden, i.e. the tax burden in the narrower sense and the administrative tax burden. The indicators used, as well as their sources, are shown in Table 1.

---

2   Austria, Belgium, Bulgaria, Croatia, Cyprus, Czech, Denmark, Finland, France, Germany, Greece, Hungary, Ireland, Italy, Latvia, Lithuania, Luxembourg, Malta, Netherlands, Poland, Portugal, Romania, Slovakia, Slovenia, Spain, Sweden.

For the tax burden in narrower sense, seven indicators were applied, and two variables were used for the administrative burden. The use of multiple variables for estimating the dimension of the tax burden allows for more precise clustering while also ensuring the results' robustness.

Table 1. Variables of the dimensions of the total tax burden

dimensions of the total tax burden	name of the variable (abbreviation)	source of data
tax burden in the narrower sense	effective marginal tax rate (EMTR)	(Spengel et al., 2021)
	effective average tax rate (EATR)	
	top statutory corporate income tax rates (including surcharges) (TSTR)	(Directorate-General for Taxation and Customs Union et al., 2022)
	total tax and contribution rate (% of profit) (TTCR)	(World Bank, 2020)
	profit tax (% of profit) (PT)	
	labor tax and contributions (% of profit) (LTC)	
	other taxes (% of profit) (OT)	
administrative tax burden	tax complexity index (TCI)	(Accounting for Transparency, 2020)
	time (hours per year) (Time)	(World Bank, 2020)

Source: author's work

3.3. Method

Taxonomic analysis allows for system clustering based on multidimensionality, i.e. using more clustering variables. Also, it is useful for categorizing entities based on their similarities (Halmi, 2016). When the sample needs to be formed into distinct groups with as homogeneous qualities as feasible, taxonomic analysis is utilized (Halmi, 2016).

The goal of the cluster analysis in question is to identify taxomes or clusters of EU member states based on the homogeneity of the total tax burden, which is characterized in two dimensions: the tax burden in the narrower sense and the administrative tax burden. The dimensions described above were assessed using numerous variables listed in Table 1. The purpose is to use cluster analysis to discover a latent association between the selected EU members on the basis of the aforementioned variables.

Given the use of numerical variables, the Euclidean distance was chosen as a reasonable measure of similarity or distance between the observed entities, implying that the variables are more similar the smaller the gap between the values. The Ward approach or the minimum variance method, which connects entities in a cluster so that the variance inside the cluster is minimized, was used to quantify the distance between individual clusters.

The clustering analysis was performed using both a hierarchical and a partition-based, i.e. a non-hierarchical method. The number of K clusters is decided based on the generated dendogram, which must be precisely defined during non-hierarchical clustering. Following in the footsteps of earlier investigations, Ravšelj et al. (2019) recognized four groups. Individual clusters determined by a non-hierarchical manner were described using descriptive statistics.

4. Findings and Discussion

Graph 1 illustrates the dendogram of EU member states in terms of total tax burden as a result of hierarchical clustering. The dendogram, while not strictly defined, denotes the presence of four clusters. This result serves as the input for the following stage, which is non-hierarchical clustering. As a consequence, four clusters were defined.

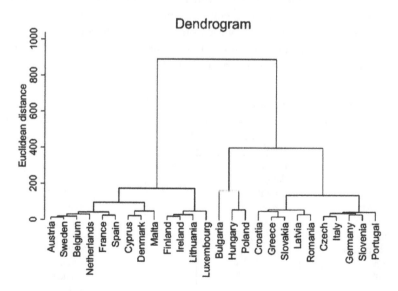

Graph 1. Dendogram of clusters of EU countries in terms of the total tax burden

Source: author's work

Table 2 presents the taxonomy of the sample of EU member states in terms of total tax burden. Graph 2 and Graph 3 compare the average results of the cluster of indicators of the dimensions of the total tax burden to the average results of all indicators in the sample. The first cluster consists of countries whose tax burden in the narrow sense is higher than the average of the entire sample, while the administrative tax burden is below average. The result of this cluster is in accordance with the results of Ravšelj et al. (2019), which characterizes such a cluster as excessive tax burden systems, whereby the above implies excessive tax burden in the narrower sense. The second cluster consists of countries whose total tax burden, i.e. both the tax burden in the narrower sense and the administrative tax burden, is below the average values of the entire sample. Also, this result is in agreement with the research results of Ravšelj et al. (2019), who characterize the mentioned system as stimulating tax systems. The third cluster consists of EU countries whose tax burden in the narrower sense is mostly below the average of the entire sample, while the administrative tax burden is above average. Although Ravšelj et al. (2019) refer to such a cluster as Excessive tax administrative burden systems, the results of the subject research differ. Ravšelj et al. (2019) include Croatia, Germany, Latvia, and the Slovak Republic in the aforementioned cluster, while this research results include Bulgaria, Hungary, and Poland. The final and largest cluster is defined by the tax burden in a narrower sense, which is above the sample average for most indicators and above the sample average for administrative tax burden. The cluster with these features is referred as burdensome tax systems by Ravšelj et al. (2019). Nonetheless, the findings of the subject research are somewhat consistent with the preceding, which applies to Italy, Portugal, and Slovenia.

Table 2. Clusters of EU countries in terms of total tax burden

cluster			
first	**second**	**third**	**fourth**
Austria	Finland	Bulgaria	Croatia
Belgium	Ireland	Hungary	Czech
Cyprus	Lithuania	Poland	Germany
Denmark	Luxembourg		Greece
France			Italy
Malta			Latvia
Netherlands			Portugal
Spain			Romania
Sweden			Slovakia
			Slovenia

Source: author's work

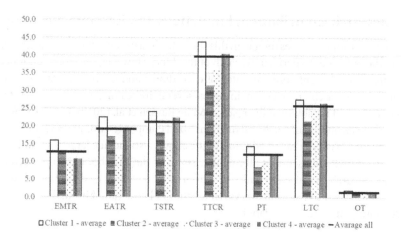

Graph 2. Cluster average results of the indicators of tax burden in the narrower sense
Source: author's work

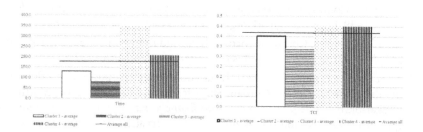

Graph 3. Cluster average results of the indicators of administrative tax burden
Source: author's work

The results agree to a greater or lesser extent with the research results of Ravšelj et al. (2019), where the consequence of disagreement with the existing results should be attributed to the time coverage of the data, the use of different variables, but also to the research sample. Namely, Ravšelj et al. (2019) include 20 EU countries in the research sample, and use only one indicator of the tax burden in the narrower sense, and one indicator of the administrative tax burden. Also, Governments implement reforms of the tax system over time, which affects changes in the total tax burden, and accordingly changes in clusters.

5. Research Contribution, Limitations and Recommendations

The current study reduces the gap in this scientific field because Ravšelj et al. (2019), were the only ones to perform research of this kind. However, the aforementioned research includes only one indicator of each dimension of the total tax burden, while the research in question includes several indicators, which ensures the robustness and reliability of the results. While Ravšelj et al. (2019) use variables to assess the tax burden of small and medium-sized companies, this research includes tax burden variables that, in addition to the above, also include large companies.

It is strongly advised that all member states of the EU should be included in future research because currently that aren't due to a lack of data. In addition, more administrative tax burden variables should be included in further studies, depending on the data availability.

References

Accounting for Transparency. (2020). *Tax Complexity Index.*

Adamczyk, A. (2012). The Effective Level of Corporate Income Tax in the European Countries. *International Journal of Economics and Finance Studies,* 4(1), 31–39. https://dergipark.org.tr/en/download/article-file/256784

Block, J. (2021, July). Corporate Income Taxes and Entrepreneurship. *IZA World of Labor 2021: 257v2,* 1–11. https://doi.org/10.15185/izawol.257.v2

Bubanić, M., & Korent, D. (2020). Efektivno opterećenje porezom na dobit u hrvatskoj. In M. Družić, Gordan, Šimović, Hrvoje, Basarac Sertić, Martina, Deskar-Škrbić (Eds.), *Održivost javnih financija na putu u monetarnu uniju* (pp. 176–197). Ekonomski fakultet Zagreb i Hrvatska akademija znanosti i umjetnosti. https://www.efzg.unizg.hr/userdocsimages/fin/hsimovic/HRZZ/Rezultati/Knjiga PuFiSuMU_2020.pdf

Buckley, A. P. (2016). Using Contribution Analysis to Evaluate Small & Medium Enterprise Support Policy. *Evaluation, 22*(2), 129–148. https://doi.org/10.1177/1356389016638625

Devereux, M., & Griffith, R. (1998). *The Taxation of Discrete Investment Choices* (No. W98/16; IFS Working Papers). https://www.econstor.eu/bitstream/10419/90851/1/wp9816.pdf

Devereux, M. P., Griffith, R., & Klemm, A. (2002). Corporate Income Tax, Reforms and Tax Competition. In *Economic Policy* (Issue October, pp. 450–495).

Dias, P. J. V. L., & Reis, P. M. G. (2018). The Relationship between the Effective Tax Rate and the Nominal Rate. *Contaduria y Administracion, 63*(2), 1–21. https://doi.org/10.22201/fca.24488410e.2018.1609

Directorate-General for Taxation and Customs Union, European Commission, & Publications Office of the European Union. (2022). *Taxation Trends in the European Union, 2022 edition.* https://doi.org/10.2778/417176

European Commission. (2020). *Tax Policies in the European Union 2020 Survey.* https://doi.org/10.2778/817571

European Commission, D.-G. for I. M. I. E. and Sme., European Innovation Council and SMEs Executive Agency, Di Legge, A., Ceccanti, D., Hortal Foronda, F., Németh, M., & Csonka, M. (2022). *Tax Compliance Costs for SMEs: An Update and a Complement: Final Report.* https://doi.org/https://data.europa.eu/doi/10.2873/180570

Halmi, A. (2016). *Multivarijatna analiza u društvenim znanostima.* Alinea.

Hoppe, T., Schanz, D., Sturm, S., & Sureth-Sloane, C. (2023). The Tax Complexity Index – A Survey-Based Country Measure of Tax Code and Framework Complexity. *European Accounting Review, 32*(2), 239–273. https://doi.org/10.1080/09638180.2021.1951316

James, S., & Alley, C. (2009). Tax Compliance, Self-Assessment and Tax Administration. *Journal of Finance and Management in Public Services, 2*(2), 27–42. https://ore.exeter.ac.uk/repository/bitstream/handle/10036/47458/james2.pdf

Kukić, N. (2006). *Efektivno porezno opterećenje trgovačkih društva u Republici Hrvatskoj* [Magistarski rad]. Sveučilište u Zagrebu, Ekonomski fakultet.

Leibrecht, M., & Hochgatterer, C. (2012). Tax Competition as a Cause of Falling Corporate Income Tax Rates: A Survey of Empirical Literature. *Journal of Economic Surveys, 26*(4), 616–648. https://doi.org/10.1111/j.1467-6419.2010.00656.x

Nicodeme, G. (2001). Computing Effective Corporate Tax Rates: Comparisons and Results. *Economic Papers, 153*, Art. 153. https://mpra.ub.uni-muenchen.de/3808/

Overesch, M. (2005). The Effective Tax Burden of Companies in Europe. *CESifo DICE Report, 3*(4), 56–63. https://www.econstor.eu/bitstream/10419/166863/1/ifo-dice-report-v03-y2005-i4-p56-63.pdf

Ravšelj, D., Kovač, P., & Aristovnik, A. (2019). Tax-Related Burden on SMEs in the European Union: The Case of Slovenia. *Mediterranean Journal of Social Sciences, 10*(2), 69–79. https://doi.org/10.2478/mjss-2019-0024

Schwab, K. (2015). *The Global Competitiveness Report 2015–2016, Insight Report.* https://www3.weforum.org/docs/gcr/2015-2016/Global_Competitiveness_Report_2015-2016.pdf

Slemrod, J., & Bakija, J. (2008). Taxing Ourselves: A Citizen's Guide to the Debate over Taxes. In *Angewandte Chemie International Edition, 6*(11), 951–952 (4th ed.). The MIT Press.

Spengel, C., Schmidt, F., Heckemeyer, J., Nicolay, K., Bartholmeß, A., Ludwig, C., Steinbrenner, D., Buchmann, P., Theresa Bührle, A., Dutt, V., Fischer, L., Spix, J., Stage, B., Weck, S., & Wickel, S. (2021). *Effective Tax Levels Using the Devereux / Griffith Methodology.* https://taxation-customs.ec.europa.eu/system/files/2022-03/final_report_2021_effective_tax_levels_revised_en.pdf

World Bank. (2020). *Doing Business 2020: Comparing Business Regulation in 190 Economies.* https://doi.org/10.1596/978-1-4648-1440-2